The Costs of Courage

Also Available from Oxford University Press

THE COSTS
OF COURAGE

Combat Stress, Warriors, and Family Survival

Josephine G. Pryce
University of Alabama

Colonel David H. Pryce
U.S. Army Retired

Kimberly K. Shackelford
University of Mississippi

OXFORD
UNIVERSITY PRESS

OXFORD
UNIVERSITY PRESS

Oxford University Press is a department of the University of Oxford. It furthers the
University's objective of excellence in research, scholarship, and education by publishing worldwide.
Oxford is a registered trade mark of Oxford University Press in the UK and certain other countries.

Published in the United States of America by Oxford University Press
198 Madison Avenue, New York, NY 10016, United States of America.

Library of Congress Cataloging-in-Publication Data

Pryce, Josephine G.
  The costs of courage : combat stress, warriors, and family survival / Josephine G. Pryce, David H. Pryce,
Kimberly K. Shackelford.
    p. cm.
  Includes bibliographical references and index.
  ISBN 978-0-190616-08-3 (pbk. : alk. paper)
  1. Veterans—Services for—United States. 2. Veterans—Mental health services—United States.
3. Veterans—Counseling of—United States. 4. Families of military personnel—Services for—
United States. 5. Family social work—United States. 6. Social service—United States.
I. Pryce, David H. II. Shackelford, Kimberly K. III. Title.
  UB357.P79   2012
  362.86'530973—dc23
                                                                              2011023196

ISBN 978-0-190616-08-3

Dedication

To America's men and women in uniform, past and present, and their families and loved ones, with heartfelt thanks and respect for their service and sacrifice.

To the memory of Commander Keith Springle, U.S. Navy, Ph.D., a graduate of the University of Alabama School of Social Work Doctoral Program, who was conducting a combat-stress treatment session in Iraq when he was killed by one of our own distressed warriors.

Contents

Preface
Yet Another Inconvenient Truth

The purpose of this book is to inspire and educate social workers, both in the classroom and in the field, on the attitudes and skill sets required for professional practice with our current generation of American warriors and their families. The authors intend to show that the social work community as a whole, with a few significant exceptions, has been slow to come to terms with the worldwide conflict in which we have been engaged for several long years with no definite end yet in sight. One needs to look no further than the 2007 Annual Program Meeting of the Council on Social Work Education for evidence of such neglect. Of the myriad sessions and offerings at that conference, not one dealt with our war veterans and their families. And our review of social work educational texts published from 1991 to 2007 reveals that only a handful of books deal even minimally with war veterans and their families. We authors are troubled by what we see, and this book highlights our concerns and offers possible solutions for the social work profession to consider.

Like it or not, the country is fighting on several fronts. Few have been asked to sacrifice anything for the war effort. Indeed, the only Americans who sacrifice are the members of our armed forces, their families, and friends. One's political position on the conflict must take a backseat to the overwhelming need to mend and strengthen our returning warriors and their loved ones. But does it? Not apparently. The physical injuries of the wounded are horrific enough, but the huge costs of mental injury are just as daunting, and estimates hold that those unseen wounds will continue to increase, threatening the very survival of the veteran and his or her family.

Our government failed to plan for the human costs of these wars, and it is struggling to make up for its lack of foresight. And its progress toward providing the health-care services essential for the recovery of our damaged warriors and their families has been less than impressive. Our country has spent billions of dollars on high-technology war-fighting equipment, much to the pleasure of the defense industry, and yet cheap homemade bombs continue to kill our men and women in battle dress. The Department of Defense (DOD) has used our warriors until they are broken, only to hustle them off active duty so it doesn't have to mend their wounds. These veterans are then dropped at the doors of our Department of Veterans Affairs (VA), whose facilities have been and continue to be overwhelmed, as a result of bureaucratic haggling and consistent underfunding by both Republicans and Democrats. This is not to say that there have not been innovative programs at both the DOD and the VA. We selectively highlight those promising initiatives as well.

We remind readers that this book is a work in progress, just as our current wars are works in progress. Casualty numbers change daily, as do statistical data.

This book shines a bright light on government successes and shortcomings and offers suggestions for professional social workers as to how to make things better for a seriously underserved population—our warriors and their families.

It is imperative that social workers in particular and other mental health professionals in general move their attention toward those who defend our freedom. One's position on the policies that have delivered us to these wars must be emotionally and cognitively separated from one's feelings for, and attention to, those who have borne war's burdens. Our young social-workers-to-be must be encouraged to pick up the torch and, with genuine enthusiasm, pursue career paths that will interact with and affect these wounded warriors and their families. To this end, we have intentionally limited the goal and scope of this book to informing social work practice. We offer no prescriptions or proscriptions to treatment models or practice techniques. When used to instruct clinical practitioners, this volume must be supplemented with a clinical text.

Also, we recognize that civilian contractors are deployed in war zones and are performing tasks similar in outcome to our warriors in uniform. The contractor culture is not the same as that of the profession of arms, and we have purposefully excluded it from our discussions herein. To the extent that the information provided may be useful to practitioners' interactions with contractors, we offer it for consideration. It is, however, up to the individual practitioner to decide whether to consider it.

We are facing a human crisis, and it's a crisis of our own making. It is yet another inconvenient truth that we must face squarely with the same commitment and courage that our young men and women face daily on the battlefield.

Acknowledgments

We offer our sincere appreciation to the following, whose support, comments, and criticism all contributed greatly to our book.

The warriors, veterans, and family members who willingly gave their time and frank commentary through interviews and conversations on the current wars and the challenges they present to all who are touched by them.

David Yancey, a wounded warrior student at the University of Mississippi, for his courage in exposing the disgraceful Walter Reed Hospital situation in 2007. Also at Ole Miss, social work students Lisa Kuklinski and Kristen O'Quinn.

At the University of Alabama: Provost Judy Bonner, Dean Cindy Roff, Lynn Tobola, librarian, Lawrence Graham, information technologist, and Fallan Frank, organizational assistant.

On the production side we offer special thanks to David Follmer, Publisher, Lyceum Books, for the idea and the opportunity to write this book. Also on the production side Lyceum editors Reese-Anna Baker and Catherine Dixon, copyeditor Katherine Faydash, and our reviewers, Jonathan Alex, Jose Coll, Dexter Freeman, Cathleen Lewandowski, Bradley Schaffer, and Peter Vaughan. We thank you for encouragement and support. Your most valuable contribution was your thoughtful criticism which has made for a better book. Hard for an old soldier to swallow sometimes, but we remain forever grateful.

Last, on a personal note, Silvey Pryce, beloved and loyal golden retriever, who seemed to know that when we had worked too long and were making too many mistakes, it was time for us to give her our undivided attention. She was not to be denied.

Introduction

Part 1: The Basics

This introduction provides a brief summary of each chapter in the order it appears in the book. We clearly identify the purpose of each chapter, as well as the premise from which we derive our reasoning.

Chapter 1 describes the nature of the current war in Afghanistan and Iraq briefly in terms of purpose, national strategy, and the nature of combat on the battlefield. We make cogent comparisons to previous wars. We introduce the physical signature wounds of the current war—wounds requiring amputation—and we introduce in more detail signature psychological and cognitive wounds: traumatic brain injury, war-induced posttraumatic stress disorder, and major depression. The disturbingly numerous reports of sexual assault involving both female and male victims, which some have described as an epidemic in and out of the war zone, receive considerable attention. Our overall purpose is to inform readers about the horrific nature of war and the human costs in terms of war trauma so that social workers and other helping professionals can begin to understand and relate to warriors and their families.

Chapter 2 is presented in two sections. The first introduces the five branches of our active duty armed forces—Army, Navy, Marine Corps, Air Force, and Coast Guard, as well as their reserve component forces (National Guard and Reserves). We explain the roles of each service. The American military is a subculture in itself. Therefore, we present selected aspects of each service's unique history and traditions to demonstrate the need for cultural competence among social workers and other practitioners. The chapter then proceeds to describe military families and their special needs, particularly family separation because of a spouse's deployment to the war zone. We introduce the general and specific stressors associated with preparing for deployment, separation during deployment, and reintegration and family reunion during postdeployment; we also mention the extraordinary potential for family violence and divorce. Social workers who seek to help military members and their families must be knowledgeable and culturally competent. The information introduced in chapter 2 is elaborated on later, in chapter 7 of this volume: "Warriors and Families Speak Out," and in chapter 8, "Social Work and Military Families."

Part 2: The Problem

Chapter 3 deals with the negative mental health effects of war on human beings, in this case combatants rather than civilians, because it is the former who must commit the decidedly unnatural act of killing fellow human beings. This chapter addresses the invisible wounds of war, specifically what have been generally acknowledged as the three signature wounds of the current conflicts in Iraq and Afghanistan. These are posttraumatic stress disorder (PTSD), major depressive episodes (MDE) and subsequent major depressive disorder (MDD), and traumatic brain injury (TBI).

Chapter 4 presents the government's response to the high incidence of PTSD among Afghanistan and Iraq War veterans. We first examine the Department of Defense (DOD) in terms of (1) the actions it takes to prepare its combatants for the possibility of war-induced stress, (2) the actions it takes to mitigate stress in the combat zone, and (3) the actions it takes with regard to veterans who have returned from the war zone with mental health problems. Readers may be surprised or even shocked to learn how the DOD treats its combatants who have mental health issues.

The discussion then addresses the Department of Veterans Affairs (VA), the government agency responsible for administering health care to veterans who have been disabled as a result of their military service. We discuss in some detail the VA mission, organization, and resources, including the Veterans Health Administration (VHA), its institutional mental health resources, and its Readjustment Counseling Service (RCS) Vet Center program. Like the DOD, the major obstacle to the provision of VA mental health care is the consistent lack of adequate funding for personnel and resources. Social work practitioners need to know what resources are, or are not, available to disabled veterans and their families to whom they may provide services.

Chapter 5 deals with suicide, a chronic and growing problem among our current war fighters. Suicide is a leading cause of death in the United States. Sadly, warriors as a group are committing suicide more often than before. The statistics demonstrate that veterans are committing suicide at a rate exceeding that of the nonveteran population. We do not know exactly how many suicides there are from war, especially the Afghanistan and Iraq Wars. Shay (2009) shares a communication with a military officer who raised a question about the number of motorcycle accidents among recently returning veterans. The officer referred to it as a "holocaust" (p. xi), and Shay suggests that these may well be suicides that go unnamed as such.

Chapter 6 deals with contemporary issues. Like any organization the military faces challenges that reflect the social and political climate. Four pressing issues are presented and discussed. Homelessness, incarcerated veterans, issues concerning military women and women veterans, and issues concerning gay and lesbian persons are addressed.

Chapter 7 reports the results of interviews with warriors and their family members. The chapter discusses common themes that were presented during these interviews, along with issues and problems that the population wanted social workers to understand. The warriors and their family members speak out about several difficulties and challenges, but they also express many positives about the military experience.

Part 3: Social Work Solutions

Chapter 8 centers on social work with military families. This unique population faces numerous challenges. Multiple deployments are taking a toll on service members and their families. The chapter covers changes in the military family and how changes in military policy affect military families. The stigma of the use of mental health services is also addressed. Issues affecting children and adolescents are also presented. The chapter also discusses secondary traumatic stress and programs that help with persons coping with death.

Chapter 9 describes the challenges student veterans face and provides ways in which social work can be part of the solution, as well as suggestions for social work educators as advocates for Soldiers and veterans as students on campus. With the advent of the new G.I. Bill, student veterans and their family members are facing hurdles in its use. Social workers can influence the policies and practice of higher education in their services to veterans and their family members.

The conclusion provides possible solutions to some of the problems discussed in the preceding chapters. Family members and warriors suggest solutions and give ideas for the improvement of services. Undergraduate social work programs should integrate information regarding the unique culture of the military and the special needs, issues, and strengths of Soldiers, veterans, and their families. This information should be integrated into courses on human behavior in the social environment; practice and policy courses; and courses such as child welfare, health, mental health, and gerontology. This population should be considered at risk; therefore, the conclusion addresses issues of social justice and oppression.

Graduate social work programs should contain the same foundation as that previously described as necessary in BSW programs, including the addressing of Soldiers, veterans, and their families in specialized courses. Clinical programs should include empirically based best practices and eclectic approaches to working with this population.

Part One

The Basics

War and Its By-Products

War means fighting, and fighting means killing.
—**Nathan Bedford Forrest**

You cannot qualify war in harsher terms than I will. War is cruelty, and you cannot refine it. You might as well appeal against the thunderstorm as against these terrible hardships of war.
—**William Tecumseh Sherman**, Letter to the Mayor of Atlanta, September 12, 1864

Background

After the devastating attacks on the twin towers of the World Trade Center and the Pentagon on September 11, 2001, the administration of George W. Bush became engaged in what it called the global war on terror (GWOT). It is a war against radical fundamentalist Islam, a stateless enemy that has sworn to destroy and then dominate the rest of the world. The enemy's weapons range from crude homemade bombs to commercial airliners, and their targets are mainly innocent civilians whom they seek to terrorize, demoralize, and ultimately subdue. Like the conflicts in Korea, Vietnam, Grenada, and Panama, the Congress has chosen not to exercise its constitutional responsibility to declare war, thus leaving the prosecution of the conflicts to the executive branch. Hence, like Vietnam before it, the GWOT has raised doubts about its legitimacy both in the United States and abroad.

Briefly examining past wars, we can draw some comparisons. Congress declared World War II, which was fought by both conscripted service members and volunteers, numbering some 16.1 million. Although it lasted only four years (1941–1945), it was the bloodiest war of the twentieth century. It is important to note that our armed forces went abroad to defeat the German and Japanese war machines. They were not sent on time-limited deployments, as is the case today. They went and did not expect to come home until it was over. The enemy surrendered unconditionally.

The Korean War (1951–1953) was fought in the context of the so-called Cold War to prevent the spread of communism. Congress did not declare war, and again the battle was borne by both conscripts and volunteers. Neither side surrendered, and officially the war continues even today under the auspices of a cease-fire that effectively divided the Korean Peninsula.

Vietnam was our longest war (1962–1975). It was fought in the context of the Cold War, in that our purpose was to contain communism in Southeast Asia. Again, both draftees and volunteers participated, rotating in and out of the war zone on twelve- to thirteen-month tours of duty, and more than fifty-eight thousand Americans lost their lives. Vietnam was fought while urban unrest was rampant in the United States. The war became extremely unpopular. Finally, the U.S. Congress refused to provide funding for our effort in Vietnam, and although our armed forces never lost a major battle, our nation lost the war. The military draft ended, and today's all-volunteer force was born. The brief Persian Gulf War (Operation Desert Storm) began and ended in 1991 and was the first war fought by the new all-volunteer force.

Afghanistan

Operation Enduring Freedom (OEF) is Pentagon jargon for the current war in Afghanistan. That country, dominated by the radical Islamist Taliban, provided safe haven for the Islamic terrorist organization, al-Qaeda, and its command structure headed by the Saudi billionaire Osama bin Laden, the mastermind of the September 11 attacks on the United States. Our purpose in going into Afghanistan was to remove the Taliban from political and military dominance, to destroy al-Qaeda, and to kill or capture Osama bin Laden and his leadership staff. Our tactics involved precision air strikes directed by small teams of Special Operations Forces and the employment of indigenous Afghan forces advised by coalition forces from Great Britain, France, and Australia (Tanielian & Jaycox, 2008).

The coalition's initial actions overwhelmed al-Qaeda and the Taliban in a matter of weeks, driving them underground and into the tribal areas of western Pakistan. A new government was elected in Afghanistan, and the coalition forces turned to military activities aimed to stabilize the new political order there. As of May 7, 2010, approximately 78,000 U.S. military personnel remain in Afghanistan, and that number will grow if the administration's war strategy continues as is: 1,046 have died and 5,730 have been wounded in continued fighting against a resurgent Taliban. The American forces are involved in the first protracted war using an all-volunteer force of both active and reserve component forces. Rather than leaving home and fighting until the enemy is defeated, American military personnel deploy to the war zone for months, usually about a year, and return home only to deploy again to fight yet another day.

Iraq

Operation Iraqi Freedom (OIF) is the Defense Department's name for the current war in Iraq. Organized Iraqi resistance was no match for American and coalition forces, and the capital, Baghdad, fell in less than a month. In May 2003, major combat operations were over, according to President Bush. However, this proclamation proved misguided and premature. Security deteriorated throughout Iraq, as Sunni and Shiite private militias fought to gain political power. The fighting quickly became a guerilla-type war that continues to this day. As in the war in Afghanistan, U.S. active and reserve component military personnel deploy for about a year to the combat zone, return home for about a year, and then redeploy to do it all over again.

The Army and Marine Corps bear the brunt of the fighting, and their ranks have been seriously depleted. As of May 7, 2010, 4,387 warriors had been killed, and 31,809 had been wounded. The unpopular nature of this protracted war has made recruiting difficult, so difficult that the Army resorted to enlisting felons for a brief period. The motives for our invasion of Iraq and the way the war has been conducted continue to be debated. As happened during the Vietnam years, the war has become unpopular. At least the American public is tending to lay the blame for the situation at the feet of politicians rather than on our warriors and their families.

Reflections on War—Sun Tzu, 500 BCE

The Chinese philosopher Sun Tzu, writing in about 500 BCE, provides us the first of the military classics that deals with the nature and conduct of war:

> His purpose was to develop a systematic treatise to guide rulers and generals in the intelligent prosecution of successful war. He believed that the skillful strategist should be able to subdue the enemy's army

without engaging it, to take his cities without laying siege to them, and overthrow his State without bloodying swords. . . . He did not conceive war in terms of slaughter and destruction; to take all intact, or as nearly intact as possible, was the proper objective of strategy. . . . He appreciated the effect of war on the economy and was undoubtedly the first to observe that inflated prices are the inevitable accompaniment to military operations. "No country," he wrote, "has ever benefited from a protracted war." (Sun Tzu, 1971, pp. x–xi)

Sun Tzu had a profound influence on Mao Tse-tung and his 1930s writings on guerrilla war. Our current conflicts in Iraq and Afghanistan are often referred to as counterinsurgencies, as was Vietnam. "Four principles define how guerrillas fight: (1) When the enemy advances, we retreat! (2) When the enemy halts, we advance! (3) When the enemy seeks to avoid battle, we attack! (4) When the enemy retreats, we pursue!" (Sun Tzu, 1971, p. 51). Each of our current conflicts disrupted our economy, and each became protracted in length. Each has polarized our population and vanquished civility from our political discourse. And each has taken its terrible toll in blood and treasure. We leave readers to their own conclusions as to what our own policymakers and generals learned or failed to learn from Sun Tzu.

The Western Way of War: The Battle

Western societies have repudiated the moderation featured in Sun Tzu's thoughts on war. Western wars have always resulted in a series of battles. And to battle we must turn to set the context for our understanding of the warrior. John Keegan (1976), a foremost student of battle, offers this discourse on the nature of battle:

Battle . . . is essentially a moral conflict. It requires, if it is to take place, a mutual and sustained act of will by two contending parties and, if it is to result in a decision, the moral collapse of one of them. How protracted that act of will must be, and how complete the moral collapse, are not things about which one can be specific. In an "ideal" battle the act would be sustained long enough for the collapse to be total. . . . [A] battle is something which happens between two armies leading to the moral and then physical disintegration of one or the other of them— and this is as near to a working definition of what a battle is that one is likely to get. . . . What battles have in common is human: the behavior of men struggling to reconcile their instinct for self-preservation, their sense of honor and the achievement of some aim over which other men are ready to kill them. (pp. 296–297)

Keegan (1976) lists the factors always present in battle that make it a singular surreal phenomenon: fear, courage, compulsion, insubordination, anxiety, elation, catharsis, uncertainty, doubt, misinformation, misapprehension, faith, vision, violence, cruelty, self-sacrifice, compassion, solidarity, and disintegration.

Killing and Warriors

The act of killing must be understood if one is to understand the effects of battle on Soldiers, and for our source we turn to Lieutenant Colonel Dave Grossman's (1995) classic book, *On Killing: The Psychological Cost of Learning to Kill in War and Society*. Drawing on the classic works of Brigadier General S. L. A. Marshall (1978), *Men against Fire*, and J. Glenn Gray (1970), *The Warriors: Reflections on Men in Battle*, and other sources, Grossman explodes the myth that soldiers have historically sought to kill their enemy in battle. Indeed, Marshall found that in World War II, only 15 percent to 20 percent of combat infantrymen were willing to fire their rifles. Since that time, however, armies have learned to train their soldiers to end their reluctance to kill. In Vietnam, 90 percent to 95 percent of American combat infantry proved ready and willing to fire their weapons and kill.

Grossman (1995) describes the predisposition of some soldiers to kill:

Predisposition consists of three factors: Training/conditioning of the soldier. . . . Recent experiences of the soldier (For example, having a friend or relative killed by the enemy has been strongly linked with killing behavior on the battlefield). . . . [Researchers] . . . proposed the existence of two percent of combat soldiers who are predisposed to be "aggressive psychopaths" and who apparently do not experience the trauma commonly associated with killing behavior. (p. 189)

Killing another human being occurs in stages. Grossman (1995) describes these stages in considerable detail:

What are the stages of killing another human being? First, before the kill, there is *concern*, particularly among soldiers newly arrived in their

unit. How am I going to do? Will I do my job, or am I a coward? Am I
going to survive? The *killing* stage is usually consummated quickly,
without much conscious thought. If the soldier is unable to kill, he will
try to rationalize his behavior or even become traumatized by his failure to do his job. Then there is the dark but very real *exhilaration* stage,
the feeling of intense satisfaction that can lead to the "combat high"
and later to "combat addiction" a condition not unlike addiction to
drugs. The combat addict must have his next fix, and that fix is more
killing. *Remorse* almost always follows the kill, particularly if it was a
close-range kill. It is common, and it will be dealt with for a lifetime.
Lastly, there is the *rationalization and acceptance* stage. The killer
needs rationalization and justification for his action. This search is a lifelong pursuit and if it fails the result will be one, two, or even all of the
negative outcomes of PTSD, major depression, and self-destructive behavior. (pp. 231–240)

Drink, and Will to Combat

Since ancient times soldiers have sought to mitigate with substances the intense
emotions that combat evokes. The Chinese of antiquity were the first to use marijuana for its psychedelic effects, and cannabis was once to India what alcohol is
today to the United States (Schaffer Library of Drug Policy, n.d.). According to
Langdale (2009), "Drug use in wartime is a topic rarely covered by the mainstream media but each war has an underlying drug culture attached to it. . . . [N]o
army in recent history has ever successfully been able to curb drug use among its
ranks. Of course not all military forces discourage the use of drugs" (p. 1).

Alcohol and drugs have historically been widely used in wartime. Soldiers
on both sides of the epic battles of Agincourt (1415) during the Hundred Years'
War, Waterloo (1815) during the Napoleonic Wars, and the Somme (1916) in
World War I all drank heavily and frequently went into battle drunk (Keegan,
1976). History records George Washington drinking with members of the Continental Army (Gates, 2009). In World War I, British soldiers were given rum in
their daily rations, and their officers often authorized additional rations of rum
before leaving the trenches for the machine-gun-raked no-man's-land. The German substance of choice in World War II was a methamphetamine designed to
keep soldiers alert for days at a time. Marijuana and heroin became the drugs
associated with the U.S. Army in the Vietnam War (Drug Policy Alliance, 2009),

and inexpensive alcohol was readily available in the rear areas, where many combat pilots and thousands of support personnel resided.

Today's armed forces have banned alcohol from the war zones, but Soldiers get it and use it anyway, as they always have (Cucullu, 2010). Experts at the National Center on Addiction and Substance Abuse's (CASA) Wounds of War conference said, "Excessive drinking [is] a huge problem among U.S. military personnel, even in combat zones in Muslim countries where alcohol is banned." At the same conference, Admiral Mike Mullen, chairman of the Joint Chiefs of Staff, said that eight years of combat was at least partially to blame for the sharp rise in heavy drinking (*Alcohol abuse*, 2009). A National Institutes of Health study found that "Reserve and National Guard personnel and younger Servicemembers who deploy with reported combat exposures are at increased risk of new-onset heavy weekly drinking, binge drinking and alcohol-related problems" (Jacobson et al., 2008, p. 663).

The current wars in Iraq and Afghanistan have produced a new wave of addiction. The prescription drugs routinely given to the Army and Marine combat troops—stimulants to keep them alert and opiates to ease stress or pain—are the culprits: "Unsurprisingly, the strains on the system have led military commanders to get men back in the fight rather than confronting addiction and mental health problems in the ranks. . . . Between 2004 and 2006, the incidence of substance abuse went up 100 percent, while treatment referrals by commanders went up zero percent" (Curley, 2009, par. 12).

Sergeant Christopher LeJeune, a veteran of fifteen months of Iraq combat, had this to say to *Time* magazine:

> Many more troops need help—pharmaceutical or otherwise—but don't get it because of fears that it will hurt their chance for promotion. They don't want to destroy their career or make everybody go in a convoy to pick up your prescription. . . . In the civilian world, when you have a problem, you go to the doctor, and you have therapy followed up by some medication. In Iraq, you see the doctor only once or twice, but you continue to get drugs constantly. . . [T]he medications, combined with the war's other stressors[,] created unfit soldiers. There were more than a few convoys going out in a total daze. (Thompson, 2008, par. 23)

Experts at the CASA conference stated that "the U.S. could face a wave of addiction and mental health problems among returning veterans of the Iraq and

Afghan wars greater than that resulting from the Vietnam War" (Curley, 2009, par. 1).

Soul Wounds

Compounding the problem of addiction, Edward Tick (2005), in *War and the Soul*, provides a perspective that views the maladies associated with the warrior's failed rationalization, acceptance, and subsequent reintegration with society as a soul wound:

> Veterans often remain drenched in the imagery and emotion of war for decades. . . . For these survivors, every vital human characteristic that we attribute to the soul may be fundamentally reshaped. These traits include how we perceive; how our minds are organized and function; how we love and relate; what we believe, expect, and value; what we feel and refuse to feel; and what we judge as good and evil, right or wrong. (p. 1)

Tick (2005) would have us think of posttraumatic stress disorder (PTSD) as an identity disorder. Jonathan Shay (1994) refers to the phenomenon as "the undoing of character" in his landmark work, *Achilles in Vietnam: Combat Trauma and the Undoing of Character*. However our understanding of combat trauma resolves itself, it is the purpose of this book to provide information and suggestions for social work education and practice.

Casualties: Visible and Invisible

As a result of vast improvements in medical skills and technology, the current wars are producing far fewer deaths among U.S. combatants than our last prolonged war in Vietnam. Wounded Soldiers are whisked from the battlefield to advanced field hospitals in the war zone, where their wounds are stabilized. Soldiers are then flown to major U.S. military hospitals outside the theater of operations, usually to Germany, where they receive more advanced treatment. If patients cannot return to combat, they are then airlifted to the preeminent military hospitals—Walter Reed Army Medical Center in Washington, D.C., and Bethesda Naval Hospital in Maryland—or one of the military hospitals specializing in treatment of certain wounds, such as the burn center at Brooke Army Medical Center in San Antonio, Texas. Many of the wounds that would have been fatal in previous wars require amputation and extensive rehabilitation.

These service members are then treated and returned to duty or, in most cases, discharged from active duty and transitioned to the Department of Veterans Affairs (VA) for further medical care, often for the rest of their lives. Such are the visible wounds of war.

War produces invisible wounds as well, and the current wars bear this out. The signature invisible wounds associated with the current conflicts require significant and often long-term treatment and readjustment and reintegration of the war veteran to society. Both the Defense Department and the VA have acknowledged the widespread scope of the problem, on the basis of several recent credible studies as well as the VA's forty years of experience with Vietnam veterans.

Three invisible signature wounds of the current war have emerged. They are PTSD, major depressive disorder and depressive symptoms, and traumatic brain injury (TBI; Tanielian & Jaycox, 2008). According to a RAND Corporation study, "Most [Operation Enduring Freedom and Operation Iraqi Freedom] veterans will return home from war without problems and readjust successfully, but many have already returned or will return with significant mental health conditions. Among OEF/OIF veterans rates of PTSD, major depression, and probable TBI are relatively high, particularly when compared with the general U.S. civilian population" (Tanielian & Jaycox, 2008, p. xxi).

Much has been learned about PTSD since the 1970s. It was first defined in the American Psychiatric Association's *Diagnostic and Statistical Manual III* (*DSM III*) in 1980, and its criteria have been refined in subsequent editions of that publication. Briefly, we know that PTSD sufferers can be affected emotionally (e.g., anger, fear, anxiety), cognitively (e.g., altered worldview), biologically (e.g., psychosomatic illnesses), and behaviorally (e.g., isolation, substance abuse), all of which combine to negatively affect interpersonal relationships with family and friends. We also know that those persons close to the veteran with PTSD can suffer secondary traumatic stress or vicarious trauma. As a result, divorce and domestic violence in some warriors' families have become commonplace.

Major depression was not considered an invisible wound of war until recently. Much needs to be learned about war-induced major depression. Certainly, the loss of friends and comrades may trigger depressive episodes. And depression and PTSD have been linked to suicidal tendencies. This book features a separate chapter devoted to suicide, as a result of the record numbers of suicides associated with our current war fighters and veterans.

Traumatic brain injury (TBI) is the third invisible signature wound of the current wars. The enemy cannot win on the conventional battlefield, so it has turned to weapons that are simple to manufacture and employ—improvised explosive devices (IEDs). Explosive material, large and small, can be fashioned into lethal weapons that can be detonated remotely to destroy vehicles and to maim or kill personnel. Persons exposed to IED blasts may develop mild, moderate, or severe brain injury, which results in temporary or permanent cognitive impairment.

The Sexual Assault Epidemic

Sexual assault and sexual harassment have been persistent problems in the U.S. military for years. They seem to pervade every activity of military life. Despite strict codes of conduct, sexual assault and harassment happen at the service academies, which produce the upper crusts of commissioned officers. They happen on the battlefield and in the rear areas of combat zones. Rear areas are logistical and administrative semipermanent support bases; service members may come under attack in those areas, but they rarely see anything but the installation where they work. They happen at military installations nationwide. They have been the subject of several official investigations, inquiries, and government hearings, and yet they persist. Sexual assault can lead to serious mental health problems, such as PTSD and depression. An understanding of the sexual assault phenomenon in the military is essential for social workers in general, who will undoubtedly encounter survivors in mental health settings.

Congresswoman Jane Harman (2008) explicitly describes the current problem:

> The stories are shocking in their simplicity and brutality; a female recruit is pinned down at knifepoint and raped repeatedly in her barracks . . . [by] her fellow soldiers. During a routine gynecological exam, a female soldier is attacked and raped by her military physician. Yet another young soldier, still adapting to life in a war zone, is raped by her commanding officer. Afraid for her standing in the unit, she feels she has nowhere to turn. (n.p.)

The real-life situations Harman describes are not isolated incidents. The congresswoman visited the West Los Angeles VA Health Center, where she met with female veterans and their health-care providers. The hospital staff reported that

41 percent of female veterans there say that they were victims of sexual assault while in the military, and 29 percent report having been raped during their military service. The women veterans reported their continued terror and the feelings of helplessness that hampered their readjustment to civilian life. Harman (2008) reiterated the sad fact that women serving in the U.S. military are more likely to be raped by a fellow Soldier than killed by enemy fire in Iraq.

Department of Defense (DOD) records show the same pattern. In 2006, 2,947 sexual assaults were reported—73 percent more than in 2004. Apparently, the DOD has been unable or unwilling to prosecute rapists. According to the department's own statistics, a mere 181 of 2,212 subjects (8 percent) investigated for sexual assault in 2007 (including 1,259 reports of rape) were referred to courts-martial. In nearly half the cases investigated, the chain of command took no action, and in the majority of those that were acted on, the offenders were assigned administrative or nonjudicial punishment. Harman (2008) calls these "slaps on the wrists" (n.p.). In more than one-third of the unpursued cases, the commander reported insufficient evidence as the reason for inaction. This is in stark contrast to the civil justice system, where 40 percent of those arrested for rape are prosecuted, according to the Department of Justice and the Federal Bureau of Investigation (Harman, 2008).

Is the Department of Defense involved in a cover-up of its sexual assault problem? Some in Congress seem to think so. During the same hearing referred to earlier, the DOD refused to allow the civilian chief of its Sexual Assault Prevention and Response Office to respond to the subcommittee's subpoena. Perhaps the DOD did not want to explain why it had taken three years to name a twelve-person civilian task force to look into the sexual assault problem in the military. The task force was appointed early in 2008 (U.S. Government Accountability Office [GAO], 2008a).

The subcommittee heard testimony from several other witnesses, including Lieutenant General Michael D. Rochelle, the Army deputy chief of staff, who serves as the Army's chief of personnel, who stated that 12 percent of reported rapes in the military involve male victims (Wright, 2008). Representative Christopher Shays stated that he had no confidence in the DOD and the armed services regarding sexual assault, and he wondered how recruiting would be affected when young women learned that their chances of being sexually assaulted were one in three and when young men learn that one in ten is raped while in the military (Wright, 2008).

In August 2008, the Government Accountability Office (GAO) released the report *Military Personnel: DOD's and the Coast Guard's Sexual Assault Prevention and Response Programs Face Implementation and Oversight Challenges*. The GAO found that, although "DOD and the Coast Guard have taken positive steps to respond to congressional direction by establishing policies and a program to prevent, respond to, and resolve reported sexual assault incidents involving Servicemembers . . . DOD's guidance may not address some important issues. . . . [I]mplementation of the programs is hindered by . . . (1) inconsistent support, (2) inconsistent effective[ness], and (3) limited access to mental health services" (GAO, 2008b, p. 11).

The GAO goes on to elaborate on these institutional shortcomings in the remainder of the lengthy report. At least as troubling as these findings, the GAO has good reason to believe that the actual number of sexual assaults in the military exceeds the rates reported. Of the 103 service members who responded to the GAO survey that they had been sexually assaulted during the preceding twelve months, 52 revealed that they did not report the incident. Many such assaults go unreported because service members think that reporting will negatively affect their career (GAO, 2008b). Other commonly cited reasons for not making a report include "(1) the belief that nothing will be done; (2) fear of ostracism, harassment, or ridicule by peers; and (3) the belief that their peers would gossip about the incident. . . . [R]espondents also commented that they would not report because of concern that they would be disciplined for collateral misconduct, such as unauthorized drinking . . . or concern that such a report would not remain confidential" (GAO, 2008b, p. 37).

The GAO provided several recommendations for the DOD and Coast Guard to remedy the discrepancies found in its report. Both agencies concurred with the GAO's findings and recommendations. Still, on March 9, 2010, the *New York Times* reported that, according to the DOD, reports of sexual assault had increased 11 percent in the preceding year, including a 16 percent increase in combat areas (Bumiller, 2010).

In December 2009 the DOD Task Force on Sexual Assault submitted its findings to the secretary of defense, which found that DOD had made progress in assisting sexual assault victims by changing reporting procedures so that law enforcement and command authority were not directly involved. The task force also recommended that Congress enact a comprehensive justice privilege to protect communication between the victim of sexual assault and his or her victim advocate. Additional recommendations are as follows:

1. Ensure service members who report they were sexually assaulted are afforded the assistance of a nationally certified victim advocate.
2. Ensure victims understand their rights, including the opportunity to consult with legal counsel to minimize victim confusion during the investigative process.
3. Improve medical care for victims of sexual assault, particularly those in deployed areas.
4. Inform victims and service members of disciplinary actions related to sexual assault.

The recommendations were derived from data collected at 60 sites worldwide. Task Force members interviewed 3,500 people regarding the problem. They included military justice legal, administrative and support personnel. (U.S. Department of Defense, Office of the Assistant Secretary of Defense [Public Affairs], 2009, December 4)

Conclusion

For any nation to successfully prosecute a war, its leaders must understand the nature of the war that they find themselves in. These protracted U.S. wars have raised questions for our leaders that are yet to be resolved. So, too, social workers who encounter survivors of war must be prepared for both the visible and the invisible signature wounds associated with these wars. With respect to the sexual assault epidemic, social workers must understand that the enemy is sometimes within the ranks of those sworn to defend our way of life and core values.

This book elaborates on such issues in the hope that all involved in this national tragedy, from policy makers to practitioners, caregivers, and indeed warriors and their families, will learn about and take heed of the costs of courage.

The American Profession of Arms

Tell my sister do not weep for me, and
Sob with drooping head.
When troops come marching home
Again, with glad and gallant tread,
But to look upon them proudly, with a
Calm and steadfast eye,
For her brother was soldier, too,
And not afraid to die.
—**Caroline Elizabeth Norton**, "A Soldier of the Rhine," 1850

Chapter Overview

This chapter is presented in two sections. The first is an introduction to the profession of arms. The latter introduces the military family as an integral inseparable part of the American profession of arms because of the unique demands of military life.[1]

The American Profession of Arms

A profession exists to serve the society from which it springs. Professions serve society by carrying out or providing specific functions that the society needs, such as the clergy, law, medicine, and the military. Academic disciplines, one being social work, are also professions. Professions are, in essence, unique subcultures with several distinct markers that identify them as apart from the greater society

---

[1]We have elevated the Marine Corps above the Navy and Air Force intentionally for the purposes of this book because the Army and the Marine Corps are performing the preponderance of ground combat functions in Iraq and Afghanistan. We intend no slight to our brothers and sisters on the sea and in the air.

they serve. Professions take on symbols that the public readily associates with the profession's unique functions. Professions also maintain and grow distinct bodies of knowledge on which they operationalize their services and functions. They set the standards for their performance and establish codes of ethics that define acceptable practice. They may even adopt certain standards of dress, as does the profession of arms.

The military is different from other professions in that success or failure in performing its duties may be the determining factor in the survival of the nation. General of the Army Douglas MacArthur (1962) said it best in his farewell address to the Corps of Cadets at West Point: "Yours is the profession of arms—the will to win, the sure knowledge that in war there is no substitute for victory, that if you lose, the nation will be destroyed; that the very obsession of your public service must be Duty—Honor—Country" (p. 3).

Military professionals, upon taking the required oath of office, accept an unlimited liability clause that means that they may be placed in danger of losing their lives when they willingly swear to support and defend the U.S. Constitution against all enemies, foreign and domestic. Note that the military professional does not swear to blindly follow any supreme leader, people, or government. The military profession is devoted to a higher calling, that of defending the Constitution. The moral principles that appear in our founding documents, the Constitution and the Declaration of Independence, form the foundation for the military profession's moral and ethical standards. Central to the profession's concept of service to nation is civilian control of the U.S. military, which since the American Revolution has been the rule in the American defense establishment.

Department of Defense

The Department of Defense (frequently referred to as the Pentagon or the DOD) is the capstone headquarters of the U.S. armed forces. The DOD is headed by the secretary of defense, a civilian political appointee who serves at the pleasure of the president. There are three departments subordinate to the DOD—Army, Navy, and Air Force—each managed by civilian secretaries whom the president also appoints. Those three departments, as well as the Marine Corps (a Navy service), are each headed by four-star flag officers. The Army, Air Force, and Marine Corps are headed by generals who constitute the Joint Chiefs of Staff. The Navy's chief of naval operations, a four-star admiral, is also a member of the Joint Chiefs of Staff. All report to their individual service secretaries, but in national emergencies they report directly to the secretary of defense and the president.

The Coast Guard is also an armed service, but it falls under the secretary of homeland security. It is commanded by a four-star admiral—the Coast Guard commandant. In war or other national emergencies, the president usually transfers some or all Coast Guard assets to the Navy. The combined all-volunteer armed services, including both full-time and National Guard and Reserve personnel, are referred to as the total force.

Total Force Demographics for Social Workers

The data contained in this section are based on the work of Watkins and Sherk (2008).

Enlisted Personnel

Contrary to common belief, the men and women enlisted in the total force in 2006 and 2007 came from middle-class and upper-middle-class family economic backgrounds. Low-income families are underrepresented in the U.S. military. In 2007, 49.3 percent of recruits came from families with incomes of more than $51,000, whereas 29 percent came from families with incomes of less than $42,000 (Watkins & Sherk, 2008).

Also contrary to widespread perceptions, enlisted recruits are not poorly educated. In 2007, fewer than 1.4 percent of recruits had not completed high school or high school equivalency, compared with 20.8 percent of American men overall between the ages of eighteen and twenty-four who had done so. Service members are not poorly educated, because military training entails intense theoretical and practical training in various fields, not unlike a university experience. Enlisted recruits typically have not completed college because they enlist before beginning their college experience, and many choose to take advantage of the military's educational benefits when they leave the service (Watkins & Sherk, 2008).

Some Americans believe that racial minorities account for the majority of those enlisted in the armed forces. However, 65.5 percent of enlisted recruits in 2007 were white, 12.82 percent were black, 3.25 percent were Asian or Pacific Islander, 1.96 percent were American Indian or Alaskan, and 3.42 percent were a combination of two or more races or declined to self-identify race-ethnicity. Hispanics are underrepresented among enlisted recruits. In 2006, Hispanics accounted for 20.02 percent of the U.S. male population age eighteen to twenty-four, whereas the percentage of Hispanics in the total recruits in 2006 was 13.19 (Watkins & Sherk, 2008).

It comes as no surprise that the strong military tradition in the U.S. South has continued: 42.97 percent of enlistees in 2007 were from that region. In contrast, the Northeast is underrepresented among enlisted recruits, with only 12.81 percent of the total number of recruits volunteering for service in 2007 from that region (Watkins & Sherk, 2008).

Officer Corps

In the United States the typical military officer comes from an affluent family and is highly educated. In the Army, both Reserve Officers' Training Corps (ROTC) and West Point graduates tend to come from high-income neighborhoods with median incomes of more than $50,000. As for new officer accessions, 94.9 percent hold at least a bachelor's degree, whereas only 25 percent of all Americans between twenty-four and twenty-seven years old could make the same claim in 2006 (Watkins & Sherk, 2008).

The racial composition of ROTC graduates in 2007 was 71.89 percent white (compared with white males between eighteen and twenty-seven comprising 70.18 percent of the population nationwide), 12.04 percent black (compared with black males of the same age group representing 9.96 percent of the population nationwide), and 7.98 percent Hispanic (among the same age group of Hispanic males nationwide). American Indian and Alaskan and Asian or Pacific Islander ROTC graduates were represented proportionately to their numbers in the general population. The numbers for West Point graduates in 2007 reflect similar trends (Watkins & Sherk, 2008).

As with enlisted recruits, with the one notable exception, the South produces the most new officers, at 36.72 percent. The Northeast follows with 24.3 percent, the Midwest with 20.20 percent, and the West with 18.68 percent of the total number of new officers.

Watkins and Sherk (2008) conclude that "the men and women who serve in America's all-volunteer military do not come disproportionately from disadvantaged backgrounds. Instead the opposite is true. Both active-duty enlisted troops and officers come disproportionately from high-income neighborhoods—a trend that has increased since 9/11" (p. 13).

Watkins and Sherk (2008) assert that America's troops are educated and highly trained, even if the lower ranks have not yet achieved a college degree. Enlisted recruits have above-average intelligence and are far more likely than their civilian peers to have a high school degree. Nearly all members of the officer corps have at least a four-year college education—far greater than the rate in the civilian population. The racial composition of the military is similar to that of the civilian population, although whites and blacks are slightly overrepresented among enlisted recruits.

Another popular misperception is that many Soldiers join the military because they lack better opportunities. This generality is wrong. In all likelihood, our Soldiers would have career opportunities in the private sector, depending on the economic climate at the time they enlist—as they would have opportunities no matter what the economic climate. The officers and enlisted men and women of the armed forces have made sacrifices to serve in the U.S. military (Watkins & Sherk, 2008).

Military Subculture

To establish credibility with warrior clients, practitioners must understand the nature of the military culture and be willing to strive to understand and accept the nature of combat, as well as the stresses it places on combatants (Kudler, 2010).

The American military subculture rests on four distinct pillars that set it apart from mainstream culture. First, strict discipline forms the basis of the military's organizational structure. Second, the military relies on loyalty and self-sacrifice to maintain order in battle. Third, rituals and ceremonies shared among warriors create common identities. Fourth, warriors are connected to one another by the military's emphasis on group cohesion and esprit de corps (Kudler, 2010).

When conversing with a warrior, practitioners should expect the use of military and sometimes service-specific acronyms and slang. Warriors will often use "military speak," and they may intertwine swear words into their communication (Kudler, 2010).

Privileges of Rank

Nowhere is tradition more evident in military culture than in its rank structure and the everyday deference of junior rank to those who are more senior. Rank insignia is worn on the uniform and reflects both experience and professional expertise. Social workers serving warriors and veterans should be very aware of a client's rank, and on initial contact, they should refer to and address individuals by their rank and continue to do so until the client indicates otherwise.

All ranks below officers refer to them as sir or madam (or ma'am) or by their rank, as their documents or uniform insignia indicate. Both second and first lieutenants are addressed as lieutenant, warrant officers as mister or "Ms.," and chief warrant officers (CWOs) as mister or "Ms." or chief. Keep in mind that the most senior CWO is technically junior to a newly commissioned second lieutenant. All generals, regardless of seniority, are referred to as Sir or Madam or General.

All noncommissioned officers (NCOs) are referred to by their insignia of rank, and they are not referred to as sir or madam. A much-repeated military adage is, "Don't call me sir. I work for a living." It is important to refer to the most senior NCOs by their rank (e.g., sergeant major, first sergeant for Army). Each service has its own labels for its most senior NCOs, which have changed over time.

Junior enlisted personnel are addressed by their rank and last name (e.g., airman, private, private first class, seaman, lance corporal). All personnel render hand salutes when outdoors to all officers, but not NCOs, who are senior to them. Officers return salutes as a sign of respect for those junior to them. Officers' and senior NCOs' spouses have no special rank or privileges because of their spouses' status in today's military. This is the policy, but it has not always been the case. The old policy that an officer's wife speaks with the authority of her husband is an old habit that has persisted despite declarations to the contrary, and it has caused consternation, frustration, and resentment among young families who have been taught that in matters of family the egalitarian model is to prevail.

For social workers who serve military members, veterans, and their families, an invaluable resource on military pay, insignia of rank, benefits, entitlements, veterans' benefits and entitlements, and other essential information is *The Annual Uniformed Services Almanac* (Gordon, Gordon, & Smith, n.d.). It is a low-cost paperback resource that should be on every practitioner's bookshelf.

Army

You may fly over a land forever; you may bomb it, atomize it, pulverize it and wipe it clean of life—but if you desire to defend it, protect it, and keep it for civilization, you must do this on the ground, the way the Roman legions did, by putting your young men into the mud.

—**Fehrenbach**, 1963, quoted in U.S. Army, 2005

The Army is the largest and oldest of the armed services. Its purpose is to protect and defend the United States and its interests by dominating the war on the ground. It does so by participating with the other armed services in joint operations. The Army is made up of Soldiers. The Army culture draws heavily on the rich history and traditions that date back to the colonial militias of the seventeenth century. History and traditions maintain Soldiers' awareness of who they are; the nation they serve; and their ties to those who have fought, suffered, and prevailed over enemies of old (U.S. Army, 2005).

The Army, as well as the other armed services, includes two components. The active component comprises full-time personnel. The reserve component comprises part-time citizen-soldiers who belong to either the U.S. Army Reserve (USAR) or the U.S. Army National Guard (USARNG). The major difference between the Reserve and the National Guard is that the former reports directly to Army Headquarters, and the latter reports to the governor of the individual state to which it is assigned, except when mobilized for federal active duty. In 2007, the Army had 47 percent of its authorized force in the active component. Citizen-soldiers make up more than half of the Army today. They tend to be older than the overall active component total force (Tanielian & Jaycox, 2008).

Today's Army is diverse. One in every seven Soldiers is female. Fifty-four percent of Army personnel are married, and 46 percent have children. In 2005, the Office of Army Demographics identified a total of 712,895 family members and other dependents of active Army personnel. The reserve component is 49 percent married, and 42 percent have an average of two children (Maxwell, 2005).

Marine Corps

Marines are sometimes referred to as infantry of the Navy. The Marine Corps traces its history to Philadelphia, where at Tun Tavern two battalions of Marines were created on November 10, 1775. Marines fought valiantly in several battles including the Battle of Princeton in the Revolutionary War in 1777. The Marine Corps' specialty is amphibious operations, which involve assaulting, capturing, and controlling beachheads. However, Marines have become involved in ground combat alongside Army forces. They currently fight in Iraq and in landlocked Afghanistan. The Marines rely on the Navy for certain logistical and administrative support. There are no medical professionals in the Marine Corps. The enlisted medics who accompany Marines on the battlefield are specially trained Navy personnel called corpsmen. In 2008 there were approximately 20,000 officers and

173,000 enlisted Marines on active duty (Marine Corps Community Services, 2008). There is no Marine Corps National Guard, but the highly trained Marine Corps Reserves are called on to support the active duty force when needed.

The Marines are generally regarded as the most tradition-bound branch of the American profession of arms. The distinctly recognizable Marines dress uniform is steeped in the history of the Marine Corps and has not been substantially modified for many years. In contrast, the other services have changed their uniform designs many times. Marines have no need to search for an identity: They know who they are. A popular slogan reminds them, "Once a Marine, always a Marine."

Navy

The Continental Congress established the Navy in 1775, when it was clear that war with England was inevitable. The Navy's role in our national defense strategy is to control the seas. The Navy can project tremendous military power through its surface ships' heavy guns and ballistic missiles and through its subsurface fleet of submarines with surveillance systems and ballistic missiles. The Navy is a major component of our nuclear deterrence effort. The Navy can project ground power through its troopships and Marines. Naval aviation aboard aircraft carriers provides close air support to ground troops and protects the fleet via air-to-air combat. The active-duty Navy comprises approximately 54,000 officers and 325,000 enlisted Sailors. The Naval Reserves provide administrative and logistical support not only to naval units ashore but also to all branches of our deployed joint armed forces, as in Afghanistan and Iraq. The Navy has no National Guard as such, but a few maritime states have formed naval militias.

Air Force

The Air Force is the youngest of the four major branches of the military. The Air Force traces its history as far back as the War between the States, when the opposing armies began using hot-air balloons to observe enemy activity. The Army controlled the fledgling air service (called by different names at different times). All that changed after World War II. In 1947, the National Security Act created the Air Force as a separate and equal partner with the Army and Navy within the Defense Department. The Air Force exists to project our national military might in air and space. It operates aircraft of all types, including fighters; bombers; and reconnaissance, troop, and cargo carriers. It is responsible for all military satellites. The Air Force controls all our strategic nuclear missile forces. Approximately 65,000 commissioned officers and 260,000 enlisted personnel constitute the force. Twenty percent of the Air Force is women. Family members of active duty personnel number more than 490,000. The Air Force is supported by highly deployable Reserves and the Air National Guard.

Coast Guard

The Coast Guard is considered a military service; however, it does not fall under the Department of Defense. It answers to the Department of Homeland Security (DHS). During times of conflict, the president can and often does transfer Coast Guard assets to the Department of Navy. The commanding officer of the Coast Guard is a four-star admiral, the commandant. The Coast Guard was formed in 1790 as the Revenue Marine. After several name changes and organizational developments, it became known as the Coast Guard in 1915.

The Coast Guard's mission includes the prevention and deterrence of terrorist attacks, the security of our maritime borders, immigration control (working with other DHS agencies), drug interdiction, and maintaining the free flow of commerce. The Coast Guard comprises a military and civilian active workforce of approximately fifty thousand and reserves numbering around ten thousand personnel. Men make up 89 percent of the force; 78 percent of the Coast Guard is white. Married officers number 37 percent, and 29 percent of the enlisted ranks are married. The Coast Guard works with various seagoing vessels, fleets of both helicopters and fixed-wing aircraft, and an abundance of high-technology surveillance equipment to accomplish its mission.

The Military Family: An Integral Part of the American Profession of Arms

The final section of this chapter introduces social workers to the unique institution that is the military family. Later in this volume we elaborate on much of what we introduce here as we deal with the effects our current conflicts have produced among our warriors and their families. What follows is based on the most recent data available as contained in Booth et al.'s (2007) comprehensive report *What We Know about Army Families: 2007 Update*. Although the other military branches have their service-specific challenges, this Army-based data can be generalized throughout the military, particularly the Marine Corps, for it is the Army and Marines who are bearing the brunt of the ground combat today.

According to the report, "the major factor influencing the career decisions of married Soldiers who leave the Army is not salary or lack of opportunities for advancement but rather an inability to balance the demands of work and family" (Booth et al., 2007, p. 5) This problem is exacerbated by the sacrifices required in recent years to contend with frequent deployments and redeployments to places like the Sinai Peninsula, Somalia, Haiti, Bosnia, Kosovo, and finally Afghanistan and Iraq.

Also important is the evolving definition of family. The military recognizes that the traditional nuclear family (husband in uniform, wife at home with the children) is not the norm, as it was twenty or thirty years ago. There are extended families, multicultural and multiethnic families, blended families, single-parent families, dual-career families, military members in committed relationships, and combinations of these. At the time of writing, Congress and the services are coping with the repeal of the so-called Don't Ask, Don't Tell law. Openly serving homosexual families will add to the diversity of family relationships.

This section is structured to briefly address (1) characteristics of Army families and Army life, (2) deployment, (3) unique issues for reserve component (RC) families, (4) well-being of Army families, and (5) children in Army families (Booth et al., 2007).

Characteristics of DOD Service Member Families

Dependent family members outnumber military members in all services. In 2009, there were 3,093,709 family members and 2,258,757 military members across the DOD. Most military children are younger than five years old. African Americans constituted 26 percent of DOD service members in 2009, and Hispanics, 10.5 percent. Women service members represent 14.3 percent of the total DOD force. Fourteen percent of female service members are single parents; 54 percent of all active-duty Soldiers are married (USDMDC, 2009).

The following demands are common for Army families: deployment and separation, intense training, war, long and unpredictable work hours, risk of death or injury, frequent relocations, and foreign residence. There is much pressure to perform to high expectations, and families are becoming more reluctant to blindly accept Army expectations (Booth et al., 2007).

Deployments, Separation, and Reunion in Active-Duty Families

Since the U.S. terrorist attacks on September 11, 2001, family separation as a result of deployment has become more frequent and unpredictable. By 2003, the

Army had surpassed the Navy in average number of nights away from family, which has negatively affected spousal satisfaction with Army life. Spouses of junior enlisted Soldiers are less likely to be prepared for deployment and separation, and the longer the deployment, the more difficult it is for them to accept. In addition, deployments with no fixed departure or return dates are the most difficult for spouses to handle.

The deployment challenges and strains the family. Families fear for the Soldier's safety, living conditions, and health. Family members become lonely and apprehensive about adapting to new and unfamiliar roles. Lack of or negative media reporting about the war effort creates even more stress. For example, during the two weeks between Michael Jackson's death and memorial service, thirteen American Soldiers and Marines were killed on the battlefield, and an unreported number were wounded. These deaths and wounds went unreported.

Particularly vulnerable to deployment and separation distress are younger families, families with a pregnant spouse, families whose Soldier deploys alone to join an unfamiliar unit in-country, and families with multiple problems and special needs.

During the postdeployment phase, when the Soldier has rejoined the family, household roles and routines have to be renegotiated. Soldiers must reconnect with their children. Because combat changes the people who survive it, the family may have to adjust to changes in the Soldier's mood and personality. Physical wounds require family support to heal, as do the invisible wounds, such as posttraumatic stress disorder, major depression, and traumatic brain injury. Sadly, but realistically, these challenges may take a lifetime of care giving, thus spawning increased incidences of domestic violence and divorce (Booth et al., 2007).

Unique Issues for Reserve Component Service Members and Families

Reserve component (RC) service members serve in all five services branches. The Army National Guard traces its history back to the seventeenth-century colonial militias. The Army and Air National Guards have a dual role of serving the individual states and augmenting the active-duty Army and Air Force when required.

Reserve component service members tend to be older and to have been married longer than active component (AC) members. They are more likely to have spouses who are employed full-time because they relocate less frequently.

Like the AC, they must handle parenting and work demands while deployed. They tend to live away from military installations, and so they have fewer available formal social support systems than are in place for the AC. This is an advantage of sorts, because RC service members tend to have closer ties with their respective communities.

During the early days of the global war on terror, RC families did not expect to experience mobilization and deployment. Many did not attend predeployment briefings. Therefore, they were not aware of how to prepare for deployments and separation. Fewer than one-third of RC spouses were knowledgeable about benefits and entitlements available to them while their service members were in federal active-duty status. They were unaware of military support services, including the TRICARE health-care coverage program. They were unfamiliar with the Uniformed Services Employment and Reemployment Act (the federal law that guarantees reemployment of RC warriors after they return from deployment and are released from active duty). Data from 2005–2006 studies show that overall preparedness among RC families has improved somewhat, as deployments among the RC have become more commonplace. Families of National Guard members report more active support and assistance than Reserve members, as reservists deploy more frequently as individuals rather than with an affiliated organization.

As the war on terror has progressed over the years, the RC and the DOD have put in place new programs, such as family assistance centers; Military One-Source (a 24/7 toll-free information and referral telephone service); and community outreach partnerships with civilian, faith-based, and veterans' organizations. These efforts have paid off: most RC family members reported that they coped relatively well in 2005–2006 studies.

Reserve component families experience much the same readjustment challenges as AC families during the transition from active to inactive status, but they require more attention to issues like transitioning from military health-care programs to VA or other civilian systems. The RC places less emphasis on reintegration than the AC, a challenge it has yet to overcome.

It is important for social workers to understand that mobilization can adversely affect RC families' financial well-being. The transition to the active-component pay system from the reserve-component pay system has not been as seamless and effective as desired. Some RC families see their monthly income decrease by more than $1,000 on entrance to active duty.

Well-Being in Army Families

According to Booth et al. (2007), "The Army takes a holistic approach in its definition of well-being and links well-being directly to organizational goals. The
Army Well-Being Strategic Plan defines well-being as 'the personal—physical,
mental, and spiritual—state of Soldiers . . . and their families that contributes to
their preparedness to perform and support the Army's mission'" (p. 4). In general,
social-psychological aspects of well-being include such factors as quality of life,
family adaptation, mental and physical health, marital satisfaction, and financial
health (Booth et al., 2007).

Quality of Life

Roughly half of Army spouses are satisfied with life in the military. Officers'
spouses are most satisfied, and spouses of lower-ranking Soldiers are least satisfied. Spouses are satisfied with the benefits of military life, such as commissaries,
exchanges, and health care. They are least satisfied with the way military life affects the balance between work and family, such as family separations because
of deployment requirements, availability of affordable child care, and pay (Henry
J. Kaiser Family Foundation, 2004).

Family Adaptation

Most (66 percent) Army spouses don't consider military demands a serious problem. However, spouses of deployed Soldiers do report more work-family conflict,
as do spouses of junior enlisted Soldiers. Also, research has linked work-family
conflict with overall marital satisfaction and decisions to leave the military (Henry
J. Kaiser Family Foundation, 2004; Segal, 1989).

Mental and Physical Health

Mental health disorders, such as clinical depression and alcoholism, among Army
spouses are low according to self-reports. Stress is a factor in mental health disorders given the nature of the Soldier's work. Young enlisted spouses consider
combat duty a serious problem, whereas the spouses of more senior Soldiers report less stress from worrying about their Soldier's participation in combat. The
lack of economic, psychological, and social support resources all contribute to
younger spouses' stress. Other spouse groups at increased risk are the foreign
born and those with young children (Booth et al., 2007).

Soldiers also report significant stress in their personal lives, although they report work-related stress to be higher than stress in their personal lives. Deployments and family separations are significant negative contributors to both mental and physical health. Those who return from war with invisible and visible wounds must be comforted and understood by their loved ones, which adds still more stress to families (Booth et al., 2007). All these factors may have contributed to the slight increase in child abuse since the current wars began. Overall, spouse abuse rates have declined, but there is a disturbing increase in severe spouse abuse that appears to correlate with deployments of more than six months and multiple deployments (Booth et al., 2007). Although divorce rates among military families was originally assumed to have increased because of deployments to Afghanistan and Iraq, a recent study by the RAND Corporation indicates otherwise (Karney & Crown, 2007).

The U.S. Department of Defense Task Force on Mental Health (2007) is committed to service members and their families. The task force's vision states: "Service members and their families will be psychologically prepared to carry out their missions. Service members and their families will receive a full continuum of excellent care in both peacetime and wartime, particularly when service members have been injured or wounded in the course of duty" (p. ES-2).

Children in Army Families

Children of military families are not much different from their civilian peers despite common stereotypes of the military brat that persist in some circles even today. They do face stressors such as deployment of parent Soldiers, family separation, and frequent moves from base to base. These are challenges that families are meeting relatively well. The most important factor in helping children cope successfully is the parent's reactions to those military-specific challenges.

Even though military children relocate more frequently than their civilian counterparts, as a group they tend to perform better in academic pursuits. Also, younger children experience fewer problems with relocations than do adolescents (Booth et al., 2007).

Military leaders must strive to create a family-friendly environment. If the Soldier's spouse believes that the military community is a good place to raise children, he or she is likely to support the service member's choice to remain in the military. If the spouse's perception is negative, the military may lose good men and women (Booth et al., 2007).

Part Two

The Problem

Combat Stress Injuries

Mental Health Stays Are Up in Military: Disorders Outpaced Injuries in 2009.

—**G. Zoroya**, 2010a

Introduction

This chapter addresses the invisible wounds of war, specifically what have been generally acknowledged as the three signature wounds of the current conflicts in Iraq and Afghanistan: posttraumatic stress disorder (PTSD), major depressive episodes (MDEs) and subsequent major depressive disorder (MDD), and traumatic brain injury (TBI; Tanielian & Jaycox, 2008).

A Government Accountability Office (GAO, 2008a) report found that significant numbers of ground-combat Army and Marine Corps service members are exposed to combat experiences, which are often associated with an increased risk of developing PTSD or other mental health conditions. According to a 2004 study, more than half of Army and Marine Corps ground combat units in Operation Enduring Freedom (OEF) and Operation Iraqi Freedom (OIF) reported being shot at or receiving small-arms fire and seeing dead or seriously wounded Americans or injured civilian noncombatants. More than half of Marine Corps service members and almost half of Army service members reported killing an enemy combatant in OIF (GAO, 2008a).

The GAO report also found that multiple deployments are associated with mental health problems. For example, a 2006 Army mental health advisory team report found that Army service members who had been deployed more than once were more likely to screen positive for PTSD, depression, or anxiety than those deployed only once (GAO, 2008a).

Today's warriors are also exposed to events such as blasts, which increase their risk of experiencing a TBI, which occurs when a sudden trauma causes damage to the brain. Traumatic brain injury can result in lack of consciousness, confusion, dizziness, trouble with concentration or memory, and seizures. Of particular concern are the aftereffects of a mild TBI that may not be readily apparent immediately. Identification of mild TBI is important, as treatment has been shown to mitigate its effect (GAO, 2008a).

Most mental health practitioners are familiar with the diagnostic criteria for PTSD that the current *Diagnostic and Statistical Manual* sets forth. In our discussion of PTSD, we have decided to share the opinion of Jonathan Shay (2009), who believes that mental health professionals should move away from thinking of combat PTSD as a disorder and toward a more reasonable construct—injury—for the following reasons.

According to Shay (2009), injury is more culturally acceptable, less stigmatizing, less of a barrier to seeking help. The relation between injury and subsequent complications is typically clearer and mind-sets more proactive than for the relationship between illness and subsequent complications of that illness. Medics and/or corpsmen and military surgeons think about preventing complications of wounds, such as hemorrhage and infection. Shay proposes that everything would be greatly simplified, and still in accordance with the facts, if we viewed the primary psychological injury as persistence into the time after danger, horror, and/or deaths of comrades has passed, as well as valid psychological and physiological adaptation to that traumatic situation.

Modern military medicine has come a long way toward controlling the complications of physical battlefield wounds. The military mental health community must find ways to control the complications of combat stress injuries, and among its highest priorities is ensuring that combat veterans do not feel dishonored by combat stress injuries.

In *Combat Stress Injury*, Figley and Nash (2007) elaborate on combat stress injury. The authors believe that Shay's (2008) logic also should apply to MDD, TBI, and PTSD. It is in this context that this chapter describes the characteristics, prevalence, and costs of these three signature wounds of our current conflicts.

Posttraumatic Stress Disorder

The *Diagnostic and Statistical Manual of Mental Disorders—Text Revision (DSM IV)* provides the diagnostic criteria (characteristics) of PTSD, an anxiety disorder:

persistent reexperiencing of a traumatic event via distressing intrusive thoughts, dreams, reliving of the event, and intense psychological and physiological distress when exposed to cues that resemble the event; persistent avoidance of thoughts, activities of the trauma, inability to recall aspects of the trauma, detachment of others, inability to have intimate feelings such as love, and no expectation for a normal life span, career, marriage, or children; and persistence of increased arousal (e.g., sleep problems, irritability or anger, difficulty in concentration, hypervigilance, exaggerated startle response). The duration of the symptoms must exceed one month. The symptoms listed here must cause clinically significant distress in social, occupational, or other important areas of functioning. The condition is considered acute if the symptoms last fewer than three months and is considered chronic if the symptoms last three months or more. Symptoms may not present until long after the stressor: PTSD is considered to have delayed onset if symptoms present at least six months after the stressor (American Psychiatric Association, 2000). It is important to understand that the effects of combat stress injuries are individualized. Many, if not most, combat veterans will not experience PTSD, but a significant portion of war fighters do. We discuss the prevalence of the disorder later in this chapter.

Major Depressive Episode

According to the *DSM IV*:

> The essential feature of a Major Depressive Episode is a period of at least 2 weeks during which there is either depressed mood or the loss of interest and pleasure in nearly all activities. . . . The symptoms must persist for most of the day, for at least 2 consecutive weeks. . . . To count toward a Major Depressive Episode, a symptom must either be newly present or must have clearly worsened compared with the person's preepisode status. . . . The episode must be accompanied by clinically significant distress or impairment in social, occupational, or other important areas of functioning." (American Psychiatric Association, 2000, p. 349)

The *DSM IV* criteria for MDE are as follows:

> Five or more of the following symptoms must be present during the same 2-week period, one of which must be (1) depressed mood or (2)

loss of interest or pleasure. **Note**: Do not include symptoms that are clearly due to a medical condition, or mood-incongruent delusions or hallucinations. Symptoms include: (1) depressed mood most of the day, nearly every day; (2) diminished interest or pleasure in all, or almost all activities most of the day; (3) significant weight change, (4) insomnia or hyper-insomnia nearly every day; (5) psychomotor agitation . . . nearly every day (observable by others); (6) fatigue or loss of energy nearly every day; (7) feelings of worthlessness or excessive or inappropriate guilt; (8) diminished ability to think or concentrate; and (9) recurrent thoughts of death (not just fear of dying) [or] recurrent suicidal ideation. (American Psychiatric Association, 2000, p. 356)

The most serious consequence of MDE is attempted suicide or suicide (APA, 2000; see chapter 5). The U.S. Department of Defense Deployment Health Clinical Center (DHCC) uses a brief acronym, SIGECAPS, to describe MDE symptoms:

S   sleep problems

I   interest deficit

G   guilt, worthlessness, hopelessness, regret

E   energy deficit

C   concentration deficit

A   appetite disorder (increased or decreased)

P   psychomotor retardation or agitation

S   suicidal thoughts or tendencies (n.p.)

The National Survey on Drug Use and Health (NSDUH, 2008) provides a useful summary of MDE and veterans:

An estimated 9.3 percent of veterans aged 21 to 39 (312,000 persons) experienced at least one MDE in the past year. Among veterans aged 21 to 39 with past year MDE, over half reported severe impairment in at least one of four role domains (i.e., home management, work, close relationships with others, and social life), and nearly one quarter (23.5 percent) reported very severe impairment in at least one of the domains. More than half (59.6 percent) of veterans aged 21 to 39 who experienced past year MDE received treatment for depression in the past year. (pp. 1–2)

Major Depressive Disorder

Major depressive disorder (MDD) is a mental condition that frequently co-occurs with PTSD (Krupnick, 2008).The *DSM IV* diagnostic features for MDD are as follows:

> The essential feature of Major Depressive Disorder is a clinical course that is characterized by one or more Major Depressive Episodes. . . . For purposes of this manual, an episode is considered to have ended when the full criteria for the Major Depressive Episode have not been met for at least 2 consecutive months. . . . Major Depressive Disorder is associated with high mortality. Up to 15 percent of individuals with severe MDD die by suicide. (American Psychiatric Association, 2000, pp. 369–371)

The University of Michigan Health System provides this description of the incidence of depression in the VA health-care system: "Nearly a third of veterans who are treated at VA health care centers have significant depressive symptoms, and about 13 percent have clinically diagnosed depression. . . . Depression is a 'very potent' risk factor for suicide among people receiving treatment for depression at the VA with a suicide rate that is three times higher than that of the overall patient population" (University of Michigan Depression Center, 2009, n.p.).

Suicide is most common among veterans between the ages of eighteen and forty-four, in contrast to both the general population and VA patients receiving treatment for depression in the VA system. The latter two comparison groups tend to be much older (Zivin, 2007).

Traumatic Brain Injury

According to the RAND Corporation, "traumatic brain injury (TBI) is getting increased consideration in the wake of the current military conflicts. TBI is associated with decreased levels of consciousness, amnesia, and other neurological irregularities; skull fracture; and intracranial lesions; and it can lead to death" (Tanielian & Jaycox, 2008, p. 6).

Explosive munitions have caused 75 percent of all U.S. casualties resulting from the wars in Iraq and Afghanistan. Such devices include improvised explosive devices, car bombs, rocket-propelled grenades, mortars, and rockets (Institute of Medicine [IOM], Committee on Gulf War and Health, 2008).

The *DSM IV* does not cover TBI. The following excerpts from the IOM Committee on Gulf War and Health's (2008) report provide introductory information for social workers to understand the phenomenon:

> Damage to the brain after trauma (for example, a blow or jolt to the head, a penetrating head injury, or exposure to an external energy source) is referred to as a TBI. A TBI may be open (penetrating) or closed and is categorized as mild, moderate, or severe depending on the clinical presentation. According to the National Center for Injury Prevention and Control (NCIPC), a mild TBI is manifest as a brief change in unconsciousness or amnesia. Mild TBI is often referred to as a concussion. (p. 14)

Higher education is striving to cope effectively with returning veterans in the university environment, as TBI can cause functional impairments in affected student veterans. Problems can be cognitive, such as slower thinking, judgment, attention span, and concentration. Perceptual problems with hearing, vision, touch, and balance may present in the classroom environment. Motor skills, endurance, headaches, and pain sensitivity may also present as physical problems. Behavioral problems such as irritability, impulse, and mood changes can affect classroom effectiveness. Some problems may be of psychiatric origin, such as paranoia, depression, hallucinations, and suicidal ideation. Some of these problems mimic symptoms of PTSD (Church, 2009).

The RAND study (Tanielian & Jaycox, 2008) provides a cogent summary of the prevalence of PTSD, major depression, and TBI among our combat troops participating in the wars in Iraq and Afghanistan:

> The assembled research to date on the prevalence of post-combat mental health and cognitive issues among Service members deployed to Afghanistan and Iraq supports five broad generalizations:
>
> 1. PTSD is more prevalent than depression among deployed Service members, and it affects roughly 5 to 15 percent of Service members, depending on who is assessed and when they are assessed; the prevalence of depression among Service members ranges from 2 to 10 percent, also depending on when assessed and who is assessed.
> 2. Many studies employ the same screening tools, making prevalence estimates across studies generally comparable. However, the criteria

used across most of these studies to identify PTSD and depression have not been validated and do not identify a substantial portion of those who actually have these conditions.

3. Because different studies have been conducted at different periods during deployment and post-deployment, comparing across studies suggests the prevalence of PTSD and depression increases as the time since returning from deployment increases.

4. Across studies, Service members who experience combat exposure and who have been wounded are more likely to meet criteria for PTSD.

5. Service members deployed to Afghanistan and Iraq are more likely to meet criteria for PTSD and depression than nondeployed troops, although those deployed to Iraq have higher rates of PTSD and depression than those deployed to Afghanistan.

If we apply the range of prevalence estimates for PTSD (5 to 15 percent) and depression (2 to 10 percent) to the 1.64 million Service members who have already been deployed, we can estimate that the number of Service members returning home with PTSD will range from 75,000 to 225,000 and with depression from 30,000 to 150,000. The precise number depends on how many of all deployed Service members are at increased risk for these outcomes—specifically those deployed with direct combat experience, those who have been wounded, and the military service of which they are a part. As we reiterate . . . we do not yet have a sound basis for estimating numbers for TBI. We hypothesize that, regardless of its cause, the need for mental health services for Service members deployed to Afghanistan and Iraq will increase overtime, given the prevalence of information available to date and prior experience with Vietnam. Policy makers may therefore consider the figures presented in these studies to underestimate the burden that PTSD, depression, and TBI will have on the agencies that will be called upon to care for those Service members now and in the future. (Ramchand et al., 2008, pp. 54–56)[2]

---

[2]One can safely supplement the word *agencies* to encompass family, friends, and associates as well. Other chapters in this volume elaborate on this issue.

Governmental Responses to Combat Stress Injuries

Let us strive to finish the work we are in: to bind up the nation's wounds: to care for him who shall have borne the battle, and for his widow and for his orphan.

—**Abraham Lincoln**, Second Inaugural Address, March 4, 1865

A man who is good enough to shed his blood for his country is good enough to be given a square deal afterwards.

—**Theodore Roosevelt**, July 4, 1903

Introduction

This chapter deals with the two major departments that have responsibility for war fighters and veterans and, to some extent, their families. Social workers need to understand the challenges service members encounter in accessing and receiving quality care from the two very different agencies charged with providing for their health care. The chapter begins with an introduction to the overall Department of Defense Military Health System, including information on how the services prevent where possible, and treat when necessary, combat stress casualties in the war zone. The remainder of the chapter provides a description of the Department of Veterans Affairs, highlighting both similarities and differences in philosophy and approach.

Department of Defense

The DOD Military Health System (MHS) provides health care to service members and their families through a variety of programs and seeks to ensure that its policies are implemented properly throughout the system. The Army, Navy (including the Marine Corps), and Air Force deliver health care directly to their members and families via military treatment facilities (MTFs) in accordance with DOD policy; the facilities employ uniformed medical personnel, who are supplemented as needed by contracted civilian health professionals.

A major component of the MHS is TRICARE. According to a study by Burnam et al. (2008) for RAND Corporation, "roughly 9 million active duty Service members, active duty family members, retirees, families of retirees are eligible to receive medical care through TRICARE" (p. 253). TRICARE provides care through MTFs and in the civilian health-care market.

Service members with mental health problems may find help from military chaplains who are embedded with operational units. The chaplain may be the first step in obtaining access to quality mental health care. What a service member discusses with a chaplain is confidential and as such can remove the stigma that often accompanies help seekers in military organizations. Chaplains often refer service members to other mental health resources, such as unit-embedded mental health providers. We have found no evidence to suggest that religiosity is a concern that service members consider when seeking assistance from a chaplain.

All of the services have begun to assign military mental health providers to operational combat units. These providers, often social workers, get to know the unit and its people. They become trusted and accepted. They know the challenges that service members face in negotiating for access to quality of care. However, practice with these providers is not confidential, and if the unit commander determines that he or she has a need to know about a service member's status, the provider is required to release it.

Counseling provided by community service programs is kept confidential. These counseling centers can be found at local military installations. Counseling sessions are not recorded in the service member's medical record. Service members found to have major mental health problems, such as major depression or PTSD, are referred to the MTF if the individual counselor deems the condition beyond his or her level of competence.

The MTF is the primary source for mental health care. Because of mental health personnel shortages across the services, active-duty service members have treatment priority. Treatment is usually outpatient, although some MTFs have inpatient programs available. The DOD is currently implementing plans to provide more mental health treatment at primary care facilities. The treatment team at such integrated facilities will include a primary care professional, a care manager, and a mental health professional. Visiting such dual-purpose facilities should work to reduce the stigma that can accompany a service member's visit to a mental-health-only clinic.

Military OneSource is an information and consultation service provided to all service members of the active and reserve components and their family members. Activation status is not considered. Retired or separated personnel and their families may use the service, which is available 24/7, for six months after separation. Callers to Military OneSource with, for example, an emotional or family problem are connected with a consultant. Consultants triage the caller's problem and refer the caller for up to twelve free counseling sessions; if consultants determine that the caller has a major mental disorder, they refer the caller to an MTF, a VA hospital or Vet Center, or a TRICARE professional. Military OneSource consultants are well educated at the master's level and licensed appropriately. Consultants follow the caller's treatment and remain in close communication until the case is concluded satisfactorily. The program is designed to help callers from all geographic locales, including rural and remote areas. Program transactions are confidential unless consultants determine that the caller is a threat to him- or herself or others.

The 2008 RAND report identified several challenges in meeting the mental health demands of service members. First, DOD outpatient care behavioral health clinics operate during standard workday hours. Given the current operational tempo, units return from deployment and begin training rigorously for the next deployment. To receive mental health treatment, service members must be absent from training to attend those appointments. Unit commanders are rightfully protective of available training time because good training saves lives. Service members are reluctant to ask for time away, given the stigma associated with the reason for absence.

Second, there are not enough uniformed mental health professionals on staff, and there is not enough funding to hire more. Funding shortfalls at the DOD make it impossible to provide adequate mental health care to service members and their families. In spite of the grueling operational tempo, the DOD has reduced the number of active-duty mental health providers in favor of civilian contractors. It is the active-duty mental health professional that accompanies units into combat, and according to the Army, 33 percent of Army providers have high levels of burnout, a situation the Army did not even consider until recent years.

Third, military providers offer much that civilian contractors cannot. They understand the culture and the social context of the services. They are the ones who can best determine fitness for duty. Both patients and commanders find it easier to trust a mental health specialist in uniform than one who is not (Burnam et al., 2008).

Social workers need to understand how the military outside the medical community handles the issue of combat stress. The underlying concepts that guide operational units are described in detail in the services' training literature. The following is from a U.S. Marine Corps (USMC, 2000) publication:

> *Combat stress* is described as the mental, emotional, or physical tension, strain, or distress resulting from exposure to combat and combat-related conditions. Controlling combat stress is a command responsibility. In terms of Service members lost from action and reduced performance, combat stress seriously affects mission accomplishment. It is every leader's responsibility to take action to strengthen Service members' tolerance to combat stress and manage it in his or her unit.
>
> Combat stress reactions (COSR) are the result of exposure to the same conditions during military actions that cause physical injury or disease in battle or its immediate aftermath, and many combat stress reactions occur in persons who are wounded or ill with disease. Rates of combat stress casualties vary greatly, with higher ratios during lengthy periods of intense combat. In Okinawa in 1945, during a peak month of battle, the combat stress casualties among Marine forces were reported as high as one for every two wounded in action (WIA). Under less lengthy periods, as suggested by data acquired from Israeli Defense Forces fighting in Lebanon in 1982, the ratio of combat stress casualties to WIA in small units can be as high as one to one. In the past, we have generally suffered as many as one battle stress casualty for every three to five WIA in heavy fighting. However, highly trained units with strong leadership and high esprit de corps have fewer combat stress casualties.
>
> This USMC publication's purpose is to inform small-unit leaders of stress characteristics and management techniques in order to *prevent, reduce, identify*, and *treat* combat stress reactions in the Service member's own unit to the maximum extent possible. A significant part of training is learning to control and cope with stress. Leaders must learn

to cope with their own stress and then assist junior personnel in managing their stress. The application of combat stress management techniques helps conserve fighting strength and provides one more step toward achieving success. (n.p.)

The Marine Corps and Army have similar combat stress control (CSC) programs. They rely on the same manuals and instructions for guidance. The CSC programs consist of three phases. The Army terms those phases *predeployment, deployment,* and *postdeployment.* The Marine Corps uses the terms *predeployment, deployment and combat,* and *postcombat.*

During the predeployment phase the focus is on rigorous training for the unit's next combat encounter. Training occurs primarily at the Marine Corps home base or Army post. This is sometimes referred to as garrison or home-station training. Predeployment training includes such activities as becoming familiar with task assignments, unit training and rehearsing for missions, conducting supply and equipment checks, and preparing for changes in sleep patterns and jet lag. Also, service members receive as much information about the upcoming deployment as operational security will allow. New members are integrated into the unit so they can quickly become team members. New significant others are introduced into the unit's family readiness network. These include all significant others, or loved ones, not just legal dependents.

Unit members are familiarized with the stressors they can expect to encounter in combat, which is immediately followed with information on how the unit is to respond to those situations. Stress reduction training should be conducted with the assistance of USMC and Army Combat Stress Control unit personnel if available (USMC, 2000).

During the deployment and combat phase, leaders work to keep the information flow going with regular meetings and briefings. Uncertainty is a major source of stress for service members. Without frequent communications encounters with unit leaders, rumors can become rampant and destructive. Leaders must provide feedback to unit members so they know that they performed well as a group. Accomplished missions help develop a winning attitude, build unit cohesion, and reduce the effects of stress.

Service members need to be ensured that their families and loved ones are being taken care of while they are away. Confidence in Service Family Support and Assistance programs, the American Red Cross, the USO, and other community organizations that provide support to families goes a long way toward relieving stress and anxiety.

Ministry teams of chaplains and chaplains' assistants are integrated into combat units. In addition to holding religious services, counseling, and administering the sacraments, chaplains provide care focusing on preventing mild and moderate combat stress reactions.

While in the war theater, during and between periods of combat the Army and Marine Corps have units and personnel assigned and tasked with preventing and managing service members who show signs of unhealthy combat stress reactions. These units are called combat stress control (CSC) teams.

The mission of the Army's CSC team is straightforward and simple: provide prevention and treatment as close to the Soldier's unit as possible to keep the Soldier with the unit. The CSC team functions as a force multiplier, which means that it focuses on preserving the fighting strength of the Soldier. Importantly, this is done with the Soldier's chain of command, always the first line of combat stress prevention. In theory, only when problems become too great for the direct line leaders do CSC teams become involved.

The guidelines (doctrine) for treating Soldiers suffering from combat operational stress reactions (COSR) follow six basic principles: brevity, immediacy, centrality, expectancy, proximity, and simplicity, or BICEPS (Moore & Reger, 2007).

The first BICEPS principle is brevity. Critical event debriefings should take no more than two to three hours. If rest and replenishment are required, they should take place for no more than three or four days. The principle of immediacy requires that CSC activities take place as soon as possible. Centrality means that if brief evacuation is called for, it should take place as close to the service member's unit as possible. Hospitalization is to be avoided unless there is no alternative. It is vital that affected service members think of themselves not as sick or as patients, but as war fighters. The principle of expectancy involves advising warriors that they are recovering from combat stress and will be rejoining their unit as soon as possible. Proximity is similar to centrality and emphasizes that treatment take place as close to service members' operational unit as possible so that they can maintain contact with their fellow warriors. The principle of simplicity means that combat stress control is not psychotherapy. The goal is to rapidly restore warriors' coping skills so they can return to the fight (USMC, 2000).

Prevention of combat stress casualties is the CSC unit's first responsibility. A CSC team performs prevention at the operational-unit level. The team normally consists of a psychologist, a social worker, and two enlisted mental health specialists. The team is mobile and is located where it is most needed as combat operations flex and adjust to new situations. Prevention is conducted through educational and informational means, such as flyers and brochures. Briefings are provided and include but are not limited to subjects such as suicide awareness, home-front issues, and stress and anger management. Enlisted CSC team members circulate among the unit and talk with enlisted service members about their concerns. These conversations are Soldier to Soldier and occur without the fear of stigmatization, which might occur if officer personnel were involved. If more extensive care is called for, the team's psychologist or social worker may become involved in a brief individual counseling program. The CSC teams can also be involved in crisis event debriefings, which allow Soldiers to process what happened in a safe environment (Moore & Reger, 2007).

The CSC units also use fitness teams when treatment at CSC facilities is required. The fitness team normally comprises a psychiatrist or psychologist, a psychiatric nurse, an occupational therapist, and mental health and occupational specialists.

The fitness concept is based on ensuring rest and replenishment. While at fitness, service members have the opportunity to sleep, through basic sleep hygiene techniques or, in more severe cases, through medication. They can receive more intensive help with stress management, relaxation training, and home-front issues. With proper rest and replenishment, most cases that fitness teams see return to their unit and are mission capable (Moore & Reger, 2007).

The postcombat (Marines) or postdeployment (Army) phase presents its own stressful challenges. Today, it is merely hours from the battlefield to the home front. Before leaving the combat theater, units should conduct end-of-tour debriefings so that service members can process their memories, good and bad, from predeployment and combat to the end of the operation. This is the time for rituals such as awards and recognition. Unit leaders, chaplains, and CSC teams should prepare service members for reunion with their families (USMC, 2000). Reunions present their own crises, as described elsewhere in this book.

Recent developments in the Army over the past decade have produced training programs designed to build psychological and emotional resilience among Soldier war fighters and their families. The original program was called Battlemind Training (BMT), "mental health training—pure and simple. . . . The model is evidence-based, experience-based, explanatory, and focuses on strengths rather than weaknesses" (Castro, 2009, p. 254).

At its beginning, Battlemind Training was a postdeployment training session. It rapidly grew to a system designed to build resilience in Soldiers and their families throughout all phases of the deployment cycle (Huseman, 2008). Battle-mind Training has been validated, and it works.

Soldiers who received BMT (p <.01) reported fewer PTSD symptoms at three months postdeployment than did Soldiers who received the standard stress edu-cation training. Depression symptoms for Soldiers who received BMT were only marginally significantly lower than for Soldiers who received stress education (p <.10; Castro, 2009).

The evidence is that BMT reduces the stigma of seeking and participating in mental health care. According to Soldiers' self-reports, participants in BMT have fewer sleep problems than those who received standard stress education train-ing (Castro, 2009).

Battlemind Training has recently evolved into resiliency training, and it is to be offered Army-wide under the umbrella program Comprehensive Soldier Fit-ness (CSF). Army Chief of Staff George W. Casey Jr. describes this new initiative as follows: "This is one of the most important programs the Army has intro-duced in a long time. . . . CSF will work because it is a program focused on self-improvement, and Soldiers are always trying to improve themselves" (Hames, 2009, par. 5). The latest on CSF is published in the 2009 U.S. Army Posture State-ment: "The Army Comprehensive Soldier Fitness (CSF) program was established to increase the resilience of Soldiers and Families by developing their strengths in all important domains: emotional, spiritual, and family, in addition to physical. The CSF will ensure that all Soldiers undergo an assessment of their total fitness. The results of the assessment will direct individualized training, intervention, or treat-ment programs as needed" (Comprehensive Soldier Fitness Program, 2009, n.p.).

One such training program deserves mention here. The Warrior Resilience and Thriving program was developed by Major Thomas A. Jarrett, the current so-cial work services chief at Fort Sill Oklahoma. The training has been presented to 850 Soldiers deployed in Iraq. The program's objectives are to enhance resiliency; to impart rational emotive behavior therapy; to promote the seven Army values (honor, loyalty, personal courage, respect, duty, selfless service, and integrity); to inspire warriors by examples of real-life role models of resiliency in the Army; to reduce barriers to care; and to reinforce those resiliency traits that warriors em-ploy daily (Jarrett, 2008). The program received high marks in immediate client satisfaction surveys.

It is too early to evaluate the effectiveness of CSF, as it is still in the devel-opment stage. Not enough time has elapsed for longitudinal studies to take place. The earlier BMT evaluations were encouraging, however. During these

early days of CSF, it is very important for social workers and other helping professionals who work with military personnel and their families to stay up to date
using Internet sources.

The Department of Defense programs for handling combat stress injuries in
the ranks are extensive but generally underfunded. The evidence is that budget
priorities lay with equipment and not with warriors. This seems an odd phenomenon, as weapons do not fire without people trained to use them, and military
efforts to maintain the fighting strength through leadership and CSC programs,
however successful because of human effort, seem shortchanged. At this point,
we move to the services and programs offered by the Department of Veterans
Affairs (VA) to identify and treat combat stress injuries.

Department of Veterans Affairs

The Department of Veterans Affairs, commonly referred to as the VA, has as its
mission serving America's veterans and their families by promoting the health,
welfare, and dignity of all veterans. Veterans' entitlements, or benefits, represent the tangible appreciation of a grateful nation. The United States has the
largest and most comprehensive system for veterans of any nation in the world.
This benefits system traces its roots back to 1636, when the pilgrims of Plymouth
Colony were at war with the Pequot Indians. The pilgrims passed a law that
stated that the colony would support disabled Soldiers (U.S. Department of Veterans Affairs, 2010a).

Separation from military service and entrance into the VA medical system
has been shown to present a major problem for some individuals who have been
receiving DOD health care. The transition to VA care is supposed to be seamless,
but in reality it is not for the all too many injured veterans who need to continue
their care uninterrupted in the VA environment. Both the DOD and the VA have
had electronic medical records systems for years, but they are not compatible
with each other. Therefore, relevant patient treatment data fail to reach the VA
system. And in certain situations, like call to active duty and deployment of a veteran receiving care from the VA back to the DOD health-care system, there are
inadequate communication systems available for the VA to provide patient data
to the DOD. Both situations threaten continuity of care (Burnam et al., 2008). The
DOD and the VA have been working on the problem for years, but the time of
this writing, the "seamless" transition was far from perfect.

The VA performs its mission through three major subordinate organizations:
the Veterans Health Administration (VHA), the Veterans Benefits Administration

(VBA), and the National Cemetery Administration (NCA). We confine our discussion to the VHA because it operates the veterans' health system.

The VHA is the largest integrated health-care system in the nation. It is organized into twenty-one Veterans Integrated Service Networks (VISNs). The VISNs offer primary and specialty care and a comprehensive pharmaceutical program. The VISNs are semiautonomous, and they develop cost-effective health-care services that suit the national VA system as well as the geographic regions for which they are responsible. The VHA operates medical centers (VAMCs) and community-based outpatient clinics (CBOCs) that provide primary and specialty care. These are staffed by VA employees and contract employees. The VHA can arrange to purchase services from private providers if required (Burnam et al., 2008).

Because the VA is funded by the discretionary budget process, it must compete with other departments for adequate operating funds from Congress each year. Therefore, by necessity, services available to veterans are prioritized. There are eight levels of prioritization: (1) veterans with service-connected disabilities, (2) prisoners of war, (3) those who have received the Purple Heart for wounds in combat, (4) veterans with catastrophic disabilities unrelated to service, (5) low-income veterans, (6) veterans who meet certain specific criteria (e.g., service in the Gulf War), (7) higher-income veterans, and (8) those who do not qualify for a higher priority.

All veterans who have served in Iraq and Afghanistan during periods of combat, except those with dishonorable discharges, are eligible to receive free VA health care for five years from the date of separation, whether or not they have a service-connected injury or illness. Social workers and other helping professionals need to encourage all veterans to enroll at the nearest VA health-care facility immediately after separation. Service members must enroll to receive VA health care. In addition, enrollment may benefit war veterans later, as many combat stress and physical injuries are detected not at separation but months and even years later, when it becomes difficult to demonstrate that an injury is indeed connected to service.

The VA provides overall guidance for mental health services within its Comprehensive Mental Health Strategic Plan, implemented in 2005, and the *Handbook on Uniform Mental Health Services in VA Medical Centers and Clinics*, published in 2008 (Katz, 2010b; U.S. Department of Veterans Affairs, 2008).

Specialized mental health services are available within the VA for PTSD. Currently, the VA offers a mix of on-site and off-site programs for evaluating and treating PTSD. The VA's approach promotes early recognition of individuals who meet formal criteria for diagnosis, as well as those with subthreshold symptoms. The goal is to make evidence-based treatments available early to prevent chronic symptoms and lasting impairment. Each VAMC offers some type of specialized expertise with PTSD, which results in a network of more than two hundred specialized treatment programs and trauma centers. In addition, many VAMCs offer walk-in clinics that provide immediate care. In addition to the national inpatient and outpatient programs, some VAMCs run their own local specialized PTSD programs (Burnam et al., 2008, p. 265).

In addition to the programs for PTSD, the VA also provides care for major depression. Services for the depressed, the second most prevalent illness treated by the VA, are found integrated into primary care settings. Only about 25 percent of patients being treated for depression in primary care environments require referral to a specialized mental health setting (Burnam et al., 2008).

The demand for mental health care has increased not only because of the numbers of service members returning from the current wars; more Vietnam veterans are seeking mental health care. Because that population is aging, the Vietnam cohort may present with physical health problems, and later evaluation may require referral to mental health services for help that they may not have known was needed or were unaware of the treatment opportunities available from the VA. As the number of veterans has increased, the number of clinic visits per veteran has decreased. This is distressing, because dropouts are not receiving time-consuming but effective evidence-based treatment regimens. Seal et al. (2010) found that "only 4 per cent of OEF and OIF veterans receiving non-PTSD mental health diagnoses and less than 10 per cent receiving PTSD diagnoses attended nine or more VA mental health treatment sessions in 15 weeks or less in the first year of diagnosis" (p. 13).

Family members of veterans are sometimes eligible for VA services. "There are three categories of family members to whom the VA may provide services: (1) family members of veterans receiving treatment for service-connected disabilities; (2) family members of veterans receiving treatment for non-service-connected disabilities . . . if such services are necessary in connection with the veteran's treatment, and (3) family members of combat veterans receiving readjustment counseling services" (GAO, 2008c, p. 3).

At a recent congressional hearing, Dr. Ira Katz (2010a), the VA's deputy chief for mental health services, reported two positive trends in the postdeployment mental health of OEF and OIF veterans: (1) suicide among veterans in VA care has declined by 12 percent since 2001; and (2) the number of homeless veterans on any given night in 2007 was approximately 154,000. The number in 2009 was 107,000, a significant decline.

Readjustment Counseling Service: Vet Centers

The Readjustment Counseling Service (RCS) offers services to any veteran who has been in a war zone, including free and confidential evaluation, education, and counseling at its three hundred Vet Centers located in communities throughout the nation. Vet Centers are not collocated with other VHA hospitals and clinics; therefore, they help alleviate stigma for help-seeking veterans.

Vet Centers are staffed with four or five personnel who are managed by a team leader. Staff include social workers, psychologists, psychiatric nurses, and sometimes paraprofessional counselors. More than one-third of all staff are OEF and/or OIF veterans. The Vet Centers have added one hundred OEF and OIF veterans to conduct outreach to their fellow war-on-terror veterans. Approximately 60 percent of staff are combat veterans who have lived through the readjustment experience themselves. Women account for 42 percent of all Vet Center staff. Each counselor is trained in standardized, proven psychotherapies, such as exposure therapy, cognitive-behavioral therapy, and cognitive processing therapy. They are also trained in TBI recognition and assessment and suicide prevention. If a veteran's problem requires more intensive treatment, he or she is referred to a VAMC (Katz, 2010a).

Each veteran receives an individualized treatment plan after a thorough assessment. The plan includes the forms of treatment thought best for the veteran's needs. This may be individual, group, or family therapy, or a combination thereof. Unlike the DOD and the VA, Vet Center records are kept confidential and completely separate from other VA medical records. Individual consumers of Vet Center services must provide permission to release their information to any outside authority. Vet Centers have reported large increases in client visits as troops return from the current wars (Burnam et al., 2008).

The following data on Vet Center use in fiscal 2009 are from RCS headquarters. The 232 Vet Centers in operation during that period saw 174,362 combat veterans and provided more than 1,188,145 visits to veterans and family members. Of all veterans receiving Vet Center services, 70,429 (40 percent) were not seen at any other VHA facility. Since the beginning of hostilities in Afghanistan and Iraq through September 30, 2009, the Vet Centers saw 424,398 OEF and/or OIF veterans, of whom 307,186 were outreach contacts seen primarily at military demobilization and National Guard and Reserve sites, and 101,133 were provided substantive readjustment counseling services at Vet Centers. Vet Centers have touched 40 percent of all separated OEF and/or OIF veterans.

In addition, Vet Centers have provided bereavement services to surviving family members of service members killed on active duty. This successful new program has provided support to more than 2,400 family members of more than 1,939 fallen warriors, 1,152 of whom were killed in action in OEF and OIF.

Fifty mobile Vet Center units have been added at locations across the country, increasing the outreach effort to provide access to services in rural and remote locations. The mobile units also are available for emergencies. Four mobile Vet Center units were dispatched to Fort Hood after the shootings there. As of early March 2010, mobile units have attended 1,472 outreach events (Batres, 2010; Katz, 2010a).

The VHA Readjustment Counseling Service's Vet Center program is more than thirty years old, and it has proved a resounding success. It has become an international model for combat veterans' readjustment in Australia, the former Soviet Union, El Salvador, Croatia, and Kosovo.

Innovations by the VHA and RCS Vet Centers

The VA has engaged in several innovations in their efforts to support veterans. The National Coalition for Homeless Veterans has worked for the past twenty-two years to end homelessness of veterans. On March 23, 2009, at a VA summit to end veteran homelessness, President Obama addressed the participants: "With this budget, we . . . provide new help for homeless veterans, because those heroes have a home—it's the country they served, the United States of America. And until we reach a day when not a single veteran sleeps on our nation's streets, our work remains unfinished" (quoted in Driscoll, 2009). A theme at the VA summit was the need to have more cooperation between the VA and other federal and community providers. The plan to do so focuses on six activities: outreach, treatment, employment and benefits, community partnerships, prevention, and housing support services for low-income veterans (National Coalition for Homeless Veterans, 2010). The goal is to end homelessness within five years.

Another innovation is the VetSuccess on Campus program, launched by the VA in 2011. The program will partner with colleges' and universities' student services and other academic units to create collaborative services so that campuses are more friendly and welcoming to veteran students. Early surveys indicate that veteran students find that an atmosphere of "welcome home" exists on only a few campuses. There will be many partnerships developed to make this collaboration work and to bring this atmosphere to more campuses. The research that emerges from these partnerships will contribute to identifying best practices for working with veteran students.

The Vet Centers are already doing outreach on college campuses with success, as a result of the confidentiality of their record keeping. If veterans hope to return to military service after they complete their education, then they don't want the DOD to be able to access their mental health records through the VA, where mental health records are not protected by legislation. This is a real fear, as veterans may be denied opportunities to return to service because of mental health issues. This issue also applies to individuals whose work requires security clearances and background checks, such as police work. The University of Alabama and the Birmingham Vet Center have collaborated through the Campus Episcopal Church, Canterbury Chapel, for more than a year to provide an office for outreach counselors to meet with student veterans on campus. The outreach counselors also use the office to provide services to veterans in rural western Alabama. Innovations such as these will contribute to the graduation rates of student veterans.

Another innovation that is showing success is the VA's outreach to veterans caught up in criminal activity or in the criminal justice system (Castille, n.d.; U.S. Department of Veterans Affairs, 2008). The exact numbers of veterans serving time in prison is unknown. It is believed that 10 percent of the individuals in state or federal prisons are veterans. According to Holbrook (2011), some estimates are that one-quarter of veterans who experienced heavy combat have been involved with the criminal justice system upon returning to the United States. It is commonly believed that the veteran's criminality is associated with PTSD. Kulka et al. (1990) compared veterans with PTSD with veterans without PTSD and found that close to half of the former had been involved in some type of criminal activity, most often involving alcohol and drug abuse. Other countries that have sent soldiers or marines to Afghanistan and Iraq are finding similar results to those in the United States (Travis, 2009). A Soros senior justice fellow at the Justice Policy Institute, Guy Gambill (2010, par. 5) writes, "Through what data we do have, as well as *anecdotal* information from around the country, it's clear that the problem of veterans returning home only to end up behind bars is colossal—and getting worse."

The VA has responded to this by collaborating with the justice system to create the Veterans Justice Outreach Initiative. The initiative aims to prevent the criminalization of mental illness by following a sequential intercept model. The first contact point with veterans is initial detention in jail and court hearings; the second is jail, courts, forensic evaluations, and commitments to treatment; the last is reentry from jails, prisons, forensic hospitalizations, community corrections, and courts. The VA carries out the initiative mostly through its transition and outreach programs. The VA medical centers and Readjustment Counseling Service (RCS) Vet Centers have established partnerships with a range of criminal justice officers, from police and sheriff's departments to judges, prosecutors, and community health providers. The veterans' courts and justice initiatives have established a deterrent to nonviolent offenses committed by veterans with mental illness, so that they are adjudicated more reasonably with interventions by the VA medical center and RCS. The Veterans Justice Outreach Initiative may also lead to better interventions and investigations of suicides among incarcerated veterans and criminal offenses that lead to the death penalty for individuals with mental illness, such as PTSD (Alvarez & Sontag, 2008; Sontag, 2008; Sontag & Alvarez, 2008a, 2008b; Wortzel & Arciniegas, 2010; Wortzel et al., 2009). The VA is also working on intimate partner violence, interventions for driving under the influence, and gambling addictions. These programs may become part of the ongoing services that the VA offers.

Both the DOD and the VA are huge bureaucracies that receive frequent criticism in the press. Some of the criticism is deserved, such as the Army's former policy of discharging Soldiers with PTSD for behavioral problems caused by combat stress. The VA has lost thousands of patient data files on lost or stolen laptop computers. Members of Congress have accused the VA of covering up the number of suicides among veterans who use VA services. Both institutions have been and are affected by the political whims of whoever sits in the White House or in the halls of Congress. Neither the DOD nor the VA has ever received the needed funding to see to the combat stress needs of warriors and their families. Nevertheless, these are systems that service members and veterans must navigate. Social workers and other helping professionals can be of great help in this effort.

Suicide and the Warrior

Soldiers killed themselves at the rate of one per day in June (2010) making it the worst on record for Army suicides. There were 32 confirmed or suspected suicides among soldiers in June. . . . Only the Marine Corps has a higher suicide rate.

—**G. Zoroya**, 2010a

Introduction

Suicide is one of the most difficult experiences for any of us to comprehend (Schneidman, 1996). It is hard to understand the depth of pain, despair, and loss of hope that the individual who commits suicide feels. Suicide is a leading cause of death in the United States. According to the American Foundation for Suicide Prevention (2011), approximately 32,000 individuals commit suicide every year, and national statistics show that 650,000 people arrive in emergency rooms each year having attempted suicide (Goldsmith, Pellmar, Kleinman, & Bunney, 2002). According the World Health Organization, more than eight hundred thousand suicides occur globally each year; some estimates are more than a million suicides per year (Krug, Dahlberg, Mercy, Zwi, & Lozano, 2002). These statistics may underestimate the true numbers, given suspicious deaths and individuals who do not go to the emergency room and consequently are not included in statistics on suicide. Historically, men in the United States are four times more likely than women to commit suicide (Dublin & Bunzel, 1933); that trend has not changed much today (Joiner, 2005). Sadly, combat veterans are increasingly committing suicide. Statistics demonstrate that veterans are committing suicide at a rate that far exceeds that of the nonveteran population (Hampton, 2007; Kaplan, Huguet, McFarland, & Newsom, 2007).

We do not know exactly how many suicides there are each year as a direct result of combat experience, most notably from the Afghan and Iraq wars. Although there are some generally agreed-on numbers, we cannot eliminate so-called accidental deaths, which may in fact be suicides. Shay (2008) shares a communication with a military officer who noted the number of motorcycle accidents that have occurred among recently returning veterans. The officer referred to the deaths as a "holocaust," and Shay suggests that these deaths may well be suicides that go unnamed as such. The DOD is so concerned about these accidents that it has begun motorcycle training and safety courses in several places.

Suicide Theory

Until recently, suicide was not a common topic of study, although it was mentioned in the literature and in religious treatises. Statistics on suicide do not reveal the true percentage of the population that commits suicide. Ivanoff and Riedel (1996) identify factors that present errors and bias in making estimations from the statistics:

> (1) The choice of statistics used to make estimates, (2) sub-cultural differences in hiding suicide, (3) the effects of different degrees of social integration, (4) the failure to keep statistics on salient subgroups, (5) significant variations in the social imputations of suicide motives, (6) the failure to assess and record accurately certain self annihilation behaviors as suicide, and (7) more extensive and professionalized collection of statistics among certain populations. (p. 2359)

Suicide is not believed to be the result of a single disease or event. Gunnell and Lewis (2005) identify several possible factors that may predict suicidal behavior, including depression, schizophrenia, psychosis, serotonin deficits, early childhood abuse, sexual assault, a family history of self-harm, access to the means of committing suicide, terminal physical illness, impulsiveness, social and environmental stressors, and war.

Durkheim (1897/1951) was the first to develop a methodology for studying suicide. He identified three categories of suicide: (1) egoistic suicide, (2) anomic suicide, and (3) altruistic suicide. He argued that the first two categories represented individuals who were poorly integrated into society and individuals who were highly integrated into society, respectively. The anomic category represents individuals who have lost social integration through trauma or catastrophe.

One of the best-known suicide theorists is Schneidman (1996), who introduced the notion that humans can be divided into two groups—suicidal and non-suicidal. He further divides the suicidal group into committed, attempted, and threatened. He argues that suicide comes from psychological and emotional pain, which he calls "psychache," which is preceded by denied or distorted psychological needs. This pain becomes intense and overwhelming. Another factor in Schneidman's suicide theory is lethality. When individuals become suicidal, they learn not to fear lethal self-harm, and they come to believe that suicide is the only solution to their psychache. Schneidman argues that to prevent suicide, we have to reduce psychache.

Beck (1991) theorizes that hopelessness is the primary antecedent for suicidal thoughts, suicidal rumination, suicide attempts, and completion. The Beck Hopelessness Scale has been applied in repeated studies, and intensity of hopelessness has been found to be a successful predictor of suicidal thinking. Beck argues that hopelessness is an acquired cognitive pattern that can be altered through cognitive therapy. He has successfully demonstrated both prediction of and reduction in suicide with cognitive therapy. Cognitive therapy can help reduce and correct cognitive distortions that lead an individual to feel hopeless. In his research, Beck found that individuals with high hopelessness scores were eleven times more likely to commit suicide than individuals with low scores.

Joiner (2005) argues that suicide is an acquired behavior: "the case is made that people desire death when two fundamental needs are frustrated to the point of extinction; namely the need to belong with or connect to others, and the need to feel effective with or to influence others" (p. 47). According to Joiner, when people get used to dangerous behavior and lose their sense of danger, then suicide attempts becomes a possibility if they have the means to commit self-harm. With practice attempts, suicide becomes the norm, overcoming self-preservation and thus making death a viable alternative to life. For Joiner, if individuals have acquired the competence and courage to commit self-harm, then suicide becomes possible through habituation. Although past suicide attempts are a major predictor of future suicide, child sexual and physical abuse are also associated with potential lethal self-harm. In addition, feelings of being a burden and of having unmet needs of emotional and psychological belonging contribute to suicide. Joiner also points out that aggression and violence are indicators of suicide in that they lower inhibitions to self-injury; for example, prisoners are at higher risk of committing suicide than are their nonincarcerated civilian counterparts.

Another type of suicide is heroic suicide, or what Durkheim (1897/1951) called altruistic suicide. Riemer (1998) argues that there are four components to heroic suicide: (1) the act occurred during combat, (2) the act involved sacrifice of one's own life for one's comrades, (3) death was certain by choosing the act, and (4) death immediately followed the act. Durkheim argued that altruistic suicide derives from an excess of social integration. Intense social integration is what military training is all about. Success in combat depends heavily on cohesion among the troops. The Medal of Honor has often been awarded to individuals for heroic suicide. There have been 3,467 such medals awarded in U.S. history. Recently, Private First Class Ross A. McGinnis saved four of his comrades' lives by covering with his body a fragmentation grenade that was tossed into the gunner's hatch. He yelled, "Grenade!" to prepare his fellow Soldiers for the blast. He didn't think, he acted, and in doing so, he sacrificed his life (Medal of Honor Citation, 2008).

Statistics

Military service members are predominately male (85 percent), and the majority are between the ages of seventeen and twenty-six. This age group is at a high risk for suicide.

The U.S. Departments of Defense (DOD) and Veterans Affairs (VA) are gravely concerned with the growing number of suicides among military personnel and veterans. In 2007, there were 108 confirmed suicides in the Army; 166 suicides were reported in Iraq and Afghanistan. According to the U.S. Army (2007) *Suicide Event Report*, the suicides were committed among young enlisted, unmarried white males. Firearms were used most often. Drugs and/or alcohol were involved in 30 percent of the suicide cases. Many of the suicides and attempts were preceded by a failed intimate relationship. It is difficult to know how to interpret this as sufficient to lead to suicide, given that many people have failed relationships and do not attempt or commit suicide. Marriage and having young children were identified as preventative. Not surprisingly, the study found a significant relationship between suicide and number of days deployed to Iraq or Afghanistan. In addition, the study found that many of the soldiers who were medically evacuated for psychiatric problems were also found to have engaged in self-harm behavior.

Stigma and Barriers to Seeking Help

The military faces a paradox between the mentality of having the right stuff and seeking help for problems related to reactions to combat. Hoge et al. (2004)

conducted a mental health assessment of Soldiers and Marines before deployment to a combat zone and then three to four months after they returned home. They found that being in combat was highly associated with generalized anxiety and major depression and that PTSD was significantly higher on return. Very few sought mental health treatment. Hoge et al. asked the Soldiers and Marines (N = 731) who screened positively for a mental health problem what prevented them from seeking help. They rated the thirteen survey items, and the results were telling:

- 65 percent of those who met screening criteria for a mental health disorder reported that they would be considered weak.
- 63 percent indicated that they were concerned that their unit leadership would treat them differently.
- 59 percent responded that members of their unit might have less confidence in them.
- 55 percent indicated that it would be difficult to get time off of work for treatment.
- 51 percent indicated that their leaders would blame them for the problem.
- 50 percent were concerned that it would hurt their career.
- 45 percent reported that it was difficult to schedule an appointment, and 41 percent reported that doing so would be too embarrassing.
- 38 percent indicated that they did not trust mental health professionals.
- 25 percent indicated that mental health care doesn't work and costs too much money.
- 22 percent indicated that they didn't know where they could get help.
- 18 percent reported that they did not have adequate transportation.

It is clear from the responses of those individuals who met the screening criteria that the greatest impediments to seeking assistance are fear of being seen as weak and fear of what leadership would think. Too many Soldiers and Marines believe that asking for help means the loss of a career.

Hoge et al. (2004) point out that the results indicate a public health problem that requires immediate attention. They argue that more attention needs to be given to PTSD and that it should be screened for along with major depression. The stigma associated with seeking assistance for mental health care can be reduced by making it clear to all military personnel that, just as physical injuries are expected in combat, so are mental health issues and PTSD. PTSD, major depression, and generalized anxiety are related to combat. The greater number of fire fights an individual experiences, the greater is the likelihood that he or she will experience PTSD, major depression, or generalized anxiety. Along with physical wounds, mental health injuries are an occupational hazard of being a combatant.

The Human Face of Suicide

As noted before, the current wars in Iraq and Afghanistan are unlike wars that we have experienced before, in that the Army and Marines have borne the brunt of combat. The wars have not proceeded as national policy makers predicted. They turned into guerilla wars, in which Soldiers and Marines never know who the enemy is—man, woman, or child. From this perspective, Iraq is not unlike Vietnam, except that the fighting is mostly located in urban areas. It is important to keep in mind that participating in war is not the same for every individual. Although all military personnel are trained to various degree for combat, not all participate in combat. Soldiers and Marines are most likely to participate in low-intensity or high-intensity combat (Castro & McGurk, 2008). The farther away you are from combat, the less likely you are to experience war-related stress, with the exceptions of certain military specialties, such as those in the medical field or mortuary workers (Kulka et al., 1990).

Castro and McGurk (2008) administered a well-being survey of Soldiers and Marines to assess their experiences. One of the most frustrating experiences they report is living within the rules of engagement (ROE). Soldiers and Marines cannot fire at the enemy until they are fired on or attacked. The rules may change often and at any time. Logically, the chances for survival go down for soldiers who are waiting to be fired on. Castro and McGurk (2008) reported that more than 650 Soldiers and Marines described an event that occurred during deployment that caused them "intense fear, helplessness, or horror" (p. 11). Their responses on their fears and the situations they encountered included the following:

- "My sergeant's leg getting blown off."
- "Friends burned to death, one killed in blast."
- "Mortars coming into your position and not being able to move."
- "A Bradley [armored fighting vehicle] blew up. We got two guys out, three were still inside. I was the medic."
- "A friend was liqu[e]fied in the driver's position on a tank, and I saw everything."
- "A huge fucking bomb blew my friends head off like 50 meters from me."
- "Marines being buried alive."

- "After my Bradley hit an IED, the driver[']s hatch wouldn't open and smoke started filling the interior."
- "Ambush on patrol & Marines caught in the open."
- "Doing raids on houses with bad intel."
- "Convoy stopped in dangerous areas due to incompetent commanders."
- "Working to clean out body parts from a blown-up tank."
- "Fear that I might not see my wife again like my fallen comrades."
- "Finding out two of my buddies died, knowing I could do nothing about it."
- "Getting blown up or shot in the head."
- "Just seeing dead people on a lot of missions."
- "I had to police up my friends off the ground because they got blown up."
- "Mortar attacks, lost a close Marine."
- "My best friend lost his legs in an IED incident."
- "Seeing, smelling, touching dead blow[n] up people."
- "Sniper fire without an obvious source."

These experiences are not "normal" and are likely to produce direct trauma, depending on the individual. The concept of transitional density (Bain, 1978) addresses the accumulation of stressful (and traumatic) events. Embedded in transitional density is the idea that each person and group (and family) has an "overwhelmed" or breaking point; at that point, a person simply can't take anymore stress and continue to function. The transitional density phenomenon is well illustrated by a statement from the director of the Army Suicide Task Force. Brigadier General Colleen McGuire said, "Our current research and prevention efforts are identifying common denominators that lead Soldiers to take their own [lives]. It's often a combination of many factors that overwhelm an individual" (quoted in Tan, 2009b, p. 25).

Combat experiences are horrifying enough, but less is said or written about how the combat experiences of our warriors with the enemy affect them. There is nothing that addresses going berserk during a combat operation. Getting into this state of mind often occurs after doing things beyond the realm of what warriors are trained to do. We have read reports of such incidents since the beginning of the wars in Iraq and Afghanistan. Sometimes such situations drive warriors to commit atrocities. According to Grossman (1995), "Those who commit atrocity have made a Faustian bargain with evil. They have sold their conscience,

their future, and their peace of mind for a brief, fleeting, self-destructive advantage" (p. 222). They will always live with their actions. The following para-
graphs discuss an *Army Times* article that featured the story of First Sergeant Jeff
McKinney, who committed suicide on July 11, 2008 (Kennedy, 2008a):

> Everything changed July 11 in the right sunshine of Adhamiya, Iraq.
> That day, while out on a simple meet-and-greet patrol, McKinney
> stepped out of his Humvee and yelled, "F—k this!"
> He raised the barrel of his M4 (carbine) to his chin and squeezed
> off two shots. The first sergeant—who sang Sesame Street songs to his
> men and teased them just enough to make them feel like family—left
> his Soldiers shattered. (p. 30)

Everyone thought it was a sniper but then realized what happened. One
witness, his driver, said, "That's not First Sergeant McKinney" (p. 30). McKinney's
family was devastated, and he had no history of mental health problems.

The family compiled information from the Army's investigation. Recent
events that McKinney had witnessed included a five-hundred-pound bomb that
killed five of his men and an Iraqi interpreter and another bomb that had almost
killed him and the soldiers around him, and he had comforted a soldier whose
leg was amputated after a roadside bomb explosion. McKinney had stopped
sleeping and eating, and he had started feeling that he couldn't protect his fellow soldiers. A soldier found him staring into space, he had noticeably lost
weight, and he had trouble during morning briefings—but he continued going
on patrol.

Several studies by the Army, the DOD, and the RAND Corporation on suicide
found that troops do not seek help for mental health problems for several reasons, including stigma and fear of being considered weak or incompetent, fear
of hurting their career, and feeling that they will abandon their fellow soldiers if
they fail to go out on patrol. Soldiers seem to believe that seeking help might
mean that they don't have the "right stuff" (Kennedy, 2008a, p. 31).

According to Kennedy (2008a), 47 percent of soldiers who commit suicide
are older than thirty. At least half are sergeants, who are experienced soldiers.
First Sergeant McKinney knew his job, and his men respected him. His good
friend pointed out that McKinney knew all 140 soldiers' names and faces, who
was married, and whether they had children. His soldiers trusted him.

McKinney's father said his son was not the same after serving in Samarra, Iraq. Sergeant McKinney told his father that when in Samarra his squad came under attack from shots fired from a school, the soldiers returned fire. Children in the school died, and the cries of their mothers haunted McKinney. He said to his father, "I'll never be the same again."

On his next assignment in Iraq he served as a tactical operations center battle captain, along with a good friend of his who was in the same position. He did not like not being with his fellow soldiers, and when someone died he assumed responsibility for that soldier's death. Casualties increased. McKinney's battalion was attacked. It was the worst attack an Army battalion had been in since Vietnam—thirty-one men were killed.

McKinney was transferred to Alpha Company, where he worked to clean up some problems with the soldiers. He took more time planning missions and encouraged the newly arrived captain. McKinney made sure his troops were taken care of. McKinney assessed each soldier when he or she returned from patrol to determine whether they had any signs of mental health problems. He experienced the same things as his soldiers. When they didn't have any air-conditioning and were low on food, he did the same. He suffered what they suffered.

On June 21, McKinney and a platoon responded to an explosion from an improvised explosive device (IED) that had blown up an armored vehicle and killed five soldiers. McKinney helped pick up the dead bodies. On June 24 another IED blew up just a few feet from him and his fellow soldiers. On June 26 another IED incident occurred, and a soldier lost a leg at the hip. When he met the soldier's father (a contractor in Iraq), McKinney cried and asked for forgiveness.

McKinney stopped eating and sleeping for long periods of time. He was taking Ambien to help him sleep. On July 7, McKinney and his men were on a night mission, and McKinney was in good spirits. Upon returning from the mission, McKinney stayed up all night preparing for a change of command, which went well the next day. Later he commented, "This place is a mess. I'm failing this company" and "I feel like I'm useless, like I don't have a real job" (Kennedy, 2008a, p. 32). His father said, "That wasn't Jeff, he was squared away. But there was . . . death all around him and he couldn't do anything about it, and he didn't want anyone else to get hurt" (Kennedy, 2008a, p. 32).

McKinney called his wife and told her, "I feel really weird. I can't think straight. I'm not doing a good job" (Kennedy, 2008a, p. 32). McKinney told the captain he was failing the company, but the captain refuted what he said. Later "he refused to sleep and on several occasions, 'zoned out' for several hours" (Kennedy, 2008a, p. 32). On July 10, the captain ordered McKinney to get some sleep. The captain thought McKinney may have incurred a traumatic brain injury when the IED exploded on June 24.

On the next mission McKinney's driver was told to keep an eye on him because "he wasn't himself" (Kennedy, 2008a, p. 33). The captain met with McKinney to go over the mission plans; he let McKinney go on patrol with the unit because he didn't want the soldiers to lose confidence in him. He seemed to believe that McKinney was competent. Later, the captain reported that McKinney shook and was confused when a call came in on the radio. For a while he played with a round from his weapon. At some point he stopped, got out of the vehicle, and yelled, "F— this!" (Kennedy, 2008a, p. 33). He then killed himself.

PTSD: A Risk Factor for Suicide

Posttraumatic stress disorder is a risk factor for suicide, and the number of warriors with PTSD has increased exponentially as each year of the war has passed. It is not surprising that symptoms of anxiety, depression, and PTSD—or mental health problems in general—are highly associated with time and intensity of combat (Castro & McGurk, 2008). Soldiers are 3.5 times more likely to experience PTSD in association with intense combat than are soldiers with noncombat experience (Castro & McGurk, 2008).

In 2007, 115 soldiers killed themselves, or 18.1 per 100,000 soldiers. Army statistics for 2008 indicate that suicide was highest among deployed (30 percent) and after deployment (35 percent) compared with personnel who had not yet deployed (35 percent) (Alvarez, 2008; Tan, 2009a). The National Institutes of Health (NIH) has begun to study suicides among soldiers; in the coming five years, the NIH will study suicide completion and suicide attempts among thousands of soldiers.

Tarabay (2010) reports that more soldiers are dying from suicide than are killed in combat. In 2009, 245 died by suicide; as of May 2010, suicides were at 163. The military has instituted many suicide prevention programs to counsel soldiers and help them identify the warning signs in their buddies. Several factors have been associated with suicides, such as prescription drugs, substance use problems, discipline, and mental health issues. The most obvious association is multiple deployments, but the military is hesitant to admit that is a cause. The rate for suicides in 2009 was twenty per hundred thousand soldiers (Lothian, 2011). Prior administration policy was to not send letters of condolence to suicide victims' next of kin. The Obama administration has changed that policy. President Obama said, "We need to do everything in our power to honor their service, and help them stay strong for themselves, for their families and for our nation" (Lothian, 2011, p. 1).

Suicide in the Army

Anyone familiar with news about the current wars knows that the Army is experiencing a rise in the tide of suicides among troops (Cavallaro, 2007; Kennedy, 2008b; Tan, 2008, 2009b). The suicide trend line is on the increase: 87 in 2005, 102 in 2006, 115 in 2007, and 143 in 2008. The Army has reported that its suicide rate has doubled since the invasion of Iraq. Tan (2009a) reported that in January 2009 the Army's suicide rate was higher than that of combat deaths. Incidents of suicide had risen from 87 in 2005 to 143 in 2008, which led the Army to initiate two- to four-hour stand-downs for soldiers to receive suicide prevention training. Initially, the Army attributed the suicide rate to relationship problems, legal and financial problems, poor job performance, alcohol and drug abuse, and belief of failure in combat (Alvarez, 2008). Many senior Army staff have made statements to the effect that disrupted and ended relationships often drive a soldier to commit suicide. In contrast to the fact that the number of suicides is related to time in combat the Army's chief of command policies and programs said, "You can't really say it's a cost of war. There are a lot of stressors that go into that," (Kennedy, 2008c, p. 10).

In 2009 the suicide rate was 20 per 100,000 soldiers, surpassing the national rate (Kennedy, 2010b). In 2010 there were 434 suicides by active-duty personnel, compared to 381 in 2009 (Donnelly, 2011). Recently, at Fort Hood in Texas there were four suicides in three days despite major efforts at suicide prevention by the Army (Gerhart, 2010; Zoroya, 2011). All of the soldiers had deployed to Iraq, and two of them more than once. The commander at Fort Hood has ordered that all brigade-level commanders assess each soldier in their unit for risk of suicide and take appropriate action. Army leadership links the suicide rates to a focus on the war that superseded the Army's focus on soldiers before 2001 (Kennedy, 2010b). This is the second year that the military reports more deaths to suicide than to combat in Operations Iraqi Freedom and Enduring Freedom (Donnelly, 2011). However, the number of suicides may still be underreported, as the services do not track suicides uniformly and are reluctant to report on the numbers.

Suicides are also occurring after deployment when soldiers return to military installations in the United States. Recent reports from various installations indicate increasing numbers of suicides. At Fort Campbell, Kentucky, the commanding general shut down the installation to engage in suicide education and prevention after eleven suicides were committed there in 2008, followed by sixty-four in 2009 (Commander shuts down Fort Campbell, 2009). In an effort to prevent and reduce suicides, the Army vice chief of staff, General Peter Chiarelli, issued the Army Campaign Plan for Health Promotion, Risk Reduction, and Suicide Prevention (Cavallaro, 2009). Army commanders are responsible for implementing the plan. Part of this plan is a response to drug testing, in which soldiers have tested positive for a range of substances. The plan includes a focus on restoring discipline among the ranks, which has declined with eight years of ongoing combat.

The stigma and shame of asking for help with psychological problems is a long-standing issue. Some leaders in charge of units still tell soldiers that going for help will interfere with career advancement, even though all services have worked to reduce the stigma. The Department of Defense continues to assert that the national rate of suicide for the same age and gender of civilians is nineteen per hundred thousand and that the Army suicide rate is lower, at seventeen per hundred thousand. An Army medic challenges this, pointing out that the Army screens potential recruits for psychological illness and that before the war, the Army had a suicide rate of eleven per hundred thousand soldiers. He points out that the suicide rate is a direct reflection of the stress of a protracted war. Given the lack of resources, especially therapists, there is dim hope that the situation will improve. At present, reports indicate that the Army's suicide rate has increased to twenty per hundred thousand soldiers (Cogan, 2010).

Recent reports indicate that suicide is the third leading cause of death for Army National Guard soldiers (Salzer, 2011; Soldier suicide rate, 2008; Studenicka, 2007). Since the policy changes that created the total force (Knox & Price, 1999), not only has the National Guard continued its state responsibilities for natural disasters but also many units have been called to duty in Iraq for support and in some cases direct combat. Many Guard soldiers have had deployments of up to eighteen months (Soldier suicide rate, 2008). Unlike soldiers who live and work at military installations, guard members live in their communities with their families and friends and may not have ready access to psychological support. Moreover, they may live at a distance from mental health providers with knowledge of military service and combat. In 2006, the National Guard Bureau initiated a suicide prevention program and appointed a manager at the national level. States have also identified part-time suicide prevention managers for the Guard. The Guard has implemented the ACE suicide prevention program—ask your buddy, care for your buddy, escort your buddy—and all ranks will be trained in and responsible for suicide prevention (Studenicka, 2007).

Currently, the Army is stretched to the limits of endurance. One of the most important interventions for suicide prevention is soldiers caring for one another, according to the Army psychiatrist and consultant to the Army surgeon general (Cavallaro, 2007). Soldiers receive "tip cards" to help them express concern for their friends and fellow soldiers that tell them to ask, "What's going on—are you thinking about killing yourself?" The cards encourage soldiers to remain calm and try to remove anything that could inflict injury (removing a gun or pistol may not be possible and should not be forced). They then should calmly take the at-risk soldier for help, and they should never leave him or her alone.

The Army is undertaking several actions as part of the Army Campaign Plan for Health Promotion, Risk Reduction, and Suicide Prevention (Cavallaro, 2009), including increasing discipline and promoting the buddy system, as well as educating to prevent self-injury. Commanders are adding reports on drug testing to their monthly reports, and they are becoming more aware of what is going on with their soldiers. Army suicide manuals from the 1980s are being updated to address issues in today's Army. The plan also includes assessments of soldiers' deployments and redeployments, as well as the moving of mental health services into hospitals to facilitate use and reduce stigma. A more direct attack on stigma is the replacement of the term *mental health* with *behavioral health*. The number of behavioral health military personnel (psychologists and social workers) will increase with an accompanying decrease in the use of medicines as a substitute for therapists. The plan also involves the use of various technological approaches to monitor the reporting of suicide risk and to increase information available to individuals who intervene in a suicidal risk situation.

Suicide is at a record high for the Army and the Marines. Deployments and redeployments and combat have taken their toll. "The greater and greater demand is destroying our military," stated Dr. Charles Figley in an interview (Tan, 2009a, p. 14). "People are starting to think, this is as good as it is going to get. . . . They're just fried" (Tan, 2009a, p. 14). Many soldiers have simply given up hope—and hopelessness is correlated with suicide.

Suicide and Deployment to Combat

There is a clear connection between combat exposure and the development of PTSD. There is also growing evidence of an increased risk of suicide for individuals diagnosed with PTSD (Guerra & Calhoun, 2010; Marshall et al., 2001; Oquendo et al., 2005; Sareen, Joulahan, Cox, & Asmundson, 2005). Using the Beck Scale for Suicide Ideation (Beck & Steer, 1991) and the Beck Depression Inventory (Beck, Steer, & Brown, 1996), Guerra and Calhoun (2010) found that the risk of suicide was uniquely associated with PTSD among 393 veterans. Interestingly, comorbidity with major depressive disorder or alcohol abuse was not found to increase suicide risk. Guerra and Calhoun found that the strongest bivariate relationship was between numbing (detachment and limited affect) and suicidality, whereas the weakest was between avoidance (avoiding particular thoughts or feelings and talking about trauma) and suicidality. The authors also found that when PTSD and MDD symptom clusters were examined together, they were positively and highly predictive of suicidality. In particular, the scores on the numbing cluster of PTSD diagnosis and the cognitive-affective dimension of depressive symptoms were highly correlated with suicidality. An important finding from this study is that persons diagnosed with PTSD should be regularly assessed for suicidality regardless of other presenting problems. Also, firearms are the most common suicide method, followed by hanging (Kang & Bullman, 2008).

Killing, Suicide, and Acquired Capability

There are few empirical studies examining the effects of killing men, women, and children on Soldiers and Marines. Fontana, Rosenheck, and Brett (1992) questioned the relationship between killing and suicide attempts among Operation Iraqi Freedom veterans. The study found that failing to prevent death or injury and killing while in combat are associated with suicide attempts. The study also found that being threatened with being killed or injured was associated with PTSD. Hendin and Hass (1991) found that feelings of guilt after combat, particularly regarding the death of women and children, were strongly predictive of both suicide attempts and suicide ideation. They also found that several suicidal veterans associated killing women and children with a state of rage or fear. Killing and its effects on people engaged in combat have not been thought of as predictive of suicidality and more studies are needed. The few studies identified are discussed later in this chapter.

In military speak, killing is an acquired capability, one of many complex factors associated with suicidal behavior. Selby et al. (2010) argued that the more experience service members have with killing, the greater is their acquired capability for suicide and their own death. Service members are taught to kill efficiently, and combat exposure affirms their capability for killing. Selby et al. also argued that repeated exposure to killing in combat desensitizes soldiers, in that it decreases the power of fear and pain and makes them less terrorizing. For example, learning to parachute with training leads to less fear of jumping out of the plane after repeated exposure and experience. In fact, this habituation may contribute a physiological rush that fills the body with excitement. Initially, service members may experience killing as profoundly stressful, which over time becomes attenuated by repeated exposure in combat (Selby et al., 2010), thus reducing service members' fear of death, even by suicide. Military training and repeated combat exposure may cause individuals to habituate to killing and death, even their own. Habituation may help explain the number of suicides by military service members.

Maguen et al. (2011) found a similar relationship between killing and suicidal ideation and desire for self-harm. In some cases, both were present. The study found that depression and PTSD symptoms contributed to suicidal ideation and killing; ironically, PTSD symptoms mediated killing and desire for self-harm. The researchers advocate that suicide assessment should include an exploration of killing experiences, particularly killing that has resulted in guilt in the context of screening for suicidal risk. Maguen et al. (2011), citing Litz et al. (2009), add that moral injury may also influence killing and suicidality. In *Achilles in Vietnam*, Shay (1994) defines moral injury as "the deforming effect on good character, caused by betrayal of what's right in a high-stakes situation by someone who holds authority that is the most damaging part" (p. 294). The act of killing may be experienced as a moral injury, accompanied by confusion between military training and personal values and morals, thus resulting in the inability to forgive oneself, guilt, and shame (Litz et al., 2009). These are complex issues that require more research, especially on the relationship of acquired capability and habituation to death through engagement in killing.

Suicide in the Navy and Marine Corps

The Department of the Navy's (DON) DON Suicide Incident Report (DONSIR) has tracked risk factors associated with Navy and Marines suicides for more than thirty years (Stander, Hilton, Kennedy & Robbins, 2004). The information is used to strengthen suicide prevention programs. Dennett (1988) has noted that there is no rigorous counting of suicides, and inconsistencies in counting make the results questionable. The Navy and Marine Corps both have directives authorizing commanders to identify a point of contact to complete the DONSIR and return the report within three to four weeks after a suicide; however, as Stander, Hilton, Kennedy, and Robbins (2004) point out, the contact may not have access to all the necessary information to complete all elements of the DONSIR. The information collected is then forwarded to the Naval Health Research Center for data entry and analysis (Stander et al., 2004).

According to Stander et al. (2004), the data collection has three primary purposes: to assess prevalence of known suicide risk factors, to gather all the psychological forensic information, and to enumerate suicide risk factors associated with being in the military. The information that constitutes the DONSIR includes military and medical records, counseling records, toxicology and autopsy reports, investigative reports, and interviews with military personnel. No significant others are contacted for information (Stander et al., 2004). Between 1999 and 2001, Navy personnel had a suicide rate lower than that of the U.S. general population. It was reported that minorities in the Navy had higher suicides than nonminority Sailors. The incidence of suicide for women in the Navy was comparable to the suicide rate of the general U.S. population. Suicides tended to occur in people's homes while they were not on duty; service members most frequently committed suicide with firearms or by hanging. As had the Army, the Navy found that relationship failures and work-related issues were common to most suicides. The DONSIR asks about behavioral and emotional maladjustment; it identified twenty-three suicide indicators, and alcohol abuse was often present. The five most frequently reported emotional indicators were depression, guilt, shame, remorse, and anxiety. Those who had committed suicide had contact with medical and mental health providers in the prior year, and in some cases within thirty days before the suicide.

In the Marines, the suicide rate among combat troops doubled from nine in 2006 to eighteen in 2007. Between 2003 and 2007, the Marines suffered a total of 143 suicides. At that time the Marine Corps did not find this alarming because the suicide rate was lower than the national rate. In a report by Walker (2008), the overall rate of suicides for all Marines rose 37 percent from 2006 to 2007. In 2009 the Marines instituted a suicide prevention program in an effort to reduce that rate. Recent statistics on suicide among Marines increased in 2010 to twenty-four per hundred thousand (Zoroya, 2010a, 2010b). As does the Army, the Marine Corps attributes suicides to relationship problems, financial and legal difficulties, and poor performance. Once again, although these factors are troubling, they are common to many young people who do not solve their problems through suicide. These suicide statistics do not account for Marines who have committed suicide at home after having been in combat. Three months after a tour of duty in Iraq, Major John Ruocco, a forty-year-old Cobra helicopter pilot, hung himself after telling his wife the prior day that he would get help (Kerr, 2007). He had lost weight; he couldn't sleep; he was numb; he had nightmares; and he was depressed, distracted, and withdrawn from his family. The following is an excerpt from the *Army Times*:

Marine Widow Describes the Pain That Suicide Brings

Kim Ruocco is the widow of Maj. John Ruocco who committed suicide three months after returning from duty in Iraq. She has a master's degree in social work and she didn't see it coming and has since become an advocate for suicide prevention. She has counseled suicidal clients and once helped her husband develop a suicide prevention presentation. The Marine Lieutenant Colonel (Lt. Col.) who asked her to speak said, "When a man's widow is standing in front of you, with [family] pictures in the background, it brings you the reality." He said, "He had everything going for him. His kids adored him. He was loved and respected. None of his friends saw it coming." She recently spoke to Marines at Camp Lejeune, North Carolina[,] about her experience. The presentation changed perceptions of suicide. The Lt. Col. said[,] "Before, they might not have gone up to someone and ask if they're OK. Now, they said they're much more likely to go up to them and ask." Kim offers her services to the Tragedy Assistance Program for Survivors (TAPS). She is now organizing a group of individuals who have lost a loved one to suicide to make presentations to troops. Her final comment was, "My husband would have given his life for any one of those Marines. Now, in a way, he has. Suicide is an ugly topic and ugly act— but, if you can save someone else's life it's not as tragic." (Jowers, 2009, p. 11)

Marine spokespersons have reported that 60 percent of the Marine Corps comprises people younger than twenty-five years old. The Marine Corps is working to identify Marines who may be at risk and get them assistance. They are developing mental health teams, with a chaplain and psychiatrist, to be assigned to units. Marines still have problems with stigma from seeking mental health assistance, and that attitude is even stronger among higher-ranking individuals. In spite of the stigma Marine suicides have come down in recent months (Walker, 2010).

Suicide in the Air Force

Air Force rates of suicide have been reduced from previous levels as a result of an innovative suicide prevention program. Increasing suicide rates affected all services during the 1980s and 1990s (Welton & Blackman, 2006). During those years the suicide rate was 11 per 100,000 in the Navy; 12.2, in the Air Force; and 13.7, in the Marines. In 2004 Air Force suicide rates increased to thirteen per hundred thousand (Caruso, 2004); however, none of the suicides involved personnel who were in or had been in war zones. The Air Force implemented a suicide prevention program that focused on reducing the stigma of actively seeking help and required participation of every service member, regardless of rank (Knox, Litts, Talcott, Feig, & Caine, 2003). The program's holistic approach encompassed eleven initiatives (U.S. Air Force Suicide Prevention Program, 2005).

The first initiative addressed leadership. Senior leaders and commanders were engaged to get the whole community involved in suicide prevention. Squadron commanders were provided training in suicide prevention and were charged with involving the whole military community. The second initiative integrated suicide awareness and prevention in all Air Force training and education. The third was to train commanders to recognize suicidal behaviors, to seek mental health assistance, and to encourage affected individuals to seek help. The fourth initiative addressed tracking community prevention efforts. In doing so, the Air Force updated the Medical Expense and Performance Reporting System

(MEDPRS), which examines prevention services and patient care efforts. The fifth initiative addressed community education. Every year, all Air Force personnel and civilians employed by the Air Force receive formal education on suicide prevention. The sixth initiative developed a policy for the actions taken following an arrest and/or an investigative interview, which is considered a high-risk period for suicide. Rather than release the individual, the investigator releases the individual to his or her supervisor. The supervisor then assesses the individual's mental and emotional state. If the supervisor concludes that there is a risk of suicide, he or she calls in a mental health provider.

The seventh initiative focuses on intervention for traumatic incidents (known as critical incident stress management). The Air Force has traumatic stress teams all over the world to respond promptly to traumatic incidents, such as suicides, terrorist attacks or serious accidents, and trauma that affects personnel in groups. The team conducts a traumatic stress intervention, which assists personnel in processing and managing their thoughts and feelings about the incident.

The eighth initiative created a comprehensive cross-organizational review to identify issues at all levels (individual, family, installations, and community) that may affect Air Force readiness. The review also examines quality of life for military personnel and families with two systems: Integrated Delivery System (IDS) and Community Action Information Board (CAIB). The goal is to resolve and find solutions to issues. Another goal is to support the installation of social agencies so that they can cohesively provide services to the military community.

The ninth initiative addresses confidentiality with military personnel. In general, information about military personnel is shared on a need-to-know basis. In the military, confidentiality about mental health problems is extremely limited. Service personnel know this, which contributes to their not seeking mental health assistance. This initiative complements the limited military patient-psychotherapist privilege established in 1999, which limits legal authorities' access to patient records. The Limited Privilege Suicide Prevention Program was developed to improve access to services, and it aims to increase confidentiality when an individual seeks mental health services.

The tenth initiative provides commanders with an IDS Consultation Assessment Tool, which they can use to determine the strengths and weaknesses of their units. They can use the information to improve the well-being of military personnel. Finally, the eleventh initiative provides for the collection of data on suicide through the Suicide Event Surveillance System. The database can be analyzed to identify risk factors that contribute to suicide for use in future pre-vention programs. The eleven initiatives of suicide prevention are elaborated in the Air Force Suicide Prevention Program (2005). Recently, the program was evaluated for its effectiveness (Knox et al., 2010); the evaluation found that Air Force suicides had decreased significantly since the program's implementation.

Postdeployment Suicide

Suicide is on the rise among veterans. At present there is no effective tracking system, so there are no official numbers. As addressed earlier in this chapter, sui-cide rates are fraught with statistical issues and biases that lead to inconclusive results. Also, the deaths of veterans who commit suicide may be classified as ac-cidents or other nonsuicide events.

As suicides among veterans have increased, family and friends have gone public about what happened to their loved ones. In 2007 CBS began investigat-ing veterans' deaths; for five months, several reporters investigated suicide among veterans (Keteyian, 2007). The researchers at CBS made a Freedom of In-formation Act request to the DOD for the number of suicides over twelve years. Between 1995 and 2007, the DOD reported that 2,200 active-duty personnel had committed suicide, not including veterans. Not satisfied, CBS approached the VA's director of mental health, Dr. Ira Katz, and asked for the same information. The researchers also contacted all fifty states for data on suicide among veter-ans. Forty-five states released the information with assurances of confidential-ity. For 2005, CBS identified 6,256 suicides by those who had served in the mili-tary (Malbran, 2007). The results also indicated that in 2004 and 2005 the suicide rate among veterans was almost twice as high as among nonveterans. There seems to have been some internal conflict at the VA about the numbers, which calls into question the reliability and validity of the numbers they had and did not want to release. The VA position has been that there is a problem but not, as others have concluded, an epidemic. Katz later wrote to CBS that there "are about 18 suicides a day among America's 25 million veterans," and 6,570 vet-eran suicides per year (Keteyian, 2008). In 2007, the DOD began monitoring the psychological and physical health of veterans (postdeployment combat person-nel and personnel who have ended military careers) at three and six months fol-lowing combat (Kerr, 2007).

Stigma remains a major barrier to seeking help and contributes to the in-crease in suicides. Kerr (2007) spoke with Shad Meshad, an Army veteran with thirty years of experience counseling veterans. He reported that he receives two or three calls a week regarding suicidal veterans or their family members. He said, "One of the biggest challenges for troubled vets is the stigma of a mental health disorder. It's very, very hard for you to reach out and say, 'I'm hurting.' It is hard for men to do it, but particularly [for] a Soldier [or Marine] who's endured life-and-death situations" (p. 3).

At the end of 2006, the pervasive stigma was well illustrated by events at Fort Carson, Colorado, and was reported in seven broadcasts by National Public Radio (Zwerdling, 2009). Fort Carson providers with requests from soldiers for mental health assistance told them there was nothing wrong with them, dismissed some as cowards, and discharged some from the service. Since that time there have been seventeen suicides. These reports led to investigations by the Senate, the Government Accountability Office (GAO), and the Pentagon. In an effort to reduce stigma, the Army started a program at Fort Bragg, North Carolina, in which they moved the behavioral (mental) health personnel into medical facilities (Kerr, 2007). A DOD task force has recommended that outreach to the troops, including screening and prevention, may get them into clinics more quickly. Even so, the military health system is overloaded and has insufficient qualified providers to promptly reach everyone concerned (Kerr, 2007). Sadly, the officers in charge of military health at the highest levels continue to say that there is no direct correlation between war and suicide.

The Veterans' Health Administration (VHA) is overwhelmed with requests for assistance for physical and mental health, and there aren't enough resources and providers. After veterans make a request, they are often told that they will be put on a waiting list, and they can end up waiting months. They may die or commit suicide before they can get help. Given the numbers of veterans who suffer from PTSD, it is likely that the deaths will continue to increase. The number of veterans making PTSD disability claims increased from 120,265 in 1999 to 215,871 in 2004, almost an 80 percent increase (Kerr, 2007). Until recently, the VA medical centers did not serve family members. A recent GAO report reveals that the VA has developed an initiative and several pilot programs to include families in psychoeducation and in support of the veteran (GAO, 2008c).

In 2008 the psychiatric researcher Thomas Insel, director of the National Institute of Mental Health (NIMH), reported that postwar suicides may exceed combat deaths (Goldstein, 2008). There are insufficient resources and providers in the health and mental health system, particularly in rural areas. In a survey of 191 military members and spouses, respondents reported that their military experience had damaged their mental health (Goldstein, 2008).

Joshua Omvig Veterans Suicide Prevention Act of 2007

One veteran's suicide led to the Veterans Suicide Prevention Act. His story is found on his memorial Web page, Joshua Omvig Life Story and Time Line (http://joshua-omvig.memory-of.com/Legacy.aspx). Joshua Omvig had completed an eleven-month tour in northern Iraq. He was twenty-two years old and had served with the 339th Military Police Company. In 2005, he was on leave visiting his family just before Thanksgiving. One week he was in Iraq, and one week later was back home. Initially, he did not speak about his experiences in Iraq. He began having symptoms of PTSD and shared his concerns with his family. Family members encouraged him to seek help, but he did not, fearing that it would adversely affect his military career. He was in pain (the "psychache" that Schneidman [1998] writes about) and shared with his mother that he felt dead inside. He later shot himself in front of his mother (Jacobs, 2006; Magee, 2006).

Omvig's parents testified before the Senate Committee on Veterans Affairs on April 25, 2007, and told their son's story to the panel. As a result of their efforts and the efforts of others, Congress passed the Joshua Omvig Veterans Suicide Prevention Act into law on November 6, 2007 (Cvetanovich & Reynolds, 2008; Lindsey, 2007). The act requires the VA to develop a suicide prevention program to address the growing number of veterans who commit suicide by requiring that all veterans' affairs staff receive mental health training, that every VA medical center have a suicide counselor, that veterans receiving care at a VA facility will have a mental health screening and receive treatment when appropriate and at the veteran's request, and that veterans have twenty-four-hour access to the VA for mental health care and an available VA suicide hotline (the VA had already put a hotline in place at the time of the prevention act).

The act is progressive. It enables the VA to do something that it has been unable to do in the past. It has a provision that states that the VA must engage in outreach and education for veterans and their family members to teach family members how to recognize when a veteran is in trouble and how to help. The act also requires the VA to conduct best-practices research on mental health care for veterans who have experienced sexual trauma (including sexual assault, harassment, and issues related to gender) while in the military. Finally, both veterans and family members can receive peer support counseling, and the VA will conduct specific research into best practices in suicide prevention in conjunction with the Department of Health and Human Services, the Substance Abuse and Services, the NIMH, and the Centers for Disease Control and Prevention (Cvetanovich & Reynolds 2008; Lindsey, 2007). There is hope that these efforts will stem the rising tide of suicides among veterans.

Finally, it is time for the DOD to accept the responsibility that it not only has the mandate to create warriors but also a responsibility to teach warriors about what can happen to them in the course of battle. Warriors must learn that killing another human being comes at a great personal cost, one that they must bear and that changes their lives forever. In *On Killing*, Grossman (1995) argues that our military service members are proficient at teaching warriors how to kill effectively and efficiently as individuals and in groups. The other side of the mission needs to be to facilitate the transition from over there to back here; Battlemind Training was created for this purpose. Veterans bring the war home, it is inside them, and they will carry it for the rest of their lives. Their worldview changes with each combat experience. Military leaders fail the troops when they assert that there is no correlation between war and the act of killing, suicide ideation, attempt, and completion.

History teaches us that after each war, veterans may or may not be able to do the final about-face alone (Butler, 1935). Veterans who have experienced intense combat will most likely be adversely affected by their experiences at some point in time, immediately or months or years later. Our culture has mythologized war and warriors, and the film industry has contributed greatly to this myth. Recent film tributes to the so-called Greatest Generation such as *Saving Private Ryan*, as excellent as the movie is, tell only one side of the story and fail to address the darker side of that generation's combat experience. In his recent book *Soldier from the War Returning*, the historian Childers (2009) documents the great suffering of World War II warriors, many from the time they returned home to their deaths. These veterans have been portrayed as coming home well adjusted with no problems and as going right back to work, getting married, and creating a good life for themselves and their families.

As Childers (2009) points out, evidence reveals something very different. Upon returning from combat, World War II veterans discovered that during the war, the country had suffered also. There were few jobs, and more than 2 million veterans were out of work. Because of a housing shortage, many had to live with relatives, friends, or anyone who would rent them a room. Many lived anywhere they could, including cars, old boxcars, decommissioned trolley cars, trailers, basements, and some lived in those places with their wives and children. Homelessness and alcoholism were rampant, and veterans were desperate and angry. Prices of food, clothing, and other necessities had increased during the war. There were shortages of meat and clothing. Many soldiers' street clothes consisted of their uniform. The country was in poor economic shape. There was no easy adjustment for many returning veterans. Many were diagnosed with psychoneurosis (later identified as PTSD). For all service members who have returned from combat in later generations, the impact of combat has not changed much. It is no wonder that the VA is the largest mental health institution in the world.

Hidden Epidemic of Female Veteran Suicides

A 2010 study of 5,948 female veterans reported that female veterans were three times more likely than women civilians who never served in the military to commit suicide (Kennedy, 2010a; McFarland, Kaplan, & Huguet, 2010). Female veterans, age thirty-four and younger, had a 13.4 suicide rate per 100,000 of women veterans, compared to 4.4 among civilian women. The gap between military women and civilians suicides was the largest for younger women who were thirty-four years and younger and smallest for older women. The rate was higher among female veterans than among male veterans, who kill themselves twice as often as civilians. The high rate of female veteran suicides was attributed to military-related sexual trauma, as well as exposure to combat and injuries such as TBI.

Social Work and Suicide Survivors

Survivors of a person who commits suicide face unending loss and the pain that accompanies it. Social workers can help survivors—spouses, children, parents, siblings, grandparents, aunts, uncles, cousins, stepparents, fellow service members and their spouses, friends—learn to live with ongoing grief. It is thought that there are at least six survivors for every suicide victim (Lambrecht, 2009), and that is likely an underestimation. One of the best resources for learning about supporting suicide survivors is the Tragedy Assistance Program for Survivors (TAPS). The program was created by Bonnie Carroll (2009), a former member of the Air National Guard who realized that there was little to no support for families experiencing the death of a service member when she lost her military husband in a tragic aircraft accident. Carroll and her colleagues, with support from federal and state agencies, created the family support for survivors program based on core principles (Burton, 2009; Carroll, 2009): to support survivors by providing emotional help, finding hope, and learning to live with loss. It is a peer-based support program with crisis care, casualty casework, and grief and trauma education resources. Today TAPS has assisted more than thirty thousand surviving family members, professional caregivers, and casualty assistance personnel to work with military family members experiencing a death. The program addresses the loss of a service member, including loss by suicide, and offers educational programs for helping professionals who work with suicide survivors, both adults and children.

A family who experiences the death of a service member is affected in some ways that are different from civilian families experiencing the death of a loved one. Never before in the history of our country have military families been so stressed by multiple deployments, which challenge the integrity of the family. To add suicide to that stress can be overwhelming and create barriers to adapting for the family. Moreover, the body of the deceased may be extremely deformed, not all there, or nonexistent because of injuries suffered in a war zone. After the burial, which may take months, the family living on post or base or in a military community usually moves back home or near relatives. This brings changes in roles for adults and possibly a loss of or change in status, and for children it brings changes in schools, friends, and familiar teachers. It may take considerable time to access benefits and adjust to a major change in lifestyle.

One of the most important services TAPS offers is helping survivors realize that they are not alone and that they can share surviving suicide loss with others who have the same experience. People benefit from being with others who are going through the same survivor experience and loss. In the case of suicide, the family most often experiences it as a sudden and traumatic, chaotic loss (LaMorie, 2010). Family, friends, and others may attach stigma to the death, which can contribute to intense and lengthy, unresolved grieving. Kim Ruocco, the surviving spouse of Marine Major John Ruocco, a decorated Marine Corps Cobra pilot who died by suicide in 2005 a few months after returning from Iraq, said, "I thought my life was over when my husband took his own life. I felt alone, confused and isolated. I didn't know anyone who had experienced this kind of loss. I felt ashamed and confused, angry and exhausted, too devastated to even look for help" (LaMorie, 2010, p. 28).

Kim Ruocco has a master's degree in social work, and she helped create the Suicide Support and Education Program that TAPS offers (LaMorie, 2010). The program provides direct support to survivors who are in crisis and need assistance with grieving after a suicide. It also provides long-term support to survivors. Both programs are directed at adapting and healing, and they emphasize peer support, spirituality, education, and remembrance of the loved one. Ruocco said of her experience with the program: "TAPS carried me through those first years by offering a multitude of support. I am now using my strength, gathered over time with the constant, loving care of TAPS, to help others" (LaMorie, 2010, p. 20). The TAPS programs help people positively channel their loss and grief. In an article on the Suicide Support and Education Program, LaMorie (2010) writes, "After the flag is folded and the day turns to dusk, the suicide death of a military service member profoundly affects the lives of those they loved and left behind" (p. 29). The TAPS program makes a difference in the lives of survivors, who move on but never away. Social workers need to be prepared to help survivors grieve, find social support, assist with practical issues, and come to accept that their loved one is dead (Hall, 2008).

Children who experience death have fewer coping resources than adults and generally cope as well as the adults who surround them (Hall, 2008). For children the loss is enormous and may affect them for the rest of their lives (Campagna & Cohen, 2010). Today the military's operational demands are constant, and children are highly aware of the risks of duty and may experience a greater awareness of loss, transition, trauma, and grief. Multiple sources reinforce this awareness, as the loss may have been public and presented repeatedly. Approximately 1.5 million school-age children have a military parent(s) on active duty, and many more have service members who are siblings, grandparents, or other relatives. Children who have parents in the National Guard or Reserve may not have other military people around them who understand their loss and sacrifice.

According to Campagna and Cohen (2010), children may experience a sense of loss of safety as the person who died is no longer there to protect them. They may become angry at the circumstances that brought about the loss. They may lose their faith, not understanding why God could let this happen. Their responses may range from very adaptive (e.g., taking pride in their parents' service) to very maladaptive (e.g., having trauma symptoms and getting "stuck" on the traumatic nature of the death). Adaptive grief means accepting the death as permanent and feeling the pain, remembering the person and holding on to memories, and accepting and adjusting to new changes. Traumatic grief reflects characteristics of posttraumatic stress. Children may act out, become depressed, have physical health problems, become angry and experience intrusive thoughts, have nightmares or greater anxiety than normal, or become withdrawn from family and friends. It is important that children receive special attention if they are having adjustment problems, and play therapy or trauma-focused cognitive-behavioral counseling may facilitate healing. Grief is a process, and it should be individualized for each child.

Social workers should become familiar with the TAPS programs and their publications for children including the quarterly magazine *Journey of Grief* for five- to twelve-year-olds. Also, TAPS holds Good Grief Camps, where adult survivors and their children come together with loss, trauma, and grief counselors and other families who have had the same experience. Social workers can learn more from the webinars that TAPS regularly offers. Social workers need to know of bereavement counseling offered in their communities and that TRICARE (military health care) does not cover the costs of bereavement counseling (Hall, 2008).

Memorial Day, 2011, marked the seventeenth year of the Good Grief Camps. The camps are safe, supportive environments for all participants to tell their story with peers of the same age. The experience reinforces an understanding that those in grief are not alone. At the camp a mentor accompanies each child through the weekend. In addition, TAPS sponsors regional Good Grief Camps throughout the states with activities for children and seminars for adults. Participants report overwhelmingly positive experiences.

If we are going to send warriors to the killing fields, we owe them the right to the knowledge of what the cost may be, and we must ensure them that transition and healing can follow. Warriors have a right to reclaim their lives. Some need more assistance in making the transition from combat to home. Ongoing assessment is required for the transition to be successful, and the social work profession has a major role to play in facilitating that transition.

Contemporary Military and Veterans' Issues

Our lives begin to end the day we become silent about things that matter.

—Reverend Dr. Martin Luther King Jr.

Introduction

This chapter introduces long-standing and ongoing issues that social workers and other helping professionals must understand to be effective with the military and veteran population. First, the problem of homelessness among veterans is a vexing one that has challenged our government and our society for generations. The chapter describes the problem of homelessness among veterans and presents current efforts to address it. Second, the chapter describes the issue of veterans who are incarcerated or elsewhere in the criminal justice system in an effort to understand why the problem exists and what, if anything, might alleviate it. Third, the chapter discusses the status of women in the military. Women are currently performing dangerous jobs both in and out of the war zones. They have made great strides, and yet there is still much to do. Fourth, the current debate on lesbian and gay persons has been in the news in recent years. Is it, or has it, been resolved? All these issues affect not only the military and veteran population but also our society.

Homeless Veterans

Between one-fourth and one-fifth of all homeless persons in America is a veteran. The latest estimate of veterans homeless on any given night is approximately 107,000 (Miles, 2010), down from the National Coalition for the Homeless's (NCH) previous estimate of between 130,000 and 200,000 in September 2009. About 40 percent of all homeless men are veterans, even though veterans account for only 34 percent of the general adult male population. More women veterans are becoming homeless as the current wars continue and the number of women in the armed forces continues to increase. The VA's current estimate is that women veterans account for 4 percent of the homeless veteran population. Veterans with disabilities, such as substance abuse, PTSD, TBI, or major depression, are at increased risk of becoming homeless. The VA and Department of Housing and Urban Development (HUD) programs do not meet existing need (National Coalition for Homeless Veterans [NCHV], 2009). According to the NCHV (2010), "about 1.5 million other veterans, meanwhile, are considered at-risk for homelessness due to poverty, lack of support networks, and dismal living conditions in overcrowded or substandard housing" (p. 1). Who are these veterans, and what is being done to solve this crucial societal issue?

The definition of *homeless veteran* warrants a brief discussion. To be considered homeless, a veteran must meet two criteria:

> First . . . a veteran is a person who "served in the active military, naval, or air service" and was not dishonorably discharged. . . . Second, veterans are considered homeless if they meet the definition of "homeless individual" established by . . . P.L. 100-77. . . [A] homeless individual is (1) an individual who lacks a fixed, and adequate nighttime residence, and (2) a person who has a nighttime residence that is:
>
> - a supervised publicly or privately operated shelter designed to provide temporary accommodations . . .
> - an institution that provides a temporary residence for individuals intended to be institutionalized . . .
> - a public or private place not designed for, nor ordinarily used as, a regular sleeping accommodation for human beings. (Perl, 2007, p. CRS-2)

In general, homeless male veterans tend to be older and more educated than nonveterans. They have more physical and mental health problems than nonveterans. Abuse of alcohol and drugs is a major problem among homeless veterans. Male veterans are likely to have been homeless for more than one year, and they are more likely to have been married than their nonveteran peers (Perl, 2007).

In general, homeless female veterans also show different characteristics from homeless nonveteran women. Like homeless male veterans, they tend to be more educated than nonveteran women (Perl, 2007). As reported by the Iraq Veteran Project:

More women are engaging in combat roles in Iraq where there are no traditional front lines. Women veterans are two to four times more likely than nonveteran women to be homeless. . . . [R]eports show extremely high rates of sexual trauma while women are in the service (20–40 percent). Repeated experience to traumatic stressors increases the likelihood of PTSD. Researchers also suspect that many women join the military, at least in part, to get away from abusive environments. Like other young veterans, these women may have no safe supportive environment to return to; adding yet more risk of homeless outcomes. . . . Until recently, the VA's research and treatment of PTSD was focused predominantly on men. (Fairweather, 2006, pp. 1–2).

Management of the federal response to homelessness resides with the U.S. Interagency Council on Homelessness (2009), which works "to create a national partnership at every level of government and with the private sector to reduce and end homelessness in the nation while maximizing the effectiveness of the Federal Government in contributing to the end of homelessness" (p. 1). The USICH comprises the secretaries of several cabinet-level agencies, including the Departments of Labor, Housing and Urban Development (HUD), and Veterans Affairs. The council produces the Federal Strategic Plan to Prevent and End Homelessness; the latest plan was submitted to the Congress on May 10, 1010.

Although Labor and HUD have their own specific programs to assist reintegration of homeless veterans into society and the workforce, the VA is the only agency that offers hands-on assistance directly to homeless persons in the United States. It offers a number of services specifically designed to help homeless veterans live as self-sufficiently and independently as possible (U.S. Department of Veterans Affairs, 2010a). The VA (2010b) offers the following fourteen programs and initiatives:

- The National Call Center for Homeless Veterans ensures that homeless veterans and veterans at risk of becoming homeless have free, 24/7 access to counseling.
- The Grant and Per Diem Program is offered annually as funding permits to provide financial resources to community-based agencies that provide transitional housing and to service centers for homeless veterans.
- Department of Housing and Urban Development (HUD) and VA Supported Housing offers permanent housing and ongoing case management and treatment services for homeless veterans who need those supports to live independently. Moreover, HUD provides Section 8 vouchers to public housing authorities for those who are eligible.

- Healthcare for Homeless Veterans involves VA social workers and other mental health clinicians performing outreach to identify eligible homeless veterans, and it assists them in accessing appropriate health care and benefits.
- The VA participates in locally sponsored Stand Downs across the country, which give homeless veterans between one and three days of safety and security, including food, shelter, clothing, VA health care, and a range of other services.
- The Compensated Work Therapy program provides temporary housing in group homes for working veterans; the VA contracts with private industry and the public sector for jobs for veterans, who learn new job skills, relearn successful work habits, and regain a sense of self-esteem and self-worth.
- Community Homelessness Assessment, Local Education, and Networking Groups (CHALENG) is a nationwide initiative in which VAMCs and regional offices work with other federal, state, and local agencies and non-profit organizations to assess the needs of homeless veterans, to develop action plans to meet identified needs, and to better understand the needs of women and families.
- Each year Domiciliary Care for Homeless Veterans provides residential treatment to approximately five thousand homeless veterans with health problems.
- Supported Housing provides ongoing case management to homeless veterans. Emphasis is on helping veterans find permanent housing and on providing clinical support to veterans in permanent housing.
- Drop-In Centers are a daytime sanctuary where homeless veterans can wash their clothes, clean up, and participate in a variety of therapeutic and rehabilitative activities.
- With VBA-VHA Special Outreach and Benefits Assistance, the VHA provides funding for twelve VBA benefits counselors to work in VHA facilities assisting homeless veterans in identifying and applying for benefits to which they are entitled.
- The VBA's Acquired Property Sales for Homeless Providers program makes all the properties VA obtains through foreclosures on VA-insured mortgages available for sale to homeless provider organizations at a discount of 20 percent to 50 percent.
- The VA Excess Property for Homeless Veterans Initiative distributes excess federal property, such as clothing, sleeping bags, and other items, to homeless veterans and programs that serve homeless veterans.
- Program Monitoring and Evaluation provides important information about the veterans served and the therapeutic value and cost effectiveness.

Eric Shinseki, the VA secretary, has placed the elimination of homelessness among veterans high on his list of priorities; he aims to achieve that goal by 2015. To break the downward spiral into homelessness, his focus will be on "medical services to confront substance abuse, depression, PTSD, TBI and other issues linked to homelessness" (Miles, 2010, p. 1). While we monitor VA's success or failure under the invigorated secretarial guidance, we must also ensure that homeless veterans do not become embroiled in the criminal justice system.

Incarcerated Veterans

Thousands of war veterans are currently in prison or jail in the United States. This complex problem is not new. After every modern war many veterans suffering from combat stress end up in the criminal justice system:

> For example, 34 percent of new admissions to 11 U.S. prisons between 1946 and 1949 were WW II combat veterans. Combat veterans from Vietnam onwards face an even greater risk of incarceration than previous generations of veterans because the U.S. now criminalizes behaviors—especially drug use—that were not covered under federal and state criminal codes until the 1970s . . . the National Vietnam Veterans Readjustment Study (NVVRS) found in 1988 that nearly half of Vietnam combat veterans afflicted with PTSD had been arrested or incarcerated in jail one or more times, and 11 percent had been convicted of a felony. PTSD and other psychological wounds of war may also emerge several years after returning from combat. Experts predict a tragic recurrence of these events as current conflict veterans return home, unless urgent, evidence-based responses to support veterans battling addiction and incarceration are implemented at the local, state, and federal levels. (Drug Policy Alliance, 2009, p. 3)

Substance abuse, mental illness, and incarceration are inextricably linked. The Drug Policy Alliance (2009) policy paper "Healing a Broken System: Veterans Battling Addiction and Incarceration" provides convincing evidence of this link:

- Approximately 30 percent of Iraq and Afghanistan veterans report symptoms of PTSD, TBI, depression, or other mental illness or cognitive disability.
- 19 percent of current conflict veterans who have received VA care have been diagnosed with substance abuse or dependence.

- 75 percent of Vietnam combat veterans with PTSD met criteria for substance abuse or dependence in a national study.
- Veterans do not qualify for substance abuse disability benefits unless they also have PTSD.
- 140,000 veterans were incarcerated in state and federal prisons in 2004.
- 46 percent of veterans in federal prison were incarcerated for drug law violations.
- 15 percent of veterans in state prisons were incarcerated for drug law violations, including 5.6 percent for simple possession.
- More than 25 percent of veterans in prison were intoxicated at the time of their arrest.
- 61 percent of incarcerated veterans met the DSM-IV criteria for substance dependence or abuse.
- More than half of veterans in federal (64 percent) and state prisons (54 percent) served during wartime.
- 26 percent of veterans in federal prison and 20 percent in state prison served in combat.
- 38 percent of veterans in state prison received less than an honorable discharge, which may disqualify them for VA benefits.
- Veterans incarcerated for drug offenses received average sentences that were one year longer than those of non-veterans incarcerated for the same offenses.
- Existing literature strongly indicates that incarcerated veterans may face a level of suicide risk that exceeds that attributable to either veteran status or incarceration alone. (pp. 2–4)

The Department of Veterans Affairs' program Health Care for Re-Entry Veterans (HCRV) strives to provide information to incarcerated veterans to assist them in planning their own reentry to society and the workplace. HCRV services include the following:

- Outreach and pre-release assessments
- Referrals and linkages to medical, psychological, and social services, including employment services
- Short-term case management assistance (U.S. Department of Veterans Affairs, 2008)

The VA has also created the position of incarcerated veterans reentry specialist within each VISN. The specialist acts as a regional point of contact for incarcerated veterans. The VA has developed state-specific resource guides to help veterans make decisions about their reentry before their release.

The Department of Labor has a program to assist veterans in reentering the workplace. Its Incarcerated Veterans Program (IVTP) addresses local, state, and federal issues that are troublesome for veterans to negotiate. The program funds, through federal grants, agencies, and individuals, direct services to incarcerated veterans and is especially focused on veterans of the current conflicts (U.S. Department of Labor, Veterans Employment and Training Services, 2010).

Most war veterans do not experience the horrible aftereffects of combat stress. They are able to avoid self-medication, criminal activity, and incarceration. Nevertheless, those not so fortunate served their country while most Americans did not. They deserve better than our society has provided them. We must remember that these incarcerated brothers and sisters are veterans first.

Women Warriors

Women have been involved in national security from the beginning of this nation. Women defended their homes in the French and Indian Wars and participated in the American Revolution and the Civil War. They served in World War I and more so in World War II. They were in Korea; Vietnam; and in the most recent international conflicts, including the Persian Gulf War, the Balkans, Somalia, and Iraq and Afghanistan. Since September 11, 2001, women have been deeply involved in all aspects of the current wars. As Meyers (2009) notes, "The wars in Iraq and Afghanistan are the first where tens of thousands of American military women have lived, worked, and fought with men for prolonged periods" (p. A1). The successful service of women has dispelled the myth that their presence would negatively affect discipline or unit cohesion in previously all-male groups.

Three factors have greatly influenced women's roles in the wars today. First, the Army has an insufficient number of male volunteers, and women have demonstrated that they can do the job alongside men and in a wide range of military occupational specialties. The military's need for military personnel supersedes their gender (Segal, 1995). Second, we are fighting a war in two Muslim countries, where culture and religion forbid male warriors from touching Muslim women. Consequently, women Soldiers and Marines are needed for this duty. As such, they become combatants when they are taken under fire. Third, we are fighting two wars with no fronts. Violent encounters can take place anywhere, which requires all warriors to stay alert and be ready to respond to hostilities no matter what their military occupational specialty, gender, or combat status. The war on terror has been called an "Equal Opportunity War" (Autry, 2008, 19). Women are dying and being wounded at war as this country has never seen before.

Women encounter several issues as they carry out their military responsibilities. In the face of performing well, women still encounter bias from men who don't believe that women belong in the armed forces, and especially in combat. They encounter different hardships, such as waste elimination when they are in the field. Women have adapted, innovated, and learned from more experienced female soldiers as any troop would do. For example, with waste elimination, according to several women's reports, they are become very skilled at finding a place or simply asking the guys to turn around. Some women carry a special urinal that catches their urine and releases it through a tube to the ground while standing. Sergeant Bradford, who went out on patrols, said, "The first time one of them [male soldiers] came around a truck and saw me peeing on a tire [using one of the urinal devices], and I thought he was going to have a heart attack" (Meyers, 2009, p. A3). Women's hygiene requirements are different from men's and discussed in *A Guide to Female Soldier Readiness* (U.S. Army Center for Health, Promotion, and Preventative Medicine, 2007). The guide addresses the particular issues women face and suggests solutions. For example, some women take birth control pills continuously while in-country, which eliminates the need to carry tampons.

In addition to hardships, female service members are often labeled "bitch," "slut," or "dyke" (Benedict, 2009; Williams, 2006). These names are only the beginning of the harassment. Women must cope with harassment in addition to living conditions that challenge any soldier, a lack of privacy, deciding whether to have sexual relations, engaging in combat operations, killing people, and seeing the horror of combat. Women live alongside male soldiers in the field and in military camps, and they manage conditions just as well. Colonel Burt K. Thompson, U.S. Army, the commander at FOB Warhorse, commented that every time he leaves the base, his patrol includes two women. Meyers (2009) writes, "Like any commander who has served in Iraq or Afghanistan, [Thompson] said that women have ended the debate over their role by their performance" (p. A6).

Sexual Harassment and Assault

The military needs women, and women can do the job. If women are doing well, why are male soldiers allowed to label women with derisive names that unmistakably demonstrate a lack of respect for a fellow soldier? Arguably, the military allows this practice with less-than-effective restraint (Benedict, 2009). Not all men show a lack of respect, but some men engage in criminal treatment of women, including sexual harassment and sexual assault. In 2006, a former Army sergeant reported that she was raped while on deployment to Afghanistan. Three years later, after seeing her rapist in the community, she sought counseling from a military chaplain who informed her "that it must have been God's will for her to be raped" (Maze, 2011, p. 12).

Previously addressed in this book are staggering numbers of women's reports of assault by their fellow soldiers, as well as assaults that go unreported because of fear of reprisal. The Army has had a campaign to end sexual assault (Cavallaro, 2008), yet the problem continues. In evaluating the implementation of sexual assault prevention, the GAO (2008a) cited several reasons for the campaign's lack of success. The GAO (2008a) also criticized the campaign for not developing criteria to evaluate the implementation of the plan or the commanders whose responsibility it is to have zero tolerance of sexual harassment and assault.

The prevalence of sexual assault is unknown. However, in testimony before Congress, the undersecretary for health policy coordination for the Veterans Health Administration of the Department of Veterans Affairs reported that about 20 percent of women and 1 percent of men reported military sexual trauma (MST; Solaro, 2006). Most of the cases were not prosecuted. The Department of Veterans Affairs found that the rates of sexual assault were consistent for all services. In a VA survey of 3 million veterans, thirty-three thousand men and twenty-nine thousand women reported having been sexually assaulted while in the military.

Article 120 of the U.S. Uniform Code of Military Justice (USMCJ, 2007) governs rape. Sexual assault is defined as follows:

> intentional sexual contact, characterized by use of force, physical threat or abuse of authority when the victim does not or cannot consent. Sexual assault includes rape, non-consensual sodomy (oral or anal sex), indecent assault (unwanted, inappropriate sexual contact or fondling), or attempts to commit these acts. Sexual assault can occur without regard

to gender or spousal relationship or age of victim. "Consent" shall not be deemed or construed to mean the failure by the victim to offer physical resistance. Consent is not given when a person uses force, threat of force, coercion or when the victim is asleep, incapacitated, or unconscious. (U.S. Army Sexual Assault Prevention and Response Program, 2010, p. 70)

The definition of assault is comprehensive; however, having a definition is useless if it is not enforced.

In 2008, the Army gathered top commanders and made it clear that ending sexual assault was a command responsibility (Cavallaro, 2008; Geren & Casey, 2008):

American soldiers are members of a band of brothers and sisters, bound by common values, and duty and loyalty to each other that sets them apart from society. They are bound by a commitment to their comrades that outsiders find incomprehensible, and a willingness to sacrifice for each other. The soldiers who committed these crimes betrayed not only their victims, but their band of brothers and sisters who counted on them. They violated a sacred trust. When a soldier fails to intervene to protect a comrade from harassment or the risk of assault, he or she has forsaken the duty to never leave a fallen comrade. (p. 62)

The problems of sexual harassment and assault apply to both men and women and are equally disgraceful. Sadly, the extent of the problem is unknown because of underreporting (GAO, 2008a). Many service members fear the potential consequences of reporting. In the GAO (2008a) study, many indicated that nothing would be done and that they would be ostracized; they were also fearful of gossip. This problem extends to the National Guard and reservists. Firestone and Harris (2009) found that the environmental culture is predictive of individual harassment for males and females, but females bear the brunt of the hostility. The problem is centered on the military culture, which overtly and covertly fails to address the problem (Benedict, 2009). It is also centered on leadership. As long as some commanders fail to enforce consequences for these behaviors, harassment and assaults will continue. It is pathetic that women, serving their country and facing all the consequences of having chosen to volunteer, must sleep with a weapon to defend themselves against assault not only from the enemy but also from their fellow soldiers. An Army reservist reported that two male soldiers raped her in Iraq (Military Rape Litigation, 2011). The men videotaped the rape and circulated the video. The victim was bruised from her shoulders to her elbows. Charges were not filed because the commander said that "she did not act like a rape victim" and "did not struggle enough." In addition, authorities did not want to delay the return home of the two alleged rapists.

Following pressure from Congress, to reduce the crimes, the Defense Department plans to respond by enhancing and expanding the required reports on sexual assault and harassment and by providing assistance for victims, with oversight by the Pentagon (Gould, 2011). Carolyn Collins, program manager for the Sexual Harassment Assault Response and Prevention program (SHARP) hopes that the added effort will help "provide a first-rate response to our victims," in addition to preventing crimes in the first place (Gould, 2011, p. 16).

The 2011 Defense Authorization Act enhances the sexual assault and prevention effort in the following ways: (1) each service must make detailed annual reports of each report of sexual assault regardless of the outcome; (2) service secretaries must explain what services and responses are made to deployed victims; (3) the Pentagon must maintain a database on reporting and documenting all sexual assaults for all services (which it failed to do in 2010); (4) the Pentagon will establish an office ensuring that all services comply with the laws and standards for sexual assault response (Gould, 2011).

The goal of SHARP in the first five years of implementation is to improve reporting assault and harassment and to increase the strength of investigative teams with the hope of improved investigations and prosecutions. Moreover, SHARP aims to reduce the stigma of reporting and to increase victims' trust in the system (Gould, 2011).

In addition to these efforts, the Judge Advocate General Corps is increasing the number of personnel with specialized knowledge in sexual assault and harassment crimes, and they will be available to assist commanders in deciding whether to prosecute the case. The Army is planning to add special victim prosecutors to assist victims with their cases. The military is counting on these actions having an effect on the problem, provided that funding is not an issue.

Sexual Assault and Harassment Lawsuit against the DOD

On February 15, 2011, a lawsuit filed in the District Court of Virginia charged the DOD with failing to prevent sexual crimes and with inadequate management of cases brought to its attention (Parker, 2011). In particular, the lawsuit charges that Secretaries of Defense Robert Gates and Donald Rumsfeld administered a military culture in which sexual crimes by military personnel were ignored and victims repeatedly suffered sexual offenses (Parker, 2011). All services are represented in the case, and the plaintiffs are fifteen women and two men. One plaintiff said, "The policies that are put in place are extremely ineffectual. There was severe maltreatment in these cases, and there was no accountability whatsoever. And soldiers in general who make any type of complaint in the military are subject to retaliation and have no means of defending themselves" (Parker, 2011, p. 18).

In a public statement, a senior spokesperson for Defense Secretary Gates said, "The Defense Department takes the issue seriously and has strengthened efforts to address the problem—which, he noted, is not confined to the military" but is a societal problem (Maze, 2011, p. 12). The spokesperson went further to state that an effective sexual abuse policy is a command priority. This statement is inconsistent with the military's past successes with social issues such as racial integration. The military is one place where behavior can be regulated and controlled, as commanders make it clear that criminal behavior will not be tolerated and there are consequences for such behavior. In today's military the consequence doesn't follow the crime, which is why women and some men fail to report sexual harassment and assault. It is reasonable to conclude that with the number of men to women (women are 15 percent of the force) in the military, there will be a handful of men who engage in unacceptable behavior—they should have to face the consequence of their conduct. When military leaders get serious about the problems, consequences will follow regardless of rank. Although it is true that sexual assault and sexual harassment are societal problems, our greater society is far more efficient at prosecution. The lawsuit alleges that the military prosecutes only 8 percent of sexual offenders, in contrast to 40 percent of civilian prosecutions (Gould, 2011). For this problem to be resolved, military culture and leadership will have to change.

Mothers in Combat Boots

Another issue that has not been much considered is the role of mothers who serve in the military. According to Iraq and Afghanistan Veterans of America (IAVA), thirty thousand single mothers have served in both wars (Eberstadt, 2010). There was a time when pregnancy meant an automatic discharge. Today the services all have maternity leave policies. In spite of these policies, the Army cook Specialist Alexis Hutchinson was ordered to Afghanistan to leave her ten-month-old son behind. She had planned to have her mother care for the child when she deployed, but that had not happened, so she was given thirty days to develop another family care plan. The single mother was unable to find a suitable caregiver in the time allowed and was arrested. Her child was placed in foster care (Eberstadt, 2010). More recently, Defense Secretary Gates has changed policy so that losing custody of a child because of deployment is preventable (Jowers, 2011). The DOD is working with the states so that deployment because of military service will not be the sole reason for losing custody rights.

American society, the military, and the social science literature have largely ignored the issue of mothers in combat. Women are needed to fill combat boots because there are insufficient numbers of volunteers. The question is not whether women can do the job; they can. In fact, women in combat support occupations were found to have significantly fewer hospitalizations than women in other military occupations (Lindstrom et al., 2006). The real issue is whether mothers, especially single mothers, should be separated from their children to serve in potentially life-threatening situations. Eberstadt (2010) raises this question as an important but ignored policy issue. She notes that children can become collateral damage in the rush to employ women in military jobs. We add to this concern that single fathers who are responsible for their children should be integrated into such discussion.

This issue needs addressing and honest disclosure. The simple fact is that there is a need to fill military roles with healthy individuals. It is also a fact that each one of us has the civic duty to serve and protect our country if we are to keep the republic we have created intact. At the same time, we need healthy children to grow into healthy adults, and the presence of a parent or both parents provides the best opportunity that children have of doing so. A healthy home front also contributes to keeping the republic. Social workers can contribute to the discussion and resolution of this issue.

Women Veterans' Health Care

The VA was not prepared for the number of women veterans who would need their services. The VA is largely a male-oriented institution that is in transition to meet the needs of male and female veterans. Women's health and mental health concerns have been highlighted with the growing number of women serving in the military. One of the main issues is the need for the VA to change the way it regards female veterans (Ostendorff & Bompey, 2011). The VA is making changes to expand and promote services for women veterans. Many medical centers did not have examination rooms allowing women privacy from gawking individuals in the hall; most restrooms did not provide female hygiene supplies. Add to these the complaints that women veterans wanted privacy when discussing personal medical problems and during gynecological exams (Hefling, 2009b). Another concern is the lack of qualified counselors able to treat sexual trauma and PTSD, as well as the need for female case managers. Women also say that they need child care to access the services they are eligible for (Autry, 2008).

Research supports the need for trauma assessments for women and treatment for PTSD. In a review of literature, Zinzow, Grubaugh, Monnier, Suffolette-Maierte, and Vrueh (2007) found that female veterans are a highly traumatized population and are more likely to meet the criteria for PTSD than their civilian counterparts. Women veterans are in need of physical and mental health services tailored to their specific problems (Kelley et al., 2008). At present too many care providers are not trained in women's health. The VA's primary goal is to "enhance the language, practice and culture of VA to be more inclusive of Women Veterans" (Hayes, 2010, n.p.).

Don't Ask, Don't Tell, Don't Pursue Law Repealed

In the past gay men and lesbians could serve in the military but not openly, because of the don't ask, don't tell (DADT) law. Belkin (2008) has argued that the previous policy "was inconsistent with public opinion, it prompted many journalists to criticize the armed forces while attracting almost no favorable media coverage, it provided a vehicle for antimilitary protesters to portray military culture as conflicting with widely accepted civilian values, and it was inconsistent with the views of junior-enlisted service members" (p. 276).

It is interesting that a person could volunteer to serve his or her country, do so successfully, and then have their service terminated because of his or her sexual orientation, even though the military was having a difficult time recruiting volunteer members. Many arguments were made against African Americans' integration into all functions of the armed forces. In 1948 President Truman ordered that the military services be fully integrated. Before that decision African Americans served, but in all-black units. Truman's order merged the groups, and there were many questions about the outcome. Over the years, as society has changed to become more integrated, so has the military, with few problems among service members today—even though racism is still an issue for some service members. Women serve in combat situations and do so successfully—this doesn't mean that all the issues have been resolved. The primary DADT arguments rested on what would happen if the policy were to change. What would happen to unit cohesion and the public's perception of the military? The military spends large amounts of tax dollars to curry favor with the public, especially with respect to recruitment and retention. To date there has been little empirical evidence with which to evaluate what the real issues are and what the implications would be now that the DADT law has been abolished.

Public opinion changes, especially as an increasing number of people have positive associations with gay men and lesbians. Many young people today have grown up with gay and lesbian friends. Such experiences have changed the way the public views sexual orientation. When the public looks at men and women in uniform, they don't pick out who is gay or lesbian or not; what they see is a body of military service members who are sworn to defend and protect the Constitution. This was demonstrated in several public polls on the issue between 2003 and 2006 (Belkin, 2008). In some cases two-thirds of respondents were found to be favorable to gay men and women serving openly. In four of the nine polls, more than 50 percent were in favor of repealing the law. In subsequent research, the DADT law did not appear to negatively affect the military's reputation (Belkin, 2008). Belkin (2008) also cited research demonstrating that most service members do not have an issue serving with gay and lesbian service members, as has been previously argued. It appears that attitudes regarding the issue may be shifting, along with the emotional intensity that has characterized the issue.

Data from service members are inconclusive and difficult to interpret, given the Pentagon's current policy regarding sexual orientation. How can service members be faithful to their service when they are supposed to support military policy regardless of what they think or have experienced? The simple fact is that, in the large body of men and women that is the military, there are gay men and women, as well as bisexual people, present and as committed to defending the Constitution as their heterosexual counterparts—and doing so honorably (Araujo, 2010).

One study of the attitudes of 545 war veterans from Operations Iraqi Freedom and Enduring Freedom demonstrated that most support allowing open service. Many service members knew of gay men and lesbians who were serving with them. Interestingly, the veterans did not associate gay service members with their ratings of cohesion or readiness. Quality of leadership, training, and quality of equipment was associated with cohesion and readiness. This is not to say that the DADT issue is resolved, but there is an apparent decline in support for it. Our society and culture are changing. More families are acknowledging and supporting gay and lesbian family members and their civil rights. And, as previously noted, young people are growing up with gay and lesbian friends, with whom they also work and socialize.

A survey conducted by *Military Times* asked three thousand military service members how they felt about gay men and women serving openly and asked gay and lesbian service members about their experience (McMichael & McGarry, 2010). The authors found support for the DADT policy among service members, who believe that there are numerous issues to address. Most service members did not feel that sexual orientation was an issue, and they cited job performance as more important. Several gay and lesbian service members of different ranks and services were interviewed. Some indicated that they would not "come out" even if the law was repealed, preferring to keep their personal lives private. Repealing the law would end the stress of living a double life and fear of being kicked out of the service. The tendency among service members is toward repealing the law once its related issues have been resolved.

In testimony before the Senate Armed Services Committee, the Chairman of the Joint Chiefs of Staff, Admiral Mike Mullen, said, "It's time for change." At present, the DOD is carefully examining all issues related to the law's repeal (Philpot, 2010). Defense Secretary Gates has indicated that there will be fewer "outings" of service members serving honorably by individuals with "a motive to harm," regardless of what happens with the law (Philpot, 2010, p. 18). The group examining the policy will consist of four DOD teams. One team will develop a survey for service members and family members. The other team members will review legislation and legal and regulatory issues, development of policy, and education and training (McMichael, 2010).

Repeal of Don't Ask, Don't Tell

On November 30, 2010, the Pentagon released a 362-page report that supported the repeal of the law against allowing gay men and lesbian women to serve openly in the U.S. Military (U.S. Department of Defense, 2010) contributing to the change in law. Secretary of Defense Robert Gates had appointed a committee on March 2, 2010 to conduct a comprehensive review of the don't ask, don't tell policy. The committee consisted of sixty-eight members (forty-nine military service members and nineteen civilian personnel from the DOD and the military services). The committee worked with professional researchers to produce a survey that was sent to four hundred thousand active-duty and reserve component service members. The survey had 115,052 respondents (a 28 percent response rate) and is the most comprehensive survey ever conducted of the military services. The survey included both military service members and their spouses. The committee also solicited the opinions of former gay and lesbian service members through a survey and interviews, and focus groups were used to produce more in-depth information. The committee also examined laws, regulations, and policies. The issue of gay men and lesbians serving in the armed forces is one of the most extensively studied issues in the history of the U.S. military.

The results of the survey demonstrated that a majority of service members did not believe that the repealed don't ask, don't tell policy would have an adverse impact on the ability of each individual and the collective to carry out the military's mission. The committee felt that the following three responses best represented the survey's findings:

- When asked about how having a service member in their immediate unit who said he or she is gay would affect the unit's ability to "work together to get the job done," 70 percent of the service members predicted it would have a positive, mixed, or no effect.
- When asked "in your career, have you ever worked in a unit with a co-worker that you believed to be homosexual," 69 percent of service members reported that they had.
- When asked about the actual experience of serving in a unit with a co-worker who they believed was gay or lesbian, 92 percent stated that the unit's "ability to work together" was "very good," "good, " or "neither good nor poor." (U.S. Department of Defense, 2010, pp. 3–4)

Interestingly, 74 percent of spouses indicated that the repeal would have no effect, at the same time that 12 percent would want their spouse to leave service because of the change in the DADT law.

The survey identified dissension over repealing the law. Thirty percent thought that repeal of the law would have adverse effects, and the results were 40–60 percent in the Marine Corps and in some of the Special Operations units. Given these responses, the committee still concluded that the overall effect of the repeal would not risk military effectiveness. For example, one Special Operations service man said, "We have a gay guy [in the unit]. He's big, he's mean, and he kills lots of bad guys. No one cared that he was gay."

The changes in policy will take effect sixty days after Congress receives written notice to proceed from the president, the secretary of defense, and the Chairman of the Joint Chiefs of Staff. The report will explain the changes in the law; according to the law repealing the act, the new policy must not affect troop readiness, cohesion, or recruitment and retention. All services have reported that each will faithfully implement the change in policy this upcoming year but that the changes will take time. Congress is expected to proceed with implementation in midsummer 2011; at the time of this writing, that has still not taken place.

Admiral Mullen publicly called for the repeal of the policy requiring gays and lesbians to keep their sexual orientation hidden. He told the Senate Armed Services Committee, "It is my personal belief that allowing gays and lesbians to serve openly would be the right thing to do. No matter how I look at this issue I cannot escape being troubled by the fact that we have in place a policy that forces men and women to lie about who they are in order to defend their fellow citizens." He also said, "To me personally it comes down to integrity, theirs as individuals and ours as an institution. I also believe the great young men and women of our military can and would accommodate such a change" (Bender, 2010, par. 3).

With the change in the policy, the Pentagon is initiating an extensive program to prepare all services for integration of gay and lesbian service members into open military service (Scarborough, 2011). Training will be delivered at the unit level regardless of where the unit is located, either in the United States or at a deployment location. Training will be provided to three groups: chaplains and other specialists, field commanders, and all 2.2 million active and reserve troops. The goal of the training is that all service members will treat one another with respect, regardless of sexual orientation. Defense Secretary Gates has assured gay and lesbian service members that, by the end of the year, they will be able to serve openly and without harm.

In this chapter we have addressed contemporary issues in the military and veteran populations. Social workers have a commitment to social justice, nondiscrimination, and support of civil rights for all citizens. These commitments are an ethical responsibility of the profession. Social workers' role should be to advocate in support of nondiscrimination policies based on empirical evidence gathered through rigorous research designs. We need to better understand the plight of homeless veterans and the growing number of women veterans in their ranks. The chapter described the epidemic of sexual assault and the military's efforts to remedy the problem. We drew attention to the need for public debate regarding mothers in combat boots and how the deployment of women has gone on without question. We included a history of the DADT law and the issues surrounding its repeal and ongoing implementation. Social workers will encounter these issues as they work with military service members and veterans.

Warriors and Families Speak Out

There was a big difference between my husband's first deployment and his second. The first time there was no information, no meetings, no [Family Readiness Group]. It got better the second time he went.

—**National Guardsman's wife**, 2010

Man has two supreme loyalties—to country and to family. . . . So long as their families are safe, they will defend their country, believing that by their sacrifice they are safeguarding their families also. But even the bonds of patriotism, discipline, and comradeship are loosened when the family itself is threatened.

—**William Tecumseh Sherman**, 1864

Warriors and their family members were interviewed by Kim Shackelford in an attempt to verify the information found in our research and to gain an understanding of the important issues from the perspective of the warriors and their families. The qualitative study "Social Work Practice with Military Personnel, Veterans, and Their Families" was conducted from April 1, 2008 to March 17, 2011. The participants in the study represented the various branches of the military and their family members. Some participants were enlisted at the time of the study and some were veterans. The following is a report of the stories and issues as told by them. The warriors and their families were willing to provide information for a book that allowed them to tell their stories and for a book that had the potential to improve the service of social workers to their population.

The current soldiers and veterans were allowed to talk about their experience without much interruption from the researcher. The study was concerned with giving the soldiers and veterans a voice concerning what they felt needed to be known by social workers. Family members were asked the same type of questions about what the experience has been like for each of them, including their thoughts and feelings. They were asked to describe the experience from their perspective.

The warriors had many questions about the use of the material and our book before they agreed to discuss the issues. It is important to note that, on first contact with warriors and while we described the research, several warriors grimaced, gave a doubting look or a shrug of indifference, or frowned at the words *social worker*. There were comments such as, "Well, I will tell you what it was like over there, but I do not know much about the social work stuff" and "I guess social workers helped in some ways." Most warriors reported not thinking about what social workers could do for them, unless they were injured and wanted help from a social worker. A common theme was that social workers had not been helpful or present in service members' lives, except in a few circumstances. The family members were more enthusiastic in discussing the need for social workers in their lives.

The questions in this research covered age; rank; and family composition at time of enlistment, on each deployment, and on return, as well as current family composition. We asked warriors about the timing, circumstances, and length of deployment. Further questions involved what the military experience had been like for each of them, what they were trained to do, their involvement in combat, and the experiences they would like to share. Another set of questions centered on social work services and what social workers did to help with situations. We asked warriors and family members about the effect of military involvement on family members. We also asked, "Knowing that a book is being written to aid social workers in their practice with warriors and their families, what do you want us to know?" and "What services or practice from a social worker would have made your experience or your family's experience better?" We cover the suggestions for improvement in the conclusion of the book.

The Military Experience

What do the warriors have to say about the military experience?

- "The military has allowed me to go places I have never been before."
- "I got to see things I never could even imagine."
- "It was rough."
- "It's different. Most people think that what they see on Fox news is what it is like and it is not like that. They always cover the bad stuff—John Wayne stuff."
- "It was scary, but not like it shows on TV."

- "I love the military. The fellowship and brotherhood that is formed is stronger than anything."
- "I love the weekend drills, the nature of the job, the fellowship and the bond with fellow soldiers."
- "I have connections everywhere I go and when I travel I can stay with people I met from all over."
- "I recommend every kid to go into the military. It is an experience like no other."
- "It sucked, but I signed up for it so I needed to make the best of it."
- "We got hit. I hit my head and some people got hurt bad."
- "I was in combat. Bombs were going off constantly. I was hit by an IED. I woke up five days later in Walter Reed Army Medical Center with my right arm and left femur torn up, nerve damage in my arm, broken ribs, a collapsed lung, traumatic brain injury and they took out my spleen. They told me I about bled to death because of my arm. I was there for two years. I found my body tag [for my dead body] filled out and in my stuff when I got home."

Difference between the First and Second Deployment

Warriors repeatedly discussed the differences between their first and second deployment:

- "The first time there were bombs, IEDs, . . . combat."
- "The first time—I would call my mom and bombs were going off—I tried to not call so much then."
- "I was on base a lot the first time and would go out during the day for 45 minutes at a time to get parts as I was in a maintenance unit. The second time I was on the road a lot at night as I was in a Calvary unit that ran at night—convoy escort. I drove 14,000 miles in 4 months. I was hit with one IED during the second time."
- "The second deployment was harder on me because of the peace agreement. I had to think twice before shooting. I felt like everything we did was under a microscope. Well, I thought twice because I did not want to end up in military prison for shooting the wrong person. I had to trust my training and hope that my judgment was right. If I couldn't identify the trigger man, if the trigger man was close to a religious shrine or in a heavy populated area, I couldn't engage."
- "The second time there was the peace agreement—if I was going south and there was a base to the east and the shooter was between us and the base, I couldn't shoot, as there might be collateral damage. He is shooting at us and we can't do anything."

- "It was a bad day. We got hit. This was during the last time. Our equipment was good it was just a bad day. We had been gone for a day and one truck had broken down and I had a blow out on my truck and no spare. We called another unit to help and it took them three hours to get there. Another truck ran hot. It was turning into a 30-hour day. Then we got hit."
- "The first time I worked for 4–5 months in a prison yard. I got TB and then I had to fly back and forth all the time as I was testing positive for TB. The second time I was on a smaller base. We were being shot at all the time."
- "The first time we had a harder time with communication with our families back home. We took turns on the computer or phone the first time but the second time we all had our own laptops and wireless so we could talk as much as we wanted to folks back home."

The families echoed this in saying that the first deployment was hard because there was less communication. During the earlier deployment, the soldier would be gone and no one was allowed to know where the unit was, where they were going, or when they would return: "There would be rumors that we had to learn to not listen to and we did not talk about our worries. We would just stay busy and pray and hope that everything was OK." The families talked about when they heard someone in the unit was hurt, they would just cry. Then they would get busy again and keep themselves from thinking about what could happen. Family members said, "You just had to think of the day when he would be home, that's all," and "I just did things to stay busy when I didn't hear from him."

The inability to know where they were going or when they would return did not change during the second deployment, but there was much more communication. The family members talked about the almost-daily contact during the latest deployments, as most soldiers had a personal laptop and access to wireless. Family members knew that soldiers would not be able to communicate for days at times, and they did not know exactly how long soldiers would be gone. If it got to be many days (longer than what they expected), they tried not to worry. If someone got hurt, no one in the unit would contact anyone at home until the soldier who got hurt (or someone for him or her) got word to the family. When one person heard that there was an injury, then the day or night would be tough and full of worry until the family members heard from their soldier. Wives of soldiers shared examples of this:

- "He was suppose to call in 48 hours and he did not call. I was just wait-ing and trying to not worry."
- "I was talking to him at 11 a.m. and he said he had to go but he would call me in 30 minutes. Twelve hours later I was freaking out. None of the spouses or girlfriends in our unit were able to communicate with anyone over there. Finally there was a message that the unit had gone on a mis-sion but it went wrong and they couldn't contact anyone. Then we were all waiting to see who was going to get a message that 'what went wrong' involved someone they loved. When the calls started coming in we would text each other or Facebook that 'my husband' knew that my friend's husband was OK and news spread quick. One wife got told her husband was shot in the head though. The Facebook messages would be 'Have you heard from your husband? Is he with my husband?' And the answer would be 'Yes, they are together' or 'No.' We couldn't say any-thing about the mission."

The difference in the communication issues was that the daily and some-times more than once-a-day communication was difficult to manage for the fam-ilies at home, especially for spouses who had jobs, school, and/or children. The following describes this situation:

I was a full-time student. I had 2-year-old twins. He is nine hours ahead of me. The timing was all off. When he was ready to talk, I was busy. It was time to feed the twins, I was ready for bed, I had to study or it was time for class. I know he wanted to talk and he wanted to know what was going on and he worried about us, our relationship, if I didn't spend a long time talking to him. It was so hard to do everything that he usu-ally did and my stuff and everything we were doing for the soldiers.

A few soldiers said that sometimes knowing what was going on at home was distracting for them, especially if it was something bad. If the soldier's spouse, girlfriend, or boyfriend was seeing someone else (romantically); if there was something wrong with the children (e.g., they were acting out, hurt, or sick); if something bad had happened to another family member; or if something needed to be fixed or taken care of in the home and the soldier would have nor-mally been the one to handle the problem, the soldier could become upset from the information from home. The overall report was that hearing about the needs of the family was sometimes frustrating. Commanding officers said that they did wonder about soldiers' ability to concentrate at times on what they were doing when their minds were on what was going on at home. More soldiers, though, liked getting the daily reports from home. They did, however, worry when they were not able to contact their families, as they realized that their family members were wondering whether they were OK when there was no communication. As one soldier said, "The constant communication—well, it helps and hurts at the same time—but I wanted it."

Effects on the Warrior

The soldiers all agreed that the experience changed them, but not always in ways that people would expect. That the military changes people for the better was an overall theme. Soldiers often reported skills training and the positive relationships as positives. Some said they picked up bad habits like smoking cigarettes, chewing tobacco, and cursing. They talked about how many had started drinking upon returning home but not while on active duty overseas. Other changes they noted included the following:

- "My perceptions have changed. I don't see things like I used to."
- "I get mad easier."
- "I can't remember stuff—even like when my wife tells me to go get something and I can't remember what she said—I do not even remember that she told me to get anything. I didn't do that before. Others say they can't remember either. We laugh and say it is the anthrax vaccine. Who knows?"
- "I am on guard for about everything. This has been different since my deployment. Is it my military training or is it PTSD? I don't know."
- "I am always watching. I check on cars going down my road. I hear a noise and I check it out. I just learned to accept that I am different now."
- "I am suspicious and hypervigilant."
- "I hate loud noises. I want to reach for my gun."
- "My view of the world has changed."
- "After the first deployment I jumped at loud noises. I still do not like loud noises. This time, I hate lasers being shined at me. There was a kid with a laser in a restaurant and I just had to leave. It made me too anxious and nervous. I really was getting angry about him shining the laser. It made me think of Iraq."

One warrior shared that a cousin had told him and his wife, "He is going to be different when he comes back." It terrified both of them, and they both talked about how scared they were that the soldier would come back so different that their marriage would not work. It was the husband's first deployment, and both remember being so worried about the different person returning from war. They each said that this terrorizing behavior was "bullshit" and that people could be prepared for what might happen without the drama and fear of believing people would be so different.

The Injured Warrior

David Yancey, one of the warriors interviewed, gave an extensive amount of information about being injured. He has also worked to improve services for injured soldiers and gave a great account of what his experience was like and the experiences of others he knew at Walter Reed Army Medical Center. He was interviewed for the *Washington Post* and the *Army Times* after working with the *Washington Post* to expose the bureaucratic system at Walter Reed Army Medical Center that was not serving injured warriors. Yancey served seventy-one days active duty in Iraq during 2005 and then spent two years trying to heal from an extensive injury after his Humvee was hit with an IED (Two months, 2007; Yancey, 2007).

Yancey and others stated that the military does not prepare them for what happens if a soldier is injured and that there is no briefing on procedures to follow if injured. There is no discussion of rights or benefits, and it is up to soldiers to find out on their own. The goal of the Army Medical Center is to get injured soldiers ready to fight again—"combat ready"—and many soldiers believe that the center attempts to keep soldiers in the dark. Therefore, it is totally up to soldiers to read, ask questions, and find out on their own how to maneuver the paperwork and bureaucracy. The warriors stated that injured warriors need help full-time while in a medical facility for everyday activities, emotional support, and wading through the mounds of paperwork about their injury and possible disability status. There is no advocacy from others in the military for injured service members except that social workers in the medical facility help get some resources like a wheelchair or clothes. Yancey gave the following as an example:

> If you are injured while on active duty, it requires a ruling that you are 30 percent or more disabled to continue on TRICARE [military insurance]. This will also enable the soldier to get monthly checks. If you have a 30 percent or more disability you are transferred from the military to the VA for services. There are so many obstacles that can be put

in the way of receiving the 30 percent disability. If you do not get this degree of disability then you get a one-time severance check and no health insurance.

Once the 30 percent disability is achieved and the soldier is able to begin with the VA—the procedures are better. I had to spend a lot of my own money to get other opinions and to achieve what was due to me. I have an arm and a leg that will never be OK—I walk with a limp, a traumatic brain injury, migraine headaches, and have severe problems concentrating and remembering. I have PTSD. At the time I would get frustrated and angry very easily.

The VA has a different rating system. There is a temporary retirement and a permanent retirement. There are requirements that must be met along the way. With the acronyms, the confusing policies, the massively detailed laws, and the people trying to keep a soldier from getting the 30 percent disability prior to getting into the VA system, many just give up or never know to fight for their rights. Some do not have the education or any idea where to start to make their way through the bureaucracy and therefore they do not get what they deserve for being injured serving their country. This is just not right.

Marriage and Deployment

One sergeant stated that he tried to tell his unit as they were getting ready to go on a four-day pass before leaving for Iraq to not get married: "Whatever you do, do not get married!" Five men got married and all five of the wives were with other people before ten months had passed. They all were divorced upon returning home, along with three others from his unit.

Another male veteran stated that he would never deploy married. He said, "I went to military training and my house was cleaned out when I got home. My wife had left with everything while I was gone. I knew then that I was not going to Iraq and leaving a woman with her name on all of my stuff. My divorce was final the day before I left for Iraq." He went on to say, "I think it would be better to have a personal assistant that you just hire to take care of your business at home."

A few soldiers discussed the distractions that occur when soldiers have a wife at home. One said, "I think it is easier if you do not have a wife while you are gone. That way you can focus on what you are doing. There are no distractions or negativity."

Overall, the warriors stated that if the marriage was good and the couple was working on something together, deployment would not harm the marriage and couples would make it through the separation. Many soldiers marry right before deployment to gain the extra pay and benefits. The military pay and benefits such as insurance help families. Sometimes it eases the financial burdens, which makes things better for the couple or the family. Many recognized that if the marriage was already in trouble, then the separation of deployment increases loneliness, adds to responsibilities, and may overwhelm the person left behind.

Family Member Experiences

Family members talked about the differences between earlier and later deployments and praised the military for changes and improvements it has made. One of the differences has already been discussed: improved communication. The second biggest improvement discussed were the family readiness groups (FRGs). Family members were appreciative of these groups, but sometimes they commented that the leadership of the groups greatly affected how much help the groups could be. Some people would not attend just because of poor leadership, or in rural communities family members knew the leader and did not want to attend. Several family members talked about how the groups brought people together and said that they do not know how they would have gotten through the deployment of a loved one without the FRG. The Yellow Ribbon meetings also were helpful. Yellow Ribbon meetings are local meetings for persons with deployed family members to receive information from local units. The groups serve to relay needed information but also as support groups for family members:

> The Yellow Ribbon Program (YRP) is a DoD-wide effort to help National Guard and Reserve Service members and their families connect with local resources before, during, and after deployments, especially during the reintegration phase that occurs months after service members return home. Commanders and leaders play a critical role in assuring that Reserve service members and their families attend Yellow Ribbon Events where they can access information on health care, education/ training opportunities, financial, and legal benefits. The DoD works in conjunction with Federal partners, including the Small Business Administration and Departments of Labor and Veterans Affairs, to provide up-to-date and relevant information to the members of the all-volunteer force and their families. The Yellow Ribbon Program is a Department of

Defense program that falls under the Office of the Assistant Secretary of Defense for Reserve Affairs. The VA's Yellow Ribbon Program is part of the Post-9/11 GI Bill and focuses mostly on partnerships with institutes of higher learning. (U.S. Department of Veterans Affairs, 2009a, n.p.)

The FRGs sometimes created smaller groups that would keep in contact and hang out together. One young wife said, "You had to be careful who you hung out with. Some of the girlfriends or wives had a reputation of not being 'true' to the boyfriend or spouse and if my husband had heard I was hanging out with 'her,' it would not be good." Jealousy or suspiciousness about activities was prevalent, but many wives stated that it was to be understood if the marriage was new or the couple was young and didn't know about trust. Many spouses stated that they were careful to not cause stress to the soldier with respect to the people they were around or what they were doing.

Family members said that it was important to not get caught up in the drama that could occur among the FRGs. The members sometimes talked about one another or gave false information. They would sometimes exaggerate information, or gossip would prevail and active-duty soldiers would receive misinformation, which could cause problems. The use of Facebook for communication was a good thing according to some and a bad thing to others. They were not to communicate anything about the soldier's mission, but at times this would slip from a soldier in another communication and then someone would put it on Facebook. One wife said, "This was frightening as we did not know who might be watching for information." Another wife said, "The good thing was that information that the soldiers were OK after a mission was gained quickly and we could communicate to each other and just be supporting friends."

The FRGs often made care packages for the units. This was a positive activity, and sometimes there was help from other community members. One of the warriors said, "I have so much deodorant from care packages that I won't have to buy any for a year!" The family members described a comradeship that occurred through participation in this activity. One wife said, however, that these types of activities sometimes brought out the worst in people. She told about an FRG collecting supplies and money at Walmart for care packages one day, and a man verbally attacked the group, saying, "Soldiers should burn in hell." The man was angry and belligerent, and they were somewhat afraid of him. She said she has been cussed out for supporting the military in Iraq and Afghanistan. She said it hurts her, and then she gets angry about it.

The general attitude was good toward the Yellow Ribbon meetings, but there was some frustration that people did not always explain the policies, rights, and benefits in detail or left out some important details. This caused the warriors and their families to not be able to take advantage of benefits. A young wife shared this example:

> I was waiting until my husband came home from Iraq to take classes at the university. I was waiting because we have small children and my childcare benefits did not come through either. I am now told that I can't transfer the benefits for the G.I. Bill when my husband is not active. He was supposed to transfer the benefits to me when he was active duty. That was an important thing that they should have explained to us at the Yellow Ribbon meeting. Now we are screwed. I can't go to school. If we had known, I would have already started and planned better.

Some family members stated that it was hard to juggle everything that needed to be done. They missed their service members, as they were an integral part of the family and filled many roles and did many jobs. One warrior talked about his dad having Lou Gehrig's disease and how his mom had to take care of him by herself most of the time, as other family members had their own families and homes. Another talked about a tree falling on his back porch during a storm and his wife having to deal with it while he was gone. This worried him.

Family members did not talk much about the exact things the service member did before deployment that were missed; discussion centered more on family problems with in-laws or persons in the extended family who could help take up the slack and pitch in but chose not to. There was an air of bitterness over needing help that was not offered or given, by in-laws especially. Several family members talked about the soldier's parents or siblings who told the soldier in Iraq that they were helping the wife and children at home but were not. These people also bragged to others in the community or at church about how much they were doing to help the soldier's immediate family or in sending care packages, but they really were not doing anything. To the contrary, sometimes they were the ones starting malicious rumors or saying negative things to soldiers about their spouse. The wives and girlfriends reported being very frustrated with this, as it was a commonality among them and a phenomenon they did not understand. One woman said:

> I just did not know how to handle this. I could not say bad things to my husband about his mom. I didn't want to cause him upset, but she did not mind causing him upset with lies about me. Sometimes she would say I was keeping the children away from her and my husband's family. Are you kidding? I needed help. I needed a babysitter. I wanted them to help me. Why would they say that?

Another spouse said:

> I needed someone to talk to about this stuff with his family. It was weird. I talked to the other wives but none of us could understand why someone would be like this. Then when he came back, his family was all about seeing him and of course, the kids. It was like they just wanted other people to think they were helping and wanted him to pay attention to them and not me. I do not know what I did to deserve this. I tried to be nice. There were others that had this same thing happen.

Some families had problems with the red tape involved in the child-care benefit. They were frustrated that they could not start using this benefit before it was time for the soldier to come home. Several families talked about the Yellow Ribbon meetings not being totally forthcoming with everything family members needed to know. They also said that it was hard to figure out everything that needed to be done to get the benefits due to them. They all agreed that that hardest times were when they could not communicate because of a mission or when someone had been hurt and there was no communication leaving the unit. Family members expressed appreciation for those who did help and for the military's efforts to make the experience better during later deployments.

The Experience of Coming Home

Soldiers commonly expressed mixed feelings upon their return home. Families had adjusted to them being gone, and when they returned, more adjustments were required for the soldiers to find their place in the family's daily routine. The following is how one young soldier explained this experience:

> It was good to come home, but it has also been hard to come home. When I left, it was just my wife and I. When I came home, we had a baby. He was born while I was gone. I wanted to be home but it was so different. We used to decide to go somewhere and we just get up and

go. Now . . . it takes one and half hours just to get out the door. My time clock is off. I want to sleep and eat at different times—like I want midnight chow. I also was used to giving orders and people just do what I say. I tried to tell my wife to put the clothes in the dryer. That did not work out as well!

The warriors talked about having to make adjustments, as the family members had their own routines and the warriors had a different routine; moreover, the family's routine at home had changed from what it was before deployment. That "things change" was a common theme that warriors expressed. Several family members said that returning warriors get mad more easily and that their short-term memory was not intact. If there was an injury, then the family and the warrior had to adjust, as they could not do the same things they did before deployment. One warrior said, "You can't just expect to walk back into your home and have it be the same. Your family will be different because they had to take up the slack from you not being there. I changed too."

Some of the warriors expressed dislike for people asking them about the experience at war. They said that they did not want to talk about it, and especially not about bad things. One soldier said, "I hated the 1,000 questions that people had about the war and being over there. Especially questions like, How many people did you kill? Did you kill anyone? Did you shoot your gun? Did you get hurt? Did anyone you know get hurt? I hated those questions. People should know not to ask about that stuff."

Our warriors are having a hard time coming home to the job market as it is in the United States. Those who did not have jobs before they left have a very difficult time finding jobs upon return. The National Guard members claim that employers do not want to hire them because of the every-month weekend drill and the two weeks of summer camp that they have to take off, as well as the potential to leave work for natural disasters. National Guard members are not receiving any help with jobs. Members of one unit talked about how many people came back within months of one another, and few had jobs to go back to, so everyone is jobless. They reported that the job centers were not helpful, and several believed that their previous employers had laid them off when they heard rumors that the unit was deploying. Many employers do not want to hold a position for them to return to the same job; they want to hire a new person in place of the deployed military person. It seems that no one is advocating for the employment or reemployment of our returning warriors.

Another issue is that the G.I. Bill has not been what the warriors and families were told. The recipients are not receiving timely benefits and have to drop out of school. Family members have been told that they cannot receive transferred benefits after the warrior is off active duty, which was not explained to them at Yellow Ribbon meetings. The G.I. Bill could be very helpful, but it is frustrating for many. Many service members said that it was hard to figure out all the rules and how to get everything paid for.

Use of Social Workers

The warriors consistently talked about combat stress. They said that many times others did not believe a person was experiencing combat stress because everyone knew that nothing bad had occurred around the person and that the person was not physically hurt. One warrior explained:

> Sometimes it was looked at like a joke—someone is whining and complaining when nothing even happened to them—if it was for something serious that happened that was OK, then nobody cared if he or she went to combat stress. We wanted the person to get help then. It was just when we couldn't figure out why they would need it—then we thought they were faking it.

When asked about the use of social workers to help with problems or issues, one warrior said, with air quotes, "for combat stress problems." He went on to say, "Most of us thought the ones using counselors for 'combat stress' just wanted to get out of work or they missed their family—what? We all missed our families and that is no reason to go to combat stress for help. No—that was not OK—we made fun of them."

Overall, service members said that there were times when they needed a social worker or counselor, like when something really bad happened. One said, "Some just had a hard time dealing with some of the really bad stuff. They needed someone to talk to about it." Many expressed concern, though, about lack of confidentiality when talking about having problems dealing with the trauma of war. The warriors reported that they did not want to talk about any problems if they knew it would go into their record. For example, "The social worker is just another station to clear. If the social worker asked me if I was thinking about harming or killing myself, there is no way I am going to say yes, as all I want to do is go home."

The warriors repeatedly said that while in the field, the only thing on their minds was going home. They said that, when they are first back in the States, no one would say that they are thinking about suicide or homicide because that might delay them in seeing the family or traveling home. One warrior explained his thoughts while he was going through debriefing: "When the social worker asked, 'Are you having thoughts of hurting yourself or others?' I am thinking about if that is a go or no go? I have *no* thoughts of suicide even if I did have or I do. I want my box checked and to move to the next station. I want to go home. . . . Have a social worker available when go back to drill after we get home. The screenings just do not do what we need, when we need it."

Some warriors said that the problem with social workers who are in the military trying to help is that they have to follow orders. If the social worker is told to not explain in detail to the warrior how to access certain benefits, then the social worker is not going to go against orders. The warriors sometimes thought about this during the interview and concluded that it must be hard for social workers to not be able to advocate for the warrior or the warrior's family. One warrior explained, "The social workers in the military are military. So they can't do anything that their commanding officer did not say they could do and they are not going against orders. So if they are told to not tell an injured soldier about his rights or benefits, it is not happening."

David Yancey, who was injured in Iraq and spent two years at Walter Reed said, "My social worker helped me to get things I needed while I was at the Army Medical Center. She helped me get clothes, my wheelchair, and items I needed. She did help but she was more like someone to just get my basic needs met. She was not one to help with making it through the maze to get my 30 percent disability ruling."

Yancey is now majoring in social work at the University of Mississippi. He talked about the ethical dilemma that military social workers face when they see a person who needs an advocate to help fight the bureaucracy and the persons trying to keep the soldier from getting the benefits they deserve. Military social workers may receive instructions as to their job duty, which does not include doing everything possible to get benefits for soldiers. Social work that is done at a minimum and does not allow social workers to go beyond the minimum, such as to help someone get benefits, causes conflicts and can be unethical for social workers. Yancey said, "It puts the military social worker in a tough place. The worker has to be a military officer first and then a social worker. This may mean the soldier's rights are not upheld or he or she doesn't get the benefits. The social worker has probably been told not to help with the paperwork or finding out the rules. This is not what a social worker should be doing—but what do you do?"

Yancey also said that social workers are needed to advocate for service members, counsel, support, find resources, help soldiers find jobs upon returning home, help families, and give guidance when soldiers try to further their education. He believes that social workers should help with developing policies about services surrounding deployments (before, during, and after return) and services to injured service members.

Part Three

Social Work Solutions

Social Work and Military Families

The reality is both the glory and the crucible of military families. It tests them to the limit. It is the source of the pride and, for many, their undoing. Nearly all military families, no matter how well informed, find themselves confronting challenges they had never imagined. They need all the support they can get.

—M. E. Wertsch

A Spartan woman, as she handed her son his shield, exhorted him saying, "Either with this or upon it."

—Plutarch, *Moralia*

He had discovered, like so many soldiers returning from the wars, that his girl had abandoned him for another man.

—Alan Moorehead, *The Blue Nile*, 1962

The military has changed dramatically in the past twenty years, and so has the military family. Most civilians think of the military family as a conservative family living on a military base or Army post in family housing. At one time that was the reality, and most families socialized within the military community. Since the creation of the total force, the military family now includes the National Guard and reservists (Knox & Price, 1995; Pryce, Ogilvy-Lee, & Pryce, 2000). The Army has significantly downsized in the past twenty years. Never before in American history has so much been asked of military family members and significant others.

Deployment Statistics

It is estimated that in the first several years of the current wars, more than 1.7 million service members deployed to Iraq or Afghanistan (Century Foundation, 2008; Tanielian & Jaycox, 2008). It is also estimated that more than six hundred thousand of those, or more than one-third, have deployed more than once, and approximately six hundred thousand reservists have been mobilized, with thirty-four National Guard combat brigades deployed to Iraq and Afghanistan at least once (Bonds, Baiocchi, & McDonald, 2010; Century Foundation 2008).

When service members are separated from their family, many people are affected daily—spouses and children and parents, brothers and sisters and their families, aunts and uncles and cousins, grandparents and great-grandparents. Darwin (2009) points out that if there were seven people in the family, then 11.8 million people would be affected. He reaches this figure by multiplying 7 (for those seven people) by 1.7 million (for the total number of deployed service personnel). If we consider extended family, colleagues, and friends, that number could grow to between 60 million and 90 million people. Moreover, we should consider service members' community. Rentz et al. (2007) reported that, in 2007, seven hundred thousand children experienced life without their deployed parent or parents. It is important that these number include not only separation and deployment for service members but also multiple separations and redeployments for family members.

Along with deployment statistics, consideration must be given to physical and psychological trauma, as well as to polytrauma, or multiple trauma, and loss of life. In any of these events, all the aforementioned individuals are affected. In some cases whole communities change, especially if a whole unit is hit during combat and several people die. In addition, statistics indicate that child maltreatment, family violence, and divorce accompany increased and repeated deployments.

Early Literature on Military Families

Families have been part of the military since the American Revolution (Albano, 1994), but military life for families has changed along with societal changes. Many of those changes are now reflected in the demographics of the military and its families. The military has more single parents, dual-career couples, and women deployed to hazardous duty and assigned to combat units than ever before. Although the military is a predominately male institution, it is no longer an all-male institution. Military children were rare before the all-volunteer service, but today they are common in today's military services. There are far more family resources and support services today, and families use them heavily. Military service has become a family affair.

Following the Persian Gulf War and the terrorist attacks of September 11, the military has experienced ongoing separations from family and deployments to Iraq and Afghanistan. Before this period, information about the impact of separation and deployment was scarce, and the literature tended to focus on the more negative aspects of military life in earlier years (Isay, 1968; Lagrone, 1978; Morrison, 1981). These studies need to be understood in the context of the time in which they were written and a general lack of knowledge about military families. This early literature also represents observations of individuals with limited data. The portrayal of military families was one of dysfunction—it was called the military family syndrome—and children were referred to as military brats.

Literature on military families has become more grounded in the realities of military life. Several books and dissertations have been published illuminating the challenges of being the spouse of a service member, the benefits, and the strengths of spouses (Biank, 2006; Daley, 1999; Hunter & Nice, 1978; Kaslow & Ridenour, 1984; Knox, 1990; Pierce, 1982; Wertsch, 1991). Most base and post exchanges offer books with guidelines and suggestions for service members' spouses (Cline, 1989; Crossley, 1990; Crossley & Keller, 2004). Today's military family social environments are less rigid and more relaxed than in the 1960s and 1970s. The Persian Gulf War and its impact on families was the focus of some of literature in the 1990s (Kaslow, 1993; Ursano & Norwood, 1996). As the military moved to outsourcing social services and counseling to nonprofit and for-profit agencies, there was a need for literature on military families that helped civilian service providers understand the culture, stresses, and strengths of families (Daley, 1999; Martin, Rosen, & Sparacino, 2000). Since the invasion of Iraq and Afghanistan more literature has been produced that provides information and guidance for social service and mental health providers working with military service members and their families, including veterans (Armstrong, Best, & Domenici, 2006; Freeman, Moore, & Freeman, 2009; Hall, 2008; Pavlicin, 2003; Savitsky, Illingworth, & DuLaney, 2009; Slone & Friedman, 2008).

The focus on the military family has changed from one of negativity to one of recognition of and respect for the strains, stresses, advantages, and strengths of being a member of a military family. Today's research is far more sophisticated than in earlier years. Sample sizes and more rigorous research designs have produced a growing body of literature that can inform civilian providers working with military service members, veterans, and their families. Research has increasingly focused on the family because of the family's relationship to service members' readiness for combat.

Changes in the Military

The military has changed in ways that dramatically impact family members. From the mid-1990s to the present, the military has experienced numerous deployments, unseen in prior years (Booth et al., 2007). Deployments include the Persian Gulf, the Sinai Peninsula, Somalia, Bosnia, Kosovo, Haiti, Iraq, and Afghanistan. National Guard units have also been deployed to natural disaster sites. Today, the majority of military families live in communities and not on military posts or installations.

The downsizing of the military was accompanied by a move to reorganize into fast and light units that can readily be deployed. The goal is to have a smaller force mostly in Europe and in smaller overseas installations. This means that service members' families will travel less overseas, and service members will experience more and longer deployments (U.S. Army, 2005). These family separations have and will continue to threaten the survival of the family as a unit.

Defining *family* is challenging because of the range of families; they can include common law or cohabiting couples, as well as single-parent and the dual-military-service parents. Some families consist of two parents and children; others may include grandparents or aunts and uncles, or even friends who serve as surrogate parents with legal guardianship. There are numerous types of families: nuclear, blended or reconstituted, single, culturally diverse, and dual-career families. The range of families means there is a wide range of family support needs. Service members are becoming more aware that their family competes for their time, which creates a challenge when the mission comes first, as it always does. According to Booth et al. (2007), this leads some personnel to leave the military because they can't meet the demands of both family and mission.

In 1989 Segal wrote about the demands of family and the military mission and how incompatible the two were. She labeled both "greedy institutions," and it would appear that they remain so today. Before the late 1960s, the military service personnel were primarily single, not married, and most spouses were officers' wives (Schneider & Martin, 1994). Military families were not considered part of the mission, which was the arena of the service member. As the number of families grew, research data began to demonstrate that families did affect military readiness (Schneider & Martin, 1994) and the ability of service members to do their job anyplace in the world. During the early 1970s, after the Vietnam

War, the all-volunteer military service emerged and the number of families grew. As the awareness increased that families do affect readiness, the military services recognized that their approach to families had to change.

In the 1980s Army spouses started organizing and planning meetings and symposia on family life, concerns, and needs. They found that various military groups shared the same concerns and needs, which led to military policy changes addressing the concerns and needs of families. In the Army, this resulted in the Army Family Action Plan (AFAP). Every year Army service members and families attend meetings that address and collect problems, concerns, and issues, which they then forward to the annual national AFAP meeting. The AFAP meeting has become a major source of information and evaluation on families' concerns and needs. Issues such as quality child care, housing, elementary and high schools, special needs children, youth services, dependent aging parents, libraries, and recreation are put into the plan, and every year the issues are revisited and evaluated until the issue is determined to be resolved or unattainable.

Major Military Policy Changes Addressing Families

A policy position paper marked the change in recognition of the importance of military families to readiness. Army Chief of Staff General John Wickham (1983) published "The Army Family," a white paper that drew attention to the importance of creating a partnership between the Army and the military family. To that end several programs emerged with the intention of contributing to stronger military families. The largest were Army Community Services (ACS) and Morale, Welfare, and Recreation (MWR). The white paper became a watershed event and acknowledged that the Army recognized the importance of families to military readiness and retention. The paper has been the foundation for Army family philosophy:

> A partnership exists between the Army and Army Families. The Army's unique missions, concept of service and lifestyle of its members—all affect the nature of this partnership. Towards the goal of building a strong partnership, the Army remains committed to assuring adequate support to families to promote wellness; develop a sense of community; and strengthen the mutually reinforcing bonds between the Army and its families. (Wickham, 1983, p. 16)

In 2003, General Eric Shinseki's white paper "The Army Family" followed. The paper recounted the history of Army families since 1983 and identified the programs and policies that the Army had implemented in support of families. It also announced that separations and deployments were likely to increase, and as such, Army families had to be proactively supported. General Shinseki introduced the Well-Being Action Plan, which would integrate the Army, National Guard, and Army Reserve seamlessly, as well as the family support and readiness programs. His plan would integrate the services into those programs.

In 2007 Army Chief of Staff General George Casey signed the Army Covenant, acknowledging that the Army family was the most "stretched and stressed" part of the force. He introduced the covenant as a response to concerns about quality housing, health and mental health care, youth services, child care, schools, and education and employment opportunities for family members, and he indicated that the Army would proactively respond to those issues. As part of the covenant, $1.4 billion has been committed to address funding and support for family programs. He also acknowledged that family and mission readiness is inherent to the success of the Army today. This support is to be anchored in the local Army family community (Bartelt, 2007; Crouch, 2010; Lorge, 2007).

In the years that followed Wickham's (1983) white paper, deployments increased, thus family separations began taking their toll. Some spouses began family support groups to take care of families at home while service members were deployed. The groups gave spouses at home places to turn to for support and help solving problems. It was a concept that grew and spread across the military. Officers' wives usually were group leaders, and volunteers carried out services for families. There was no standard format for the groups and no training. Simple problems had simple solutions. However, the lack of training and the complexity of some families' problems were overwhelming to leaders and groups, and so went unresolved. In addition, without a standardized organization, the groups differed greatly from unit to unit. Well-intended volunteers attempted to solve problems beyond their expertise. There was also inconsistent communication between the Army and the support group, which left family members to hear rumors and speculation about the status of the military unit and service members. The military recognized that this was compromising mission readiness.

Military Readiness: An Ongoing Issue

During and after Operation Desert Storm, the Army realized that family readiness was an ongoing issue and that the family support system needed a more standardized structure. During this period, too, many soldiers and their families were not prepared for deployment. Dual-career couples had to leave children with relatives, as did single-parent soldiers. These caregivers had challenges that were not easily solved. Many soldiers did not have family care plans or the accompanying legal papers, like guardianship for children. Some spouses knew little about managing finances, including how to use a checkbook. Many spouses were not familiar with managing home finances or did not know where legal papers were. Some spouses in the Guard and Reserve did not know what military supports and resources they had when service members were activated for federal duty. There were numerous issues that the Army realized that it needed to incorporate into family readiness.

Interestingly, in 1987, before Desert Storm, the Department of Defense funded the fledgling National Guard Family Program (NGFP) to facilitate National Guard families' readiness as part of the total force (Personal communication, Dorothy Ogilvy-Lee, chief of family programs, National Guard, LCSW, October 10, 1992). The program was a marker in the development of support for total-force families. During Desert Storm the NGFP was enormously successful in setting up more than six hundred family assistance centers (FACs) across the nation. In the initial stages of the Persian Gulf War, 3,436,626 family members were served at a FAC. When the troops returned, 2,532,046 of them received services (Knox & Price, 1995). The FACs were the only such place providing resources that were available to any reserve component. Their effectiveness was such that they quickly expanded to meet the reserve component's support needs as well as those of active-duty families who were not living near a military installation. The FACs provided services to all branches of service. As a result of the FACs' success, the National Guard was formally and officially charged with providing family support and assistance for all military families not living near a DOD installation.

The NGFP was created by a social worker. Every state and territory has a state family program coordinator, some of whom are social workers. The state programs are decentralized, diverse, largely self-help organizations that depend heavily on thousands of volunteers, both Guard members and civilian supporters. The NGFP works with communities and community programs to meet its mission goals. It has formed partnerships with the Veterans of Foreign Wars, American Veterans (better known as AMVETS), Disabled American Veterans, the American Legion, and the USO. The state NGFPs have programs for children and youths, as well as community contacts for various types of social support, from counseling to parenting, preparing for deployment, redeployment, reintegration, bereavement, and loss.

Following the Persian Gulf War, the Army Community and Family Support Center recognized the need for formal family support and readiness education to improve in light of increasing deployments for service members. The solution was the development of a program that educated families and military service members about preparing for deployment, surviving deployment, coming home, and being reunited. One of the most important components of the program was the integration of information regarding the National Guard service members and reservists, including information about the NGFP. The curriculum, called Operation READY (Resources for Educating about Deployment and You), was developed in 1993 by three universities: Texas A&M University, the University of California at Berkeley, and the University of California at Riverside (Knox & Price, 1995). The curriculum had several components, including the *Army Family Readiness Handbook*, predeployment, postdeployment, family assistance center, and family support group (advanced training), and the program materials were accompanied by training videos (Knox & Price, 1995). The Army has often used these materials, and they are also used by other programs, such as Army Family Team Building, which emerged from the lessons of Desert Storm. Family readiness became an integral part of mission readiness. Family support groups became known as family readiness groups (FRGs). The education and team building ensured that service members could deploy without a moment's hesitation and knowing that their family was equally prepared for the separation.

The concept of the Operation READY psychoeducational program was groundbreaking and provided families with a standardized structure to organize family support programs, with some uniformity across the military. The curriculum addressed all aspects of predeployment, deployment, postdeployment, and reintegration. Families could move from one military community to another and find a family readiness group. The Army recognized the need to make timely revisions to the original materials to reflect the dynamic changes in the demands on families. As the years have passed and the Army has grown smaller, and deployments and redeployments more numerous, the Operation READY program materials have been revised, in 2002 and 2007, so that they now incorporate eighteen years of changes since the inception of the program. The materials are available for downloading online at Military OneSource (http://www.armyone source.com), and they have been repackaged with new graphics and new videos and DVDs, as well as CDs, that address more recent issues. The materials will continue to be revised as military families' needs change. The other military services have developed similar curricula and family support and readiness programs tailored to their needs.

Since the development of Operation READY numerous materials and Web sites have added to the military's deployment curriculum. The ultimate goal of these efforts is to build resiliency in service members, their family, and the military community. Resilience can be thought of as hardiness, or the ability to adjust during and following challenges and difficulties. The military has come to understand that resiliency is a major key to family readiness and that resiliency can be learned. Several factors influence resiliency. Two of the most important are perception of organizational culture and personal characteristics.

The military has made changes to organizational culture as it has acknowledged the need for family readiness. In addition, multiple deployments have created a need to build more resiliency in the service members. Although the military has been moving to promote seeking help when service members need it, there are still service members who fail to understand or do not get the message. Some still believe that if you have the right stuff, you can handle anything. There is much work to be done to reduce and even eliminate this barrier to seeking help. Social workers can help the military to make this change.

Social workers can help service personnel, families, and communities build and sustain resiliency. Using the materials developed by the military, social workers can educate families about resiliency and how to build and sustain it. Counseling is another opportunity to help individuals develop personal skills that contribute to resiliency. Through community organizing, social workers can help military communities, on or off base, understand and develop the support networks that promote resiliency and sustain it. Social workers can also contribute to ongoing resiliency campaigns in the community, with simple activities such as making resiliency visible by posting information on billboard or passing out pamphlets.

Paton, Violanti, and Smith (2003) identify several characteristics that can be learned that lead to sustained resiliency. Each individual can identify what social support means to them, as well as how they give social support through personal relationships and in relationship to their community. Individuals can also strengthen their communication and coping skills.

An important factor is developing a philosophy regarding crisis. The Chinese have a saying that crisis is a dangerous opportunity—embedded in this wisdom is the understanding that crisis can lead to disaster and pain, or it can lead to growth and understanding. Another factor is understanding that change in life is a constant and affects every part of life. Given that the military is predominately made up of young people, social workers can present resiliency building as a lifelong developmental process and the idea that each individual brings all of his or her experiences to their framework for resiliency. In some cases it may be necessary to nurture individuals into believing in themselves and learning to take a positive perspective as often as possible. It is possible to reinforce acceptance and growing with the "new normal."

The process of building sustained resilience is ongoing, and it should not be portrayed as Pollyannaish, where everything is fine and wonderful. Military life comes with harsh and hard realities that many civilians will never know or experience. Military life is not for everyone. Social workers who are able to acknowledge and share the difficulties and pains as well as the positives and pleasures of this life are more likely to be accepted into a military community. By using the strengths perspective and seeing the positive attributes, talents, and resources of the community, social workers can emphasize these abilities in their work with the military and can become an asset to the military community.

Common Characteristics of Military Life

Regardless of the branch of service, all military service members and their families share certain characteristics (Booth et al., 2007). Military lifestyle has much to commend it, especially to young people. First, families benefit from stable employment and ongoing training for upward mobility. Military experience is an asset to many employers, who give military veterans preference in employment. Health care is readily available for the whole family, including parents, if they should become dependent on the military member. Housing on installations and housing allowances are provided to service members for civilian community housing. Assistance is provided to families seeking housing. Service members earn thirty days a year of paid vacation that they can take as requested, depending on the military unit's needs. Most military posts and installations have recreation facilities, churches, an exchange for household and personal tax-free purchases, package stores for alcoholic and nonalcoholic tax-free beverages, a commissary for nontaxable food purchases, dry-cleaning services, various social clubs, mental health services and counseling, child-care centers, youth services, schools, employment assistance, beauty and barber shops, and movie theaters. Many installations operate parks and pools for summer recreation. There are many benefits provided for a good quality of life.

There are also many challenges to military life. Military families often experience frequent relocation from one post or installation to another. Often, they live at a distance from their relatives and may live outside the United States, in places like Turkey, Japan, or Germany. Being in the military means long hours, and sometimes unexpected time away from family. Military service members and their families have separations, deployments, and redeployments to national and foreign locations and to combat zones. The risk of various injuries and death is constant. Service members often work long hours away from contact with their family. The military service members and their families are pressured to conform to military life and expectations, whether or not they live on the military installation. They may find themselves living in a foreign country and in that local community if an installation is not present. Military spouses face challenges in seeking child care and employment. As the number of families has increased, there has been a growing reluctance for family members to accept the military lifestyle and expectations. In some cases spouses have careers and children and do not want to leave familiar communities that compete with service members' relocation requirements. As stated earlier, some service members choose to leave the military because of competing demands of family and a military career.

Before the advent of the all-volunteer military force, fewer than one-fourth of enlisted service members were married (Booth et al., 2007). It was far more common for noncommissioned officers and upper-ranking officers to have wives. As the years passed, increasing numbers of spouses of both groups began to identify military life as more stressful than that of their civilian counterparts. Research supports the idea that military life does incur an unusual amount of stress on family members (Amen & Jellen, 1988; Black, 1993; Bowen, 1989; Burrell, Adams, Durand & Castro, 2006; Finkel, Kelley, & Ashby, 2003; Harrell, 2002; Kelley, 1994; Kelley et al., 2001; Knox & Price, 1995, 1999; Orthner, Bowen, & Beare, 1990). The primary stressors are separations and deployments (Knox & Price, 1995), especially deployments with unknown departure and return dates. Families are expected to adapt to separations, deployments, and reintegration at postdeployment. There is empirical evidence that the strain of these experiences on service members and families is the source of marital stress and dissatisfaction, poor parental relations, and impaired communication and relationships (Blount, Curry, & Lubin, 1992; Burnam, Meredith, Sherbourne, Valdez, & Vernez, 1992; Martin, 1984; Mozon, 1987; Padden, 2006; Peebles-Kleiger & Kleiger, 1994; Perconte, Wilson, Pontius, Dietrick, & Spiro, 1993; Pierce, 1982; Rosen & Carpenter, 1989; Rosen, Westhuis &

Teitelbaum, 1994; Rothberg & Koshes, 1994; Wheeler, 2009). It is the parent, grandparent, relative, or designated caregiver who must take on the responsibility for preparing for the separation, filling the parental role for the departed service member and becoming a single parent, organizing and managing all family events (e.g., births, birthdays, holidays, school events), and maintaining discipline and morale during the separation. It is also that parent's responsibility to manage home maintenance and finances and repairs on auto and home appliances, to make decisions about major purchases, and in many cases to successfully maintain their own employment. Also, he or she has to manage communication with the deployed service member if communication is possible. In addition to all of the foregoing, some parents have concerns about aging parents or special needs children who may require around-the-clock care. All of this is expected of the spouse who remains at home.

In the past there was an expectation that upper-ranking military spouses would be unemployed and give considerable time to volunteer work for the military. There was an unstated understanding that officers' spouses and enlisted spouses did not associate with one another. As Schneider and Martin (1995) point out, this has resulted in diminished support for many young and inexperienced families, especially single parents, who need it the most. In the 1980s the evolution of family readiness groups (FRGs) included all unit spouses, which increased the potential for support to younger families and all families experiencing deployments. Family stresses originating from spouses and/or children impede the ability of the service member to focus on the mission and compromise military readiness. In more recent years commanders and small-unit leaders have been pressured to keep their families informed and mission ready as part of their normal duties and evaluations. This represents a serious policy shift. These leaders are also responsible for maintaining clear factual communication with the FRG leadership.

The stress and strain of military life has increased with the length of the wars. This is reflected in the increase in reports of family violence (Alvarez & Sontag, 2008) and divorce rates (Jelinek, 2008; McMichael, 2008; Zoroya, 2010a). In addition, child maltreatment has been rising among military families (Gibbs, Martin, Kupper, & Johnson, 2007).

Military Families Seeking Help for Mental Health

There are a variety of sources of formal help for military family members in need of mental health services. Service members and families have access to counseling on the military post or installation. The services also offer Military OneSource to service members and their families. Military OneSource is an online service that can identify a list of mental health providers in service members' community who can offer twelve prepaid counseling sessions. They can also make referrals for more serious problems. The services provided are confidential unless the situation is life threatening to the client or others.

A barrier to seeking help is the stigma attached to having a mental health problem. Burnam et al. (2008) identify three factors that interfere with service members and veterans using mental health services: (1) personal beliefs, or an individual's perceptions; (2) social beliefs, or the perceptions of the immediate group to which one belongs and how that perceives mental health; and (3) cultural factors, or long-standing beliefs embedded in a large group of people that guide what is acceptable collective behavior. Corrigan and Penn (1999) define stigma as a "negative and erroneous attitude about a person, a prejudice, or negative stereotype" (p. 765). The military culture has a long-standing belief that if service members have the right stuff, they and their families will not experience mental health problems. There is a widespread belief that seeking mental health services will negatively affect promotions and upward mobility. There is an ongoing effort by the Department of Defense (U.S. Department of Defense Task Force on Mental Health, 2007) to dispel and discourage barriers to seeking mental health services.

Burnam et al. (2008) discuss the three types of stigma identified by Corrigan and Watson (2002). The first type is the perception of the public and public responses to an individual who has mental health issues, which is referred to as public or societal stigma. Often, the public believes and reinforces negative perceptions of mental health issues. This makes it difficult for individuals who have mental health concerns to seek help or to adhere to interventions that help.

The second type of stigma can become individualized when a person shares and believes the public negative perception of mental health. Such beliefs can be internalized, and individuals with mental health problems may perceive themselves as weak and worthless. This negative internalization can also lead to hopelessness.

The third type of stigma is institutional stigma. In this instance, public policy practices negatively regard the use of mental health services, in such a way as to become a barrier to access. There is a long-standing belief in the military that a person in need of mental health services is no longer an asset and may be an impediment to mission readiness. This belief is contagious and spreads to families who become concerned about how they would be perceived for seeking help. Any promotion of mental health well-being should address all three ways that stigma creates a barrier to use of services.

Hoge et al. (2004) identified the responses from service members who were deployed and had mental health issues. The three most common responses were, "I would be seen as weak," "Unit leadership might treat me differently," and "Members of the unit would have less confidence in me." The following three most common reactions were, "It would harm my career," "[It would be] difficult to schedule an appointment," and "[It is] too embarrassing." The final and least reported response was "[I] don't trust mental health professionals." The first four responses are locked into military culture; the remaining reasons are person individualized beliefs. The last statement is most likely a result of ignorance of mental health services or poor experiences with mental health providers. Family members may think as the service member does and fear the impact of seeking help on the service member's career (Hoge, Castro, & Eaton, 2006).

In a recent mental health study of 250,626 military spouses experiencing a deployment compared with military spouses not experiencing deployment, it was found that deployments are correlated with psychological and emotional problems, as well as family functioning (Hoge et al. 2006; Mansfield et al., 2010). In the first study, the authors drew data from medical records of spouses using mental health services between 2003 and 2006. The results demonstrated that a one- to eleven-month deployment was associated with depressive disorders, sleep disorders, acute stress reactions, and adjustment disorders. When deployment was longer than eleven months, there was an increase in all such disorders. Longer deployments were clearly correlated with increases in mental health disorders.

Hoge et al. (2006) found, consistent with other literature, an association between Soldiers' and Marines' combat service and social and family dysfunction. In their postdeployment twelve-month study, they found associations with increased spouse abuse, intention to divorce, and marital dissatisfaction. Spouses reported experiencing moderate to severe emotional and family problems and alcohol use. Interestingly, spouses were more likely than service members to seek help from their primary care physician or a mental health professional. The primary barrier to seeking mental health services was getting off of work and needing child care.

A mental health provider can work to educate a person in need of mental health services. One possibility is to find ways to affiliate in a nonprofessional way with service members and their families. Just as mental health providers are available and have a presence in military units as combat stress control teams, mental health providers at home need to be part of the military community. By making casual contact at units' family functions, attending school events, and making presentations at the FRGs, mental health providers can reduce barriers that would keep family members from seeking services when needed. Mental health providers can also engage family members in nontraditional ways, such as by starting a mental and physical wellness group that incorporates mental health into exercise. The provider's creativity contributes to lowering the barriers to services. Darwin (2009) reports that mental health providers' attendance at FRG meetings increased spouses' contact with mental health services. Green-Shortridge, Britt, and Castro (2007) advocate that leaders and supervisors can dispel stigma and myths about mental health proactively and normalize mental health well-being. Also, implementing mental health policies and practices in the organizational culture will positively change perceptions of asking for help.

Transitional Density and Family Survival

Transitional density is an important concept for understanding how a family can get to a breaking point at which survival as a family is not possible. Bain (1978) argues that the ability of a family to cope with a transition (e.g., separation, deployment) is "directly proportional to the stress on the family generated by the transitional density" (p. 678) that they have been experiencing. When we consider "normal" transitions that a family experiences, it does not take long to observe incremental stresses accumulating and strain beginning to occur. For example, when two individuals marry, they transition into becoming a couple, with roles and responsibilities that accompany the transition. When a child is born, another transition takes place as the couple becomes not just husband and wife but also parents, mother and father. As each transition takes place, additional roles are acquired. In essence each individual has multiple roles and experiences multiple transitions. This process can be stressful, but usually people adapt and cope with the changes, and even grow as individuals and as a family. Most families successfully move through a lifetime of transitions and role changes. However, when separations and deployments and redeployments become part of the process, the stresses and strains threaten family survival, and in some cases, the strain is too great for the family or a couple to survive.

One of the potential outcomes of reaching maximum strain is maladaptive coping. This was one of the lessons learned following the Persian Gulf War, and it was addressed in the psychoeducational materials produced for Operation

READY. Specifically, the *Army Family Readiness Handbook* (U.S. Army Community and Family Support Center, 1993, 2002) identifies the stresses and strains of separation and deployment, and provides recommendations for positive coping choices. It makes recommendations for single deployments, not multiple deployments, and raises questions about the reality of coping with multiple deployments. Every couple and family has breaking points. A deployment of fifteen months is fertile ground for divorce, as is a deployment of thirty or sixty months. Families are not meant to be separated like this.

Predeployment, Separation, and Postdeployment and Reintegration Periods

It is always important to individualize work with military families. They are not all alike and too often are treated as though they were. The range of military families is as diverse as the communities in which they are located. Some families have a long, intergenerational history of military service, but for others it is a completely new experience. Of greatest concern are young families with children. Too many of these families live below the poverty line, and many rely on food stamps and have inadequate housing. For young people without deployment experience, the stresses and strains can be great.

Another aspect of war today is the overwhelming amount of media covering the war in multiple forms: television, radio, newspaper, journals and magazines, and movies. In addition to a family being constantly reminded about the two ongoing wars, deployed service members have access to various ways to contact family members. Laptop computers, video cameras, phone calls, Facebook, Twitter, and texting all make it possible for deployed service members to stay in touch when they are not in remote areas. Service members and their families have to be careful about how much information and what kind of information they share. It remains to be seen whether a lot of contact and communication is beneficial or helps anyone cope more effectively.

Mobilization and Predeployment

When service members are notified of an impending deployment, family members have many reactions. Protest against the loss of the service member to the deployment is natural, as are despair, detachment, and return adjustment (Pincus, House, Christenson, & Adler 2010; U.S. Army Community and Family Support Center, 1993, 2002, 2006). Feelings of tension, anger, fearfulness, anxiety, and doubts are experienced and require strong coping skills. It is not unusual for a couple to have significant arguments during this period (Pincus et al., 2010). This information is shared in FRGs so that service members and their spouses can anticipate these feelings and be prepared proactively to cope.

Psychoeducation programs have been developed to prepare military families to understand what kinds of emotions they may experience and how everyone in the family will change. The programs also help them anticipate ambiguous loss (Boss, 1980, 1999, 2007), which is characterized by uncertainty, lack of clarity, vagueness, and indeterminacy. For example, service members may be physically absent or psychologically present, or just the reverse, physically present but psychologically absent. Both situations leave family members frustrated and frozen in uncertainty. Each family member may express this experience in a variety of ways, including unhealthy ones. Families are chronically aware also that service members are going into harm's way, which is the greatest uncertainty.

Separation, Deployment, and Sustainment

While the service members are away, families have a range of positive and negative experiences. They begin to learn to function without the presence of the deployed service member. For some families these separations are common, and they are familiar with the "new normal." But for some families, especially those who have not experienced deployments, it may come as a shock. Either way families learn to cope or do not. If not, this could lead to maladaptive coping behaviors. The uncertainty contributes to the emotional roller coaster that some families may experience (Pincus et al., 2010). For many families the ups and downs lead to positive growth. The central theme during deployment is that everybody is changing at home, and so is the service member. This is the new normal for everyone. During this time, service members and spouses (or significant others) may have contact, and they are advised to keep it positive (Pincus et al., 2010). Problems are best solved where they occur, and the distance makes the other person's involvement impossible. During deployment, the caregiver at home seeks support from friends, family, and FRG members. Rumors are one issue that everyone needs to guard against. With ready communication, it is easy for misinformation to occur and do great harm.

Reunion, Postdeployment, and Reintegration

Reunion of the family and the service member is complex and includes both positive and negative emotions. Most of the literature written for military families encourages them to understand that everyone has changed and that it will take some time to reintegrate into a changed family (Pincus et al., 2010). Much of the literature identifies some of the ways in which family members and service members grow. The programs of the various service branches tailor lessons learned from prior separations and deployments to prepare service members and families for what to expect during reintegration and to have realistic expectations. There are numerous resources available to assist civilian and military providers in helping prepare service members and families for successful reintegration. The primary goal is to support the family to create another new normal.

When a Warrior Deploys, the Family Also Serves

Never before in our history has so much been asked of military families as part of the total force. This is especially true of the National Guard and reservists, whose families more often than not live away from installations and ready access to family readiness groups. In fact, a handful of National Guard service members and reservists may be attached to a military unit in an entirely different state and deploy with that unit. The families at home are at a distance from the FRG, and although they may find out some information on the unit online, there is little proximity to the physical and emotional support that may be needed. Often, families must cope with a deployment the best they can.

Until recently, the impact of deployment on the mental health of military spouses has gone unstudied. Mansfield et al. (2010) studied the wives of 250,626 Army service members between 2003 and 2006 in a review of electronic records. The researchers controlled for social, demographic, and mental health history of the spouses and compared mental health diagnosis with the number of months of deployment to Iraq or Afghanistan. The spouses were compared with spouses of service members who had not deployed. Spouses whose service member was deployed for one to eleven months had a significant number of mental health issues. Diagnoses of depressive disorder, sleep disorders, anxiety, acute stress reactions, and adjustment disorders were common. Also, the longer the deployment was beyond eleven months, the greater was the increase in all mental health issues. The researchers concluded that the longer the deployment, the greater was the incidence of mental health problems.

In working with families experiencing ambiguous loss, Boss (1999) found that people can cope and grow: "the goal for families is to find some way to change even though the ambiguity remains. This is yet another paradox—to transform a situation that won't change" (p. 119). Families use their ability to master the situation while remaining aware of the deployed service member.

Boss identifies several factors related to families' power of mastery over their situation. Social workers can support families by helping them claim their identity as a military family and recall the situations they have mastered in the past. Getting families to talk about their roles, rules, and rituals and past family events, can help them anchor themselves in who they are in the face of ambiguity. Social workers can remind families that they have the ability to adapt, change, and grow. Spirituality can also help families find meaning in their experience with deployment and remain optimistic that their family will survive the separation and deployment.

Children and Adolescents

Military children make many sacrifices when either or both parents deploy. At the end of 2008, 1.7 million service members had been deployed (National Center for PTSD, U.S. Department of Veterans Affairs, 2010). Approximately 40 percent are National Guard and Reserve service members, and it has been suggested that deployment is particularly difficult for them (Chartrand & Siegel, 2007). In addition, the number of children and spouses is greater than the number of service members. The majority of children are five years old or younger (Barker & Berry, 2009). The VA's National Center for PTSD (2010) reports on research identifying how deployment affects children and families, and it has identified several issues that both face. According to the report, 43 percent of active-duty service members have children. In fact, an estimated 2 million children have experienced a deployment, and many have experienced the death of a parent. As of 2006, approximately 1,600 children had lost a parent, with unknown numbers having parents return home with serious injuries (Chartrand & Siegel, 2007). The extent to which service members' injuries affect the family and how is still unknown. A preliminary study has examined the effects of combat injury of service members on their families (Cozza et al., 2010). The researchers found that the stress the family experienced before the injury was associated with child and family distress after the injury. They did not find the severity of the injury to be related to child distress but to the degree to which the injury disrupted an already-stressed family. More research is needed on this issue.

Ryan-Wenger (2001) found a high degree of awareness among perceptions of war in fifty-seven children. When asked how they felt about war, most said "bad and afraid." When asked what they thought about the United States getting into a war, most responded, "people [are] killed or dying, and it's not right." When asked what they liked about war, all children responded, "Nothing."

Families with extended family, friends, and community support tend to manage deployment with success. A major issue the family at home faces is how changed the deployed service member is and how they will reintegrate with that person. In one study of children, the average number of months the service member spent away from the family was eleven (Chandra et al., 2010). This is particularly challenging for children who developmentally have limited coping resources (Barker & Berry, 2009). It is important to consider the age and development of the child when supporting military families. Consistent with other literature, the mental health status of the parent at home was reported to be the strongest predictor of how children fare during deployment (National Center for PTSD, U.S. Department of Veterans Affairs, 2010). Veterans affected with PTSD have reported wanting to have the family involved with their care (Batten et al., 2009). Hefling (2009a) reported that military children are seeing mental health counselors in record numbers. In 2003, 1 million children had contact with a mental health professional, and that number had increased to 2 million by 2008.

Reservists' families are most often found in communities and may be living among people and service providers who do not have an understanding of military culture or current events (Chartrand & Siegel, 2007). Civilian service providers may not understand what a deployment means to a family or how best to support them. There is a need for research to better understand how deployment affects these families and how they are best supported.

One thing that deploying service members should never do is tell a child at home that he or she will be the man or woman of the house while they are gone. This can have negative consequences for children. Children and adolescents need the security of knowing that their caregiver is in charge while the service member is gone and will meet the child's needs.

Another important point is that children will do as well as the parent (caregiver) left in charge. If the parent is angry or depressed, it will affect the child (Pincus et al., 2010). Military Family Services, the FRGs, and social workers should pay particular attention to caregivers providing for children while service members are away. It is important to include children in deployment planning and communication about the upcoming separation. At first children may act out and behave in ways that reflect their distress and anxiety at being separated from the service member, especially if both parents are deploying. A child's distress and anxiety need to be addressed with support and calmness. Children need specifics about the deployment, such as where, when, how, and why. Older children can be helpful with younger siblings' concerns about deployment.

The age and developmental stage of the child is likely to have a great influence on how they manage the deployment and cope (Barker & Berry, 2009). Young children may experience behavior and mood problems. Also, increased demands for attention, discipline problems, and sadness may occur. Children in the process of attachment formation may not recognize their deployed parent on his or her return (Barker & Berry, 2009), which can be very distressing to the parent. As with other studies, Barker and Berry (2009) found that longer deployments were associated with increases in problems for children. Toddlers were more affected than infants (Barker & Berry, 2009). In a study by Chartrand, Frank, White, and Shope (2008), three- to five-year-old children with a deployed parent had greater behavioral problems and symptoms than did children with no parent deployed. They also found that children between the ages of one and a half and three years responded differently to deployment than did the children between the ages of three and five.

Chandra et al. (2010) studied military children between the ages of eleven and seventeen. Telephone interviews with children and surveys of the caregiver ($N = 1,507$) at home were conducted and compared with a national sample of same-age children. The results demonstrated that children with a deployed parent experienced more emotional difficulties that did the comparison group. Specifically, females and older adolescents had school-, family-, and peer-related difficulties ($p < .01$). Length of deployment was significantly associated with having problems and with reintegration of the parent ($p < .01$). Problems were also significantly associated with caregiver mental health status: the poorer it was, the greater the number of problems ($p < .01$). Living in rented housing was also associated with having a greater number of problems. This may be attributed to being in the civilian community versus living on the military installation, where there is strong community support. Chandra et al. (2010) recommended targeting ongoing support and developing support programs for caregivers with poor mental health. Rosen and Teitelbaum (1993) found similar results in the Persian Gulf War.

Some studies have found troubling results. In one study adolescents with a deployed parent were found to have higher heart rate and perceived stress than adolescents without a deployed parent (Barnes, Davis, & Treiber, 2007). Huebner,

Mancini, Wilcox, Grass, and Grass (2007) found that adolescents expressed feelings of loss and uncertainty, which the authors associated with difficulties in development.

At the third Family Forum of the Association of the U.S. Army, an Army psychiatrist reported that the increased mental health needs of military children are challenging service delivery (Collins, 2009). The psychiatrist went on to say that the number of mental health visits increased from 800,000 in 2003 to 1.6 million in 2008. Mental health professionals are finding higher rates of anxiety and depression in military children. This increase has been attributed to the constant and repeated deployments of parents, which have gone from months to years. These problems are associated with dropping out of school, academic problems and academic failure, and problems with socialization. One response by the Army has been to create the Military Child and Adolescents Center of Excellence at Madigan Army Medical Center, at Fort Lewis, Washington. The center is staffed with a multidisciplinary team, including social workers, psychologists, and child and adolescent psychiatrists whose mission is to examine the research and interventions for improving services and intervention programs. It is hoped that the center will contribute to finding ways to improve the mental health issues that military children and adolescents face.

A related problem is the increase in prescription drugs for military children with mental health problems (Jowers & Tilghman, 2011). Children younger than eighteen, who are covered by TRICARE, received more than three hundred thousand prescriptions for psychiatric drugs in 2009. Since the beginning of the invasion of Afghanistan, the military has seen a 76 percent increase in the use of psychiatric medicines by military service members. The prescription increases for both children and adults are associated with repeated deployments. Tricia Radenz, a military spouse and emergency room nurse, attributes her son's suicide to the prescription of a psychiatric drug, Celexa. A psychiatrist prescribed Celexa to Radenz's son, Daniel, for mood swings and anxiety, as he had become withdrawn and had difficulties with his grades (Jowers & Tilghman, 2011). While his father was deployed, Daniel began cutting himself. During a band class he had hallucinations and was found in a hall scratching his face and hitting himself. Daniel hanged himself from his bunk bed on June 9, 2009—he was twelve years old.

Deployment clearly affects children in a variety of ways. It may also put children at risk for maltreatment. Research on child abuse in the military services is complicated by irregular and contradictory factors (Chamberlain, Stander, & Merrill, 2003). Military families do experience strain and stresses, as well as low incomes among enlisted personnel, especially for younger service members in the lower ranks. However, at the same time, at least one parent has stable employment and multiple benefits that can buffer the stress of military life. Before the Afghanistan and Iraq wars, it was believed that child maltreatment in the military was lower than national levels. As deployments to those wars have increased, reports of child maltreatment have increased (Campbell, Brown, & Okwara, 2011; Gibbs et al., 2007; Rentz et al., 2007). Among deployed enlisted service members, the rate of substantiated child maltreatment was 42 percent greater during deployment than when soldiers were not deployed. The rate of moderate or severe maltreatment was 60 percent greater during deployment. In another study of one state's military children, substantiated cases of child maltreatment doubled after October 2002. This calls attention to the need to increase support to families with young children during deployments. Family advocacy programs are located in military communities to address family problems that may lead to child maltreatment. In addition, FRGs and FACs can provide support and referrals to community services as needed. Service providers can also identify at-risk families and help build support networks to lessen the strain.

Secondary Traumatic Stress

Much has been written about posttraumatic stress and service members. In contrast, secondary traumatic stress (STS) in family members has not received the same attention. Caregivers at home are vulnerable to STS by witnessing the experience of service members. Although there are many caregivers involved with service members (Bride & Figley, 2009), especially those injured in combat with physical or invisible wounds, the focus in STS is on family, parents, spouses, children, and other close relatives and friends.

Figley (1995) describes STS as a phenomenon that occurs when the caregiver of a traumatized person becomes indirectly traumatized. The caregiver may experience the same or similar symptoms of trauma. They may experience hyperarousal, emotional distress, avoidance, and sleep and perception disturbance. They may also experience a disruption in normal functioning. McCann and Pearlman (1990) refer to this as vicarious traumatization. We believe that vicarious traumatization produces secondary trauma (Pryce, Shackelford, &

Pryce 2007), which is believed to result from empathic engagement with a traumatized person (Figley, 1995). Secondary traumatic stress should not be confused with burnout. Burnout is produced by few rewards in the provider's work
and stressful demands that an organization places on the provider (Pryce et al.,
2007).

Family members of injured service members face numerous challenges. Most
especially, they preserve the link to the former life of the service member, and
after an injury, they have the responsibility of creating a new "normal" for their
family. Most often the spouse of the injured service member is in that role, although others, such as parents or siblings, may be involved also. Spouses bear the
emotional challenge of helping service members heal and reintegrate, and
through spouses' empathic engagement with a service member, they may experience symptoms of STS (Calhoun, Beckham, & Bosworth, 2002). Franciskovic et
al. (2007) studied STS in fifty-six veterans' wives through interviews and ques-
tionnaires. The authors describe living with a veteran who suffers from posttraumatic stress:

> The veteran's difficulties in everyday life mostly affect his family, while
> the family is expected to provide all the supports he needs. The wife
> and children witness his sleepless nights, restless dreams, and absent-
> mindedness that sometimes lasts for hours or even days, and avoids up-
> setting him as much as possible. His low frustration threshold, lack of
> patience with children, inability to carry on with his family role, great
> expectations, and verbal and physical aggressiveness heavily influence
> the relationship with his spouse, children, parents, and the rest of the
> family. (Franciskovic et al., 2007, p. 178)

In their study, Franciskovic et al. (2007) found that more than one-third of
women married to war veterans had symptoms of STS. The spouses of the veterans who were married the longest were the most affected by STS. It is natural,
and possibly inescapable, that empathic responding to an injured spouse or parent results in secondary trauma and STS symptoms. Other studies have produced
similar results (Batten et al., 2009; Ben Arzi, Solomon, & Dekel, 2000; Dekel,
Solomon, & Bleich, 2005; Harkness & Zandor, 2001; Koic, Franciskovic, Muzinic-
Masle, Dordevic, & Vondracek, 2002). Further research is needed into STS and
family members of service members and veterans who are diagnosed with PTSD.

Psychoeducation of family members can help them understand the person with PTSD, their own responses and reactions to that person, and how to cope and use social support (Batten et al., 2009). Comprehensive treatment programs guidelines for PTSD recommend the inclusion of marriage and family counselors (Riggs, 2000).

VA Caregiver Support

The VA (U.S. Department of Veterans Affairs, 2011) has a new program that provides support to family caregivers of post-9/11 veterans with serious injuries, such as TBI, psychological trauma, or some other mental disorder as a result of military service. The program was created in recognition of the toll that caregiving may take on the caregiver and to support veterans receiving the best services possible. The new services provided to caregivers of veterans whose injuries interfere with their activities of daily living include a monthly stipend, travel expenses, access to health insurance, mental health services and counseling, comprehensive VA caregiver training, and respite care.

Tragedy Assistance Program for Survivors

An important resource for social workers working with military families is the Tragedy Assistance Program (TAPS) for survivors (U.S. Department of Veterans Affairs, 2011; for more information, visit http://www.taps.org). The TAPS program was incorporated in 1992 (Carroll, 2009), and since then it has helped thousands of families, especially children, grieve and bereave the loss of a service member. The organization offers the following services:

- Peer-based emotional support for survivors from a national network of trained volunteer supporters who have also lost someone serving in the military
- Grief and trauma resources and information to educate family and friends, as well as benefits information, workshops, and webinars
- Assignment of a casework assistance officer to work with families and to help them through their grieving in any way the officer can
- 24/7 crisis intervention to connect family members who have experienced loss with a support person who quickly arrives at their home; through this service, TAPS has prevented many suicides
- Regional military survivor grief camps for children, where children can come together to be with others who have similar experiences

Resources for Social Work with Warriors and Their Families

The resources available to social workers are numerous and can be found in all forms of media, especially on the Internet. Social workers are cautioned to check out sources before they make a referral for families, service members, or veterans to ensure the quality of the referral. To that end, social workers can develop a network of resources in their location to assist military families. Slone and Friedman (2008), in *After the War Zone*, have developed an extensive list of resources that assist in helping families. There are also several books that can help social workers better understand the military services.

Since the first white paper on families was produced (Wickham, 1983), the military has made considerable progress in valuing the family's contribution to military readiness, as evidenced by programs such as Operation READY, which aims to facilitate family and military readiness. In addition, paid family readiness officers help alleviate the stress of spouses during deployments and homecomings. Some military communities and schools have on staff paid family life consultants who can provide confidential assistance to children and family members. Military OneSource offers confidential counseling for both service and family members; it is available twenty-four hours a day, seven days a week. In addition, a spouse tuition assistance program is available, which is especially effective for helping spouses find transferable careers. A tutoring program has also been developed (www.tutor.com/military). These efforts go a long way toward making military life manageable.

The present-day military family is complex. Social work has a long history of working with the American military, dating back to the 1896 U.S. Sanitary Commission. Smith College was created in 1918 to educate social workers to work with World War I veterans (Basham, 2009). Another program with a focus on social work with the military and veterans was developed at the University of Southern California in October 2008. In recent years, the Department of Defense has increasingly hired civilian social workers as government employees or as contractors, nationally and internationally. Social workers need to learn about the total force and American military culture and to prepare to work with a diverse population (Knox & Price, 1999; Savitsky et al., 2009). Social work has much to offer the military families who give so much to our country.

Veterans' Higher Education
Challenges and Opportunities

> What veteran-friendly colleges don't do is coddle veterans. Instead, they create environments in which vets have the tools to engage in debate and make use of resources.
> —**Luke Stalcup**, Army combat veteran and Georgetown University student, American Council on Education, 2008

The new G.I. Bill brings a wealth of resources to military personnel and veterans. Social workers and social work educators need to be informed about these students and the resources available to them. Since 9/11 less than 1 percent of the U.S. population has been serving the country to ensure the safety of all our citizens from terrorism. The director of the program Supportive Education for the Returning Veteran (SERV), John Schuup (personal communication, April 18, 2009) estimated that about 2 million service members have been involved in maintaining the safety of U.S. citizens. Many of them committed to the military as the means to obtain a college education. The new post-9/11 G.I. Bill is likely to encourage many service members to pursue degrees from institutions of higher education. Social work can be involved in advocating for these students and in identifying policy and practice changes that will enhance their education experience and contribute to retention and graduation. Social workers have a long history in social justice and advocacy. They can use those values and skills to persuade education administrators to examine their educational policies and practices to determine whether they are vet-friendly. Schools of social work can also examine their own policies and practices to ensure that they are vet-friendly.

Military Service Members and Veterans

There is a range of male and female service members and veterans. Active-duty military personnel are presently in one of the armed services and may or may not have been in combat, either as a direct combatant or as a combat support person. They may be eligible for educational leave and may be deployed or required at periodic training drills during the semester. This disruption calls for institutional policies to be in place to preserve the educational investment of the student and to facilitate reentry to education as soon as possible or to excuse the student from classes.

Veterans may be on active duty, Guard or Reserve duty, or may be out of service altogether. Veterans may have served as combatants or as combat support persons. The range of roles could be from infantryman or calvary scout, involved in direct combat, to a specialist who is part of a medical unit or a clerk in a combat support unit. All carry weapons (except conscientious objectors) and are trained to use them on the field, and some may or may not off the field. Veterans who are out of service usually have some combat experience or combat support experience. Both groups bring their unique military experience to the educational setting.

Educational Characteristics

Active-duty military members and veterans bring an array of characteristics to colleges and universities, which make them potentially strong students. Many colleges recognize this, and recruiters are encouraging applicants to consider their programs. The G.I. Bill covers most or all of service members' and veterans' tuition, which may be supplemented by the Yellow Ribbon program. For most of these individuals, finances are not as formidable a barrier as they may be for the student population in general. As beginning students in their first year in college, most veterans are more mature in many ways than the typical fresh-out-of-high-school student. In addition, military students bring a practiced discipline to their studies and a goal-oriented attitude that supports their achievements in college. Military students and veterans are accustomed to a chain of command and are clear about taking orders from leaders. They also have leadership skills that may serve them well in doing group work in the classroom or in social clubs. These students have shouldered major responsibilities, from learning to use and care for highly sophisticated and expensive equipment to teaching new recruits about their responsibilities as members of the military. In many cases they may have dealt with choices and decisions that greatly affected the lives of the people around them, including life and death.

Military recruits have to meet both physical and intellectual standards, which make them good candidates for higher-level education. Common characteristics of service members and veterans are that they are dependable, responsible, dedicated, respectful, and punctual. These factors are true of most military personnel and veterans. Both groups have much to offer an educational setting. They know pressure and expect to be challenged, and they often excel beyond expectations.

Social workers will encounter veterans in a variety of educational settings. It is important for social workers to be knowledgeable about several factors that influence access to higher education for veterans. At this point, only 40 percent of veterans are taking advantage of the G.I. Bill. John Schuup (personal communication, April 18, 2009) identifies several factors that serve as barriers to accessing education for veterans. These factors identify and address what service members and veterans may bring home from their deployment experience in a war zone.

Readjustment Experience

Soldiers, Marines, and others have left what has become their normal environments and relationships to forge a new way of living and experiencing home and the educational environment. It may be a challenge for many and a difficult transition to make. The individual's worldview and physiology in the military in an ongoing threat situation is different from being in a safe situation where keeping alert and hypervigilant are not required. Service members or veterans may find that they continue to be hypervigilant, which may lead to difficulties in communications at home and in the classroom or relationships. It is also the case that veterans may find the pace of an academic setting frustrating and have limited patience for anyone who they perceive as "wasting their time." Most often service members and veterans have changed in ways that people in their new surroundings have not, and both find it hard to understand and cope with the changes or lack of changes. This may be particularly true of relationships with significant others and close friends. It is often difficult to understand that service members and veterans have changed in ways that few people without their experience will understand. Frequently, the returning service personnel will say, "It's just not the same." Often military students may be more comfortable with other veterans and military service members, given what they have in common, places they have been, and what they have done. When military personnel and veteran students come to campus and the classroom, they bring their experiences with them and may find it a challenge to relate to other students and their educators because of social and cognitive dissonance.

Mental and Physical Health Issues

Any student can bring mental and physical health challenges to his or her education. With the assistance of a medical or mental health professional, students can obtain assistance from the college's or university's office of disability services. With proper documentation, accommodations can be made for a wide range of issues, from assistance with note taking to taping lectures or being able to take a test in a quiet room or being given additional time to complete assignments. Some colleges can provide assistance in diagnosing learning disabilities and providing students with recommendations to improve their performance in the classroom. Students' information is kept confidential and is shared with classroom instructors only when necessary.

Policies and Practices of the Educational Environment

In addition to learning challenges, students who are veterans may benefit from knowing about services that the university's student counseling center offers. Professionals who staff these centers need to be educated about the mental health issues that veteran students may present. Often counselors in university settings have specialized education and training particularly for veterans and their concerns. They may be skilled in leading groups to give veteran students opportunities to share and discuss their past and present experiences. These professionals should also be informed about VA outreach programs. Either can be a source for psychoeducation (Briere & Scott, 2006) and interventions for issues that veterans experience and believe pose problems to their educational progress.

Educational institutions can do much to become veteran-friendly sources of higher learning and will realize the financial benefits by expanding their student bodies to include veterans who use the G.I. Bill and, in some cases, the Yellow Ribbon program to pay their tuition. There are a range of improvements that colleges and universities can make to support veterans and military personnel. Recently, six educational organizations collected data from 723 higher education institutions to identify how veteran-friendly colleges and universities meet the needs of their student veterans. More work in this arena remains to be done (Wright, 2009).

Three actions were deemed as extremely important to schools being veteran-friendly. One way is to become informed about the G.I. Bill, both the Montgomery G.I. Bill and the Post-9/11 G.I. Bill, to maximize benefits to veteran students. Part of this effort is to create a network of accessible veterans' affairs contacts who can assist when questions arise or unusual situations occur. The second is to award curriculum credit for military training. This is a challenge; however, several universities have successfully accommodated the challenge. They can assist other colleges and universities by sharing their experiences. The third practice is to develop a policy that addresses deployment during the semester and to develop a refund policy, to maintain the individuals as students, so they don't have to go through the process of readmission. This can be done with respect to time limitations that institutions must impose.

The Vet-Friendly Campus

In a survey of 723 educational institutions, more than half acknowledged that responding to the needs of veterans and service members was included in their long-term goals (Wright, 2009). In addition, more than half reported actively recruiting both active-duty and veteran students. The survey also found that public institutions were more proactive on behalf of military veterans than private institutions, although the latter seem to be moving in that direction. An interesting finding was that most campuses are planning vet-friendly changes. Of those changes, the most pressing are the education of staff and faculty regarding the education of veterans and increasing knowledge about the issues that veterans bring with them. Another priority for these schools is to obtain funding to provide campus programs for veterans.

The survey found a high rate of diversity in the provision of services and programs for veterans and service members (Wright, 2009). There was no consistency in the campus location of services or providers. The events of September 11, 2001, were a marker in national changes toward educational institutions being friendlier to veterans and service members. Two types of financial support were addressed. Public institutions often offered in-state tuition to veterans and their family members. Private institutions offered financial discounts for tuition for veterans and family members. Almost all the institutions had policies addressing tuition refunds for service members who deploy. Work remains to be done on facilitating the reenrollment of military members in school. Many still have policies that require students to apply for readmission and enrollment. The services most frequently offered were financial aid, employment assistance, and advising.

Additional services were mental health counseling and disability assistance for visible and invisible injuries and learning challenges. Most institutions gave academic credit for military education and training. Another crucial service provided was establishing a location where veterans and military personnel can gather and interact. The information exchanges and camaraderie that occur in these gatherings contribute greatly to adjustment to campus life. These activities may take many forms from gathering at lunch to talks and meetings for student veterans and military personnel.

Not surprisingly, the size of the campus and student enrollment of veterans and military members and families influences the services provided to veterans. The larger the veteran and military service population, the greater was the likelihood of services and policies friendly to this population. However, smaller education institutions are also making headway in meeting veterans' and service members' educational needs (Wright, 2009).

The Counseling Center: A Critical Contact

Counseling centers on campus may find that veteran students present a challenge in that they can be expected to increase the number of students seeking assistance. Counseling services may consider developing a cadre of veteran student peer counselors who can lead groups and do one-on-one counseling. Veterans are prone to open up to fellow veterans over nonveterans, especially to student veterans whose military occupational specialty was behavioral sciences and who served in a mental health setting. When a nonveteran counselor provides groups for veterans, having a veteran student peer counselor as a co–group leader can be an asset. In addition to training veteran students to provide peer counseling, it is important to clarify boundaries for them and how to maintain them.

University Office of Veterans Affairs for Warriors and Family Members

A key indicator of a vet-friendly campus is having an office for services for veterans and military service members. Veterans view dedicated space as a concrete, visible sign of institutional commitment. Almost half the institutions in the survey had such an office (Wright, 2009). Institutions with a dedicated office were also found to have made additional changes in policy and practices to improve veterans' and service members' educational experience. They also were more likely to support veterans and military personnel campus social organizations.

The personnel in a dedicated office are informed about VA and Vet Center services and can offer meaningful referrals for warriors and their family members.

The final part of Wright's (2009) survey reported on findings from focus groups with veterans and military service personnel regarding higher education. The focus groups identified services and programs that they felt were needed. A frequent point was the need for staff to be informed about the old and new G.I. Bill and benefits. They also found it important to have deployment policies that are supportive of military service members and to excuse absences when a member of the National Guard or Reserve has drill and will be gone from campus. Overall, the focus groups identified further needs that administrators could address to make campuses more vet-friendly and supportive of service members and veterans.

A Vet-Friendly Web Page

Service members often depend on the Internet to connect with colleges and universities for information on their education programs and veteran-friendly status. The American Council on Education (2008) has identified several actions that make a campus veteran-friendly. Potential students in focus groups indicated that finding information on educational benefits can be a challenge and presents a barrier to accessing education, especially when they separate from military service. In one focus group, a participant suggested that the university home page should include a label "Veterans" that links to a site for veterans and military personnel to access information and names of individuals to contact.

Another feature that would contribute to being veteran-friendly is to identify faculty who are themselves veterans or vet-friendly and may serve as advisers or contacts for applicants. Schools can make peer support available by linking veteran student volunteers enrolled in education programs with potential students on the Web. A range of information can be provided to potential students, from how to obtain credit for military education and training to navigating the Montgomery G.I. Bill and the Post-9/11 G.I. Bill.

Educating Faculty, Administrators, and Staff

Essential to a vet-friendly campus are faculty, administrators, and staff who are knowledgeable about veterans. When students seek information and services, it is important that referrals be accurate and that the person making the referral knows where and to whom students should be sent for assistance. An example of education for campuses is Maryland's Montgomery College Combat2College

(C2C) initiative. This program is available to veterans, faculty, administrators, and staff. The goal is to make faculty, administrators, and staff across campus knowledgeable and able to respond to needs as they occur. Referral tip sheets promote accuracy, and this information could also be included on a separate Web page for veterans.

Student Veterans of America

The national organization Student Veterans of America encourages and supports veterans in forming a chapter of the organization on their campus. Members participate in a variety of activities, from peer support to advocating and making referrals to appropriate staff and administrators. In addition to helping fellow vets get through the university paperwork and find offices they need, they can help one another navigate the VA Medical Centers and Vet Centers. They can provide assistance with a variety of concerns, from how to use the G.I. benefits to purchasing a house and getting tax breaks for pay earned in the combat zone. The Midwest regional director of Student Veterans of America, John Mikelson, points out that there is much the university can do for veterans, but there is also a lot the veterans can do for one another and themselves beyond the university administration, staff, and faculty.

A Model Vet-Friendly Center

One indication of veteran-friendly campuses is having a space dedicated for student veterans to hold meetings and other opportunities to gather with other veterans. This space should be available during the day and in the evenings to students and may be staffed by students on the Department of Veterans Affairs work-study program.

A good example of a clear point of contact is the Sonny Montgomery Center for America's Veterans at Mississippi State University in Starkville, Mississippi. This is one of the oldest programs for student veterans. The center provides services to veterans, and the center's staff also provides assistance to military service members and dependents. The center has a director, veterans' benefits and program coordinator, veterans' transition coordinator, veterans' outreach coordinator, and an administrative supervisor and administrative assistant. Each team member is dedicated to facilitating veteran students' entrance into educational programs and retention until graduation.

The center building has administrative offices, a computer lab with printers, and a room dedicated to student veterans. The center offers a full array of services to veterans, including counseling, academic guidance, course selection, registration, assistance with the G.I. Bill, mentoring, and graduate school advice. The director also has built relationships with key administrators and units on campus who have designated a point of contact for each person in their department, including financial aid and counseling. The director of the center explains that all the key individuals are "infected" with knowledge about veteran students and are able to provide appropriate services (personal communication, A. Reardon, September 14, 2009). Students are referred to the individuals from the center, and if students experience problems, they can obtain assistance from the center's staff. Veteran students do not receive special treatment and follow the same processes as other students in the academic setting. In addition, faculty and staff are educated about the challenges these students face and are encouraged to be helpful when problems arise. The center also coordinates the veterans' work-study program. Students are provided with part-time work and are trained to assist other students with veterans' administration programs, paperwork, and related issues.

The center coordinates with the MSU Career Center to facilitate the transition to careers for veteran students. The center helps students develop resumes that integrate their military experience with their academic degrees. The two centers work together to enhance students' interviewing skills and to promote employment, especially in state and federal careers.

The G.I. Bill of Rights, 1944, 1984, 2009

In 1944, the Servicemen's Readjustment Act passed with much controversy (U.S. Department of Veterans Affairs, 2009b). It may be one of the most important pieces of federal legislation in U.S. history, and it was largely responsible for the creation and growth of the middle class after World War II. Veterans returning from World War II were provided with an opportunity to attend college for the first time. At that time, attending college was a privilege of the wealthy, as was home ownership (Childers, 2009). The bill was signed into law on June 22, 1944, with provisions for education and vocational training, loans for purchasing a home or business (including farms), and unemployment benefits. The bill allowed for mass entry into the education system and was an alternative to scarce employment. According to the Department of Veterans Affairs (2009b), in the history of the 1944 G.I. Bill, 2.2 million of 16 million veterans joined the ranks of university students, and 5 million signed up for vocational training (Alvarez, 2008). At the same time, home ownership became a reality for millions. The original bill came to closure on June 25, 1952. There are two G.I. Bills for veterans to consider, and they need to make an informed decision about which bill is most appropriate for their particular situation.

It was not until 1984 that the Montgomery G.I. Bill was introduced as a revision of the former bill (U.S. Department of Veterans Affairs, 2009b). Military.com is an excellent source, and we used it to make the following comparisons of both G.I. Bills. The Montgomery G.I. Bill can be used for a variety of educational programs, including college, business, and vocational courses; online, distance, and correspondence courses; certification tests; apprenticeship job training; and flight training. It has a nationally set monthly payment rate ($1,321) and does not cover other expenses such as books and supplies. To be eligible, you have to have joined the military by the end of June 1985 and paid the enrollment fee ($1,200). The educational benefits are good for ten years after military discharge, and the bill has restricted family benefits. As with any legislation, the bill is subject to changes.

The Post-9/11 Veterans Educational Assistance Act of 2008 is very generous in its benefits. It has the potential of applying to more than 2 million eligible veterans. At present it covers the costs of any public institution's college program, and payments go directly to the institution. It allows for living expenses comparable to the enlisted pay grade E5 with family in monthly stipends, and it covers books and supplies ($1,000 per year). To be eligible, service members have to have been on active duty for ninety days or more since September 11, 2001. The benefits expire fifteen years after the last ninety days of continuous service. Service members who are eligible may transfer benefits to family members. Unlike the Montgomery G.I. Bill, there is no enrollment fee for the Post-9/11 G.I. Bill. At present, payments to postsecondary institutions are slow because of the large numbers of applicants. The VA is working to correct the delays (Maze, 2010).

Yellow Ribbon Program

Part of the Post-9/11 G.I. Bill is the Yellow Ribbon program (U.S. Department of Veterans Affairs, 2009a). This program assists veterans when an educational institution's tuition and expenses are more than the state's public universities' tuition for undergraduates, which is often the case for private colleges and universities. The college or university, whose tuition and expenses exceed the state's public costs, can offset half the difference, and the VA covers the other half. This allows student veterans broader access to all colleges, public or private.

The college or university participating in the Yellow Ribbon program has several responsibilities. They agree to respond to requests for this assistance and provide the assistance throughout the time the student is in college and making satisfactory progress. The institutions are also to report on the number of students they assist and the amount of assistance provided to each student. The institutions identify the number of students they will assist with offsetting costs beyond what the Post-9/11 G.I. Bill provides. In addition, the college or university selects the amount it is willing to offset.

Students who are eligible for the full benefit amount (100 percent) are entitled to request this funding to offset additional costs not covered by the full benefit. For example, a student who is an out-of-state resident and is eligible for full Post-9/11 G.I. Bill benefits may have nonresident costs reduced through the Yellow Ribbon program. This assistance began on August 1, 2009, for those colleges and universities that volunteered to participate. The university or college notifies the VA that the eligible student has submitted a certificate of eligibility and is enrolled in the program.

Veterans Upward Bound

The U.S. Department of Education is aware that there are veterans interested in education but who may not have been in an academic setting and are unsure about pursuing higher education. The Veterans Upward Bound (VUB) program has the collective goal that no potential learner will be left behind and that quality educational opportunities be available to student veterans (Curtin & Cahalan, 2005; Oxendine, 2005). Many potential students may not equate all the military training they have received and what they have learned in the military as education. It is important to encourage them that if they can survive the military, they can do well in an academic setting. In some cases, veterans enter military service without a high school diploma, although they most likely will have obtained a General Education Diploma during active duty. There currently are forty-eight VUB programs in the United States, and they are funded through a grant from the Department of Education. This program, almost forty years old, has the goals of assisting veterans in becoming eligible for postsecondary education, in being successfully retained in an educational program, and in graduating to go on to employment in their career choice (National Veterans Upward Bound Program, 2009; U.S. Department of Education, 2009).

The VUB program provides services to veterans who separated honorably from service after January 31, 1955, as shown on their form DD-214 (certificate of release or discharge from active duty) and who have completed at least 181 days of active-duty service. The student may be a first-generation college applicant or may be qualified by low-income criteria. The program is free to el-igible individuals who are specifically in need of higher education academic preparation. The VUB addresses the needs of high-risk veteran students to re-tain them and to promote graduation.

The VUB services a wide array of academic assistance and skill development, with the specific goal of assisting veterans in completing a program that will achieve the equivalent of a high school diploma and facilitate entrance to a col-lege or university (National Veterans Upward Bound Program, 2009; U.S. Depart-ment of Education, 2009). The range of VUB services include assessment of aca-demic skills and refresher courses, assistance with college application paperwork, and G.I. Bill requirements and applications, tutoring and mentoring, and assis-tance with study skills. The VUB program has broad discretion to determine how to best assist each and every eligible student veteran. One dissertation studied 495 veterans in a state VUB program to find that social and organizational inte-gration into the campus community was strongly associated with academic suc-cess (Petriccione, 2001). The students were able to relate to younger, nonmilitary students, faculty, and the institution. High-quality academic skill instruction and college survival skills contributed greatly to academic success. Clearly, feeling like one belongs on campus and can learn skills for academic work makes a differ-ence to student success.

Difficulties in Obtaining an Education beyond High School

Kevin Crum experienced a head injury while he served in Iraq. He suffered from seizure disorder, had frequent doctors visits, and took endless medications with numerous side effects. He has experienced as many as eight seizures in a day. In addition, Kevin came from a difficult and abusive childhood and joined the mil-itary to find a career. The head injury ended that endeavor.

In spite of his injuries, medications, and experiences with frustration and de-pression, and some educators who have no sympathy, Kevin refuses to give up. He keeps on doing his class work and is now a senior with a social work major at Western Kentucky University. As a VA work-study student he has encouraged, mentored, and helped other veterans in the VUB office (Wilson, 2009).

The VUB program supported Kevin throughout his education and is a re-source on university and college campuses for student veterans who meet the re-quirements. Kevin's story is testimony that an education may be achieved under extremely challenging circumstances.

Veteran Students with Disabilities

Sadly, every war the United States has been involved in inevitably results in tragic wounds. The wars in Iraq and Afghanistan have resulted in multiple types of wounds, including invisible wounds. The three signature invisible wounds of the current wars, PTSD, TBI, and major depression and their symptoms, are discussed in detail elsewhere in this book. The Student Office of Disability in universities and colleges can anticipate increased numbers of differently abled student veterans seeking assistance.

The *Journal of Postsecondary Education and Disability* dedicated a special issue to veterans with disabilities. In his introduction to the special issue, Madaus (2009) stated that "disability service providers face a new set of challenges in ensuring that veterans with disabilities receive access to education they deserve. . . . [T]he field is at a crossroads, but in rising to meet these challenges, the disability services profession can emerge as a leader in campus initiatives and in the promotion of civil rights of all students with disabilities" (p. 6). The new disabilities act broadly defines what can be considered a disability in both ways, obvious and hidden.

The American Council on Education's Vet-Friendly Campus Checklist

In June 2008, a presidential summit was held at Georgetown University. The theme of the conference, sponsored by the American Council on Education (ACE), was "Serving Those Who Serve: Higher Education and America's Veterans." The conference featured an open forum on the barriers that veterans encounter to obtaining higher education (ACE, 2008). The summit was attended by a cross-section of college administrators and representatives, student veterans, upper-ranking military personnel, and interested individuals. Participants worked to find solutions to the problems that veterans experience in seeking education. The ACE offers a checklist that can be used as a starting place for making universities and colleges vet-friendly:

- Campus homepage has a welcome for vets and link to veterans' resource page.
- Evaluate admissions and other processes and policies to determine their impact on veterans.
- Host a forum to explore avenues for enhancing and streamlining services for military veterans.

- Explore why veterans choose not to participate in higher education and come to campus.
- Veteran resource information is posted at key locations on campus.
- Identify campus and local resources that are available to veterans and their dependents and disseminate the information to them (e.g., e-mail, mail).
- Create a veterans club.
- Create a veterans' resource team.
- Establish a veteran peer mentor program.
- Employ activities that demonstrate a vet-aware and friendly campus:
  - Host an event to welcome veterans and their dependents each term.
  - Post signs that welcome veterans to campus and can be found in employee offices or cubicles.
  - Host a vet info day or fair with VFW, American Legion, VA, WorkSource, and other veteran personnel.
  - Celebrate Veterans' Day, Armed Forces Day, and Memorial Day.
  - Challenge Coin (a military tradition in which coins are minted with unit and service information; military members and veterans exchange them, and commanders and leaders give them informally for a job well done).
  - Erect a monument or Memorial.
  - Host a freedom run, a patriotic race like the Marine Marathon.
  - Post stories and photos on a Web site or dedicated wall.
  - Establish an audio-video history project to interview and record veterans' stories.
  - Develop a list of all campus employees who are vets or dependents of vets.
- Partner with veteran-related community organizations.
- Create transitional support programs.
- Create a psychoeducation course on PTSD or military culture.
- Provide training to campus employees about Battlemind, military culture, and issues particular to the transition from military to civilian life.
- Identify additional information and training resources to further develop knowledge, skills, and abilities related to the retention of recently returned combat veterans, particularly PTSD, TBI, and related issues and services.
- Educate faculty and staff about Post-9/11 G.I. Bill Benefits.

- Create a study skills course specific to veterans.
- Provide vets only introductory courses.
- Create a tuition-waiver program and eliminate nonresidency tuition.

Social Work Advocacy for Student Veterans

Social work educators are in a good position to advocate for the student veteran population in their colleges and universities. These educators must prepare to welcome veterans into their programs. Social work educators can infuse knowledge about the military and veterans into their curricula. Many of these students will be seeking social work degrees to return to the military and work with service members and their families or to return to civilian settings, where they can provide services for veterans, either with the VA, Vet Centers, or community services.

Conclusion

We shall not cease from exploration. And the end of all our exploring
will be to arrive where we started and know the place for the first time.
                                        —**T. S. Eliot**, *Little Gidding*, 1943

In past years social work has neglected military service members, veterans, and
their families, as is illustrated by the lack of books, publications, and educational
curricula addressing this population. We have been at war in Afghanistan for
over ten years and in Iraq for approximately eight years and were involved in
many previous conflicts. Our review of textbooks found little information on veterans and less on military families.

Smith College held a conference titled "Combat Stress: Understanding the
Challenges, Preparing for the Return," from June 26 to 28, 2008. It was sponsored by the School of Social Work and Give-an-Hour, and supported by the
Brown Foundation. There is a need for more conferences like this across the
country. Smith College published articles from the presentations at the conference in a special issue of their journal. We found one publication, that of Savitsky et al. (2009), addressing social work with the military and veteran population.
There is a need for more social work literature like this and empirical research to
improve practices.

The University of Southern California's School of Social Work and Fayetteville State University in North Carolina have partnered with the U.S. Army to produce social work students to work with the military. The two schools of social
work offer a master's degree with a concentration in military service members
and veterans and their families.

The University of Southern California requires students to have two to five
years of clinical practice. The curriculum prepares social workers to provide a
range of services for military service members and their families, as well as

veterans and their families. The focus is to help military families cope with stress, especially constant and repeat deployments and reintegration stress that affects the transition home. The program is partnered with the Center for Innovative Research, which is creating patient-based virtual-reality modules to provide students with an avatar simulation of military service members and veterans with whom they can interact regarding combat stress. The program offers a six-hundred-hour field placement in a military setting.

Fayetteville State University has a master's program that also focuses on providing services to military families. They have partnered with Fort Sam Houston, Texas, to increase the number of social workers prepared to work with the military population. In addition to the standard social work graduate curriculum, the learning outcomes include engaging in research-informed practice and practice-informed research in the military community, engaging in policy practice in the military to advance social and economic well-being and to deliver effective social work services, and responding to and shaping the ever-changing professional context of the military. The Army officer graduates serve as clinical social workers in a wide range of positions as behavioral science officers. The Department of the Army's collaboration with Fayetteville State will contribute to meet the growing need for the increase and expansion of military social work services.

Finally, the Council on Social Work Education (CSWE) has addressed this population and called for the inclusion of this group in social work curricula (CSWE, 2009). The Joint Task Force on Veterans' Affairs produced a final report in October 2009 with several recommendations:

Social Work Education

- Overall curriculum goals should strive to build the capacity of social work veterans to effectively work with veterans and their families.
- At the baccalaureate level, attention to the preparation of generalist social workers who will work in remote settings is crucial.
- At the master's level, military-related content should be incorporated into social policy, human behavior and social environment (HBSE) and fieldwork, and/or a complete concentration developed.
- At the doctoral level, dissertation and general research on military social work and veterans' services supported by academic institutions, private foundations, and governmental agencies should be fostered.

Research and Assessment

- To what extent are social work education programs preparing social work students to assist veterans in pursuing educational career opportunities.
- To what extent are social work educators consulting with the DOD, VA, and civilian providers to identify and promote evidence-based practices associated with successful transition of service members from the military services and the coping and recovery of veterans hampered by mental health problems.

Family Behavioral Health

- Raise awareness of the multifaceted needs of veterans' families.
- Convey specific practice knowledge within social work programs.
- Address assessment protocols within agencies.

Collaborative Partnership and Agency

- Advocate for legislative initiatives that transcend organizational boundaries.
- Partner with organizations to provide social work education that attends to biopsychosocial issues of active-duty personnel, recent veterans, and their families.
- Facilitate the entry of recent veterans and their family members into social work education programs.
- Urge NASW to add members of the military, veterans, and their families to its specialty practice credentialing program.
- Foster ties with community agencies to help prepare social workers for working with veterans, raise awareness of veterans' issues, and examine policies pertaining to veterans.

CSWE-Specific Recommendations

- Add a section to the CSWE Web site for resources.
- Encourage member institutions to link with other groups serving returning veterans and their families.
- Identify and join with other social work education and practice groups that have a common interest in quality-of-life issues for veterans.

- Convene a work group to develop a statement of advanced practice behaviors for MSW concentrations in military social work.
- Continue to host an open forum during the Annual Program Meeting (APM). (pp. 1–5)

The complete version of the recommendations can be found on the CSWE Web site. These are good recommendations to begin the process of educating social workers to respond to service members, veterans, and their families.

In reviewing the recommendations, we found no mention of sexual orientation, which is an issue that social workers will encounter. At present, the DOD is exploring all the issues that will need to be addressed before the repealed ban on gays serving in the military is implemented. Social workers need to be educated about the issues pertaining to gay, lesbian, and bisexual service members openly serving if they are to be fully prepared to work with the military and veterans.

The warriors and family members who were interviewed for this book gave several recommendations for improving social work practice with warriors and their families. The resources of Military OneSource and MyHealthVet.com are helpful and have made finding and using resources better. Many claimed that the previous automated system was not helpful. They felt like they got the runaround and had a different person on the phone or were sent from person to person until they became so frustrated that they gave up. For example, several families of one National Guard unit did not receive child-care benefits until a month before the military members returned home, and the benefits were not retroactive. The spouses reported trying for ten months to receive the benefits and never succeeded. The direct extension for specific needs is necessary, and having a list of persons' names, e-mail addresses, and phone numbers for specific needs in a state or area would be very helpful. Social workers in nonmilitary agencies in communities in which military service members and families live (everywhere in the United States and many places overseas) should keep an updated resource list readily available for use with clients who are service members, veterans, and their families. Along with this, the warriors and family members want a Web site with correct information on rights and benefits and how to apply for the benefits, and the Web site needs to be kept up to date with all the changes for soldiers and veterans and injured soldiers and veterans.

The warriors and family members also stated that the following are needed:

- A list of military acronyms with meanings
- A counselor in the area where they live for family and marriage problems, and emotional support
- More information on how to find a counselor for the family at home, for things like problems with in-laws and children acting out
- More predeployment information and services, and more about what to expect and how to handle separation
- Advocates for warriors' rights and to help in the receipt of benefits due, especially while injured and before going to the VA
- A stronger Iraq/Afghanistan Veterans of America group, with chapters in rural areas (e.g., "We just do not fit in the VFW and the American Legion")
- Debriefing at weekend drills after we have been home from the war and continued questions about suicide and problems (e.g., "We are not listening or talking about our problems at the four-hour debriefing when we want to go home")
- Enlisting the services of a volunteer coordinator who could recruit volunteers and maintain a list of e-mail addresses and phone numbers of community members who can help with numerous needs, such as yard work, emergency child care, finding various resources, caregiving to elderly parents, and help if a military spouse is sick

A veteran who was attending university classes described one more way for social work educators to help:

I have TBI. I have to read and reread everything so many times to understand it. I can't be distracted during tests and I need more time. Use [the] blackboard and announcements on e-mail to help me keep on track. I need reminders, as my memory is not very good. Please follow what is said on the syllabus and do not change things and confuse everything. I have everything written down and a comment in class that changes things—well, I might not even get it that it changed. I need communication and everything to be clear. The person who is the Veterans' Affairs officer on campus needs to be culturally competent and understand the needs of the veteran.

In a 2010 op-ed, Omar Domenech, an Iraq War veteran and social work student, wrote:

> The need for social workers trained to deal with veterans' issues is critical. The social worker's challenge is to convey both to the veteran and the military chain of command that it's ok for a soldier to ask for help, and that acknowledging a need for help makes you a stronger person and better soldier. The social worker must also point out to veterans that they are entitled to certain services and benefits and they should not be shy in asking for them. Equally important, our government needs to provide a wide array of services to help meet the challenges that returning veterans have. More social workers need to be trained to work with returning veterans. Family members of troubled veterans could also benefit from specialized counsel.

Our hope in writing this book is to bring attention to the needs of warriors, veterans, and their families and to evoke interest in the education of social workers, as well as the development of services for this underserved population in institutions of higher education, service agencies, and communities. It is also our hope that the various branches of the military and our government will continue to improve on the services provided to our warriors, veterans, and their families. More research is needed for social workers to be competent in our provision of services to build resiliency and hardiness, to prevent suicide, to facilitate transitions, to successfully reintegrate families, to respond appropriately to visible and invisible injuries, and to facilitate positive change for this population. Serving our country in this capacity will change service members and their family and friends. War is hell. It is our responsibility to not forget the debt we owe to the men and women who fight our battles—before, during, and after the battle.

> Our God and the soldier we alike adore
> Ev'n at the brink of danger, not before:
> After deliverance, both alike requited,
> God is forgotten, and the soldier slighted
> —**Francis Quarles**, *Emblems*, 1635

Let us not let this happen again.

Glossary
Common Military Speak and Slang

AAFES	Army Air Force Exchange Service
AAR	After Action Review
ACS	Army Community Service
ACR	Army Combat Uniform
AFTB	Army Family Team Building
AFU	All fucked up; pronounced "ah-foo"
AG	Adjutant General
AGI	Annual General Inspection
AIt	Advanced Individual Training
AK	Kalashnikov Assault Rifle
AMVETS	American Veterans Organization
ANG	Air National Guard
Angels	KIAs who die in the military while undergoing care
AR	Army Regulation
ARCOM	Army Commendation Medal
ARTEP	Army Readiness Training and Evaluation Program
ASAP	As soon as possible
AUSA	Association of the U.S. Army
AVF	All-Volunteer Force
AVN	Aviation
AWOL	Absent Without Leave
Back-door draft	"Stop loss," or being held past the end of your enlistment so that you can deploy to Iraq or Afghanistan
BAH	Basic Allowance for Housing
BAQ	Basic Allowance for Quarters
BAS	Basic Allowance for Subsistence

Battle rattle	Body armor
BDU	Battlefield Camouflage Field Uniform
BEQ	Bachelor Enlisted Quarters
Blue canoe	Portable latrine
BNCOC	Basic Noncommissioned Officers' Course
Bongo	Small flatbed truck driven in the Middle East
BOQ	Bachelor Officers Quarters
Bust a cap in his ass	Shoot the bad guy
BX	Base Exchange
CAV	Cavalry
CBOC	Community Based Outpatient Clinic (VA)
CENTCOM	Central Command
CG	Commanding General
CGSC	Command and General Staff College
CHAMPUS	Civilian Health and Medical Program of the Uniformed Services (TRICARE)
Cherry	A first-timer, also a "newbie"
CINC	Commander in Chief
Citizen-soldiers	Reserve and National Guard Service members
CO	Commanding Officer
COB	Close of Business
COLA	Cost of Living Allowance
CONUS	Continental United States
COSC	Combat Operational Stress Control
COSR	Combat Operational Stress Reaction
CP	Command Post
CPO	Civilian Personnel Office
CQ	Charge of Quarters
CSM	Command Sergeant Major
DA	Department of the Army
DACOWITS	Defense Advisory Committee on Women in the Service
DAV	Disabled American Veterans
DCINC	Deputy Commander-in-Chief
DEERS	Defense Enrollment Eligibility Reporting System
DEROS	Date of Estimated Rotation from Overseas Assignment

DFAC	Dining facility; current term for mess hall
DHS	Department of Homeland Security
DIVARTY	Division Artillery
DOD	Department of Defense
DODDS	Department of Defense Dependent Schools
DODEA	Department of Defense Education Activity
Down range	Deployment Area
DPCA	Director of Personnel and Community Activities
DROS	Date of Rotation from Station
Dwell time	At-home time between deployments
Echelons above reality	Higher HQ, where no one has any idea what is really happening
Embeds	Media reporters embedded with a coalition unit
Embrace the suck	"The situation is bad, but deal with it"
EOD	Explosive Ordinance Disposal
EUCOM	U.S. European Command
FA	Field Artillery
FAC	Family Assistance Center
FCP	Family Care Plan
Fire fight	Armed combat
FLO	Family Liaison Office
FM	Field Manual
FOB	Forward Operating Base
Fobbits	Derogatory term for soldiers who never leave an FOB
FOD	Field Officer of the Day
FORSCOM	Forces Command
FRG	Family Readiness Group (Army)
FSG	Family Support Group (Navy, Coast Guard)
FST	Female Search Team; vital component when operating in a Muslim country; female soldiers search female suspects
FTX	Field Training Exercise
GI	Government Issue (service member)
GO	General Officer
Grunt	Infantry Soldier

Gunship	An attack helicopter (e.g., Apache) or a USAF C-130 Spectre gunship
GWOT	Global War on Terrorism
Haji	An Iraqi, but any Middle Easterner who hails from a predominantly Muslim country (derogatory)
HESCO	A Hesco barrier, a large wire frame and cloth box filled with dirt to provide protection against mortar and rocket shrapnel; alternative to sandbags
HHC	Headquarters and Headquarters Company
Hooah	Army slang, usually a shout; signals approval or solidarity; means most anything except "no"
HQ	Headquarters
HRAP	Health Risk Appraisal Program
Humvee	Highly Mobile, Multipurpose Vehicle
IAVA	Iraq and Afghanistan Veterans of America
ICAF	Industrial College of the Armed Forces
IED	Improvised Explosive Device
IG	Inspector General
IN	Infantry
JAG	Judge Advocate General (Law Office)
JCS	Joint Chiefs of Staff
JUMPS	Joint Uniform Military Pay System
KP	Kitchen Duty
KSP	Key Spouse Program (Air Force version of FRG)
KVN	Key Volunteer Program (Marine version of FRG)
Leave	Vacation
LES	Leave and Earnings Statement
LOI	Letter of Instruction
LZ	Landing Zone
MAC	Military Airlift Command
MACOM	Major Army Command
MCEX	Marine Corps Exchange
MEDAC	U.S. Medical Activity
MEDBOARD	Medical Board (determines fitness for duty)
MDD	Major Depressive Disorder

MDE	Major Depressive Episode
MEDEVAC	Evacuation of Sick and Wounded
MFLC	Military and Family Life Consultant
MI	Military Intelligence
MILCOM	Military Community
MILPERCEN	Army Military Personnel Center
MOPH	Military Order of the Purple Heart
MOS	Military Occupational Specialty
MP	Military Police
MRE	Meals Ready to Eat
MTF	Military Treatment Facility
MWR	Morale, Welfare, and Recreation
NATO	North Atlantic Treaty Organization
NCO	Noncommissioned Officer (E4–E9)
NCOER	NCO Efficiency Report
NCOIC	Noncommissioned Officer in Charge
NEO	Noncombatant Evacuation Order
NEX	Naval Exchange
NTC	National Training Center, Fort Irwin, California
OBC	Officer Basic Course
OCONUS	Outside Continental United States
OCS	Officer Candidate School
OD	Officer of the Day
OEF	Operation Enduring Freedom, Afghanistan
OER	Officer Efficiency Report
OIC	Officer in Charge
Oo-rah	Marine cheer; means anything except "no"
OPREADY	Operation READY, Resources for Educating About Deployment and You
OPSEC	Operational Security, or being careful what you say about operations
OPTEMPO	Pace of an Operation
OT	Occupational Therapist
OTS	Officer Training School
PA	Physician Assistant

PAC	Personnel Administration Center
PAO	Public Affairs Officer
PC	Primary Care
PCC	Pre-Command Course
PCS	Permanent Change of Station
PLDC	Primary Leadership Development Course
PNOK	Primary Next of Kin
POC	Point of Contact
POG	People Other than Grunts; used by grunts as a derogatory term for everyone else
PSYOPS	Psychological Operations
PT	Physical Training
PTSD	Posttraumatic Stress Disorder
PX	Post Exchange (Army)
QRF	Quick Reaction Force
RA	Regular Army
Ragheads	Derogatory term for Arabs, Iranians, and Afghanis
RCS	Readjustment Counseling SVC (Vet Centers)
RIF	Reduction in Force
RON	Stay Overnight
ROTC	Reserve Officer Training Corps
SATCOM	Satellite Communications
SBP	Survivor Benefit Plan
SECDEF	Secretary of Defense
Semper Fi	Marine motto (Latin *Semper Fidelis*, "Always Faithful")
SHAPE	Supreme Headquarters Allied Powers Europe
SITREP	Situation Report
SOP	Standing Operational Procedure
SQT	Skill Qualification Test
SUPCOM	Support Command
TA-50	Regulation Field Equipment Issued to Soldiers
TBI	Traumatic brain injury
TD	Temporary Duty
TDY	Temporary Duty Assignment
TLA	Temporary Living Allowance

TLE	Temporary Lodging Entitlement
TMP	Transportation Motor Pool
TO&E	Table of Organization and Equipment, issued to a unit
TOC	Tactical Operational Center
TRADOC	Training and Doctrine Command
Twat	Slang for a tanker without a tank; an armored unit member operating as Infantry
UCMJ	Uniformed Code of Military Justice
UMT	Unit Ministry Team
USA	U.S. Army
USAF	U.S. Air Force
USCG	U.S. Coast Guard
USMC	U.S. Marine Corps
USN	U.S. Navy
VA	Veterans Affairs
VAMC	Veterans Affairs Medical Center
VBA	Veterans Benefits Administration
Vet Center	Community Based Readjustment Center (RCS)
VFW	Veterans of Foreign Wars
VHA	Veterans Health Administration
VISN	Veterans Integrated Service Network
WESTCOM	Western Command; Hawaii
XO	Executive Officer
YAC	Youth Activities Center
Zoomie	Anyone serving in the Air Force

References

Albano, S. (1994). Military recognition of family concerns: Revolutionary War to 1993. *Armed Forces and Society, 20*(2), 283–302.

Alcohol abuse on the rise among U.S. soldiers. (2009, June 20). Retrieved from http://www.armybase.us/2009/06/alcohol-abuse-on-the-rise-among-us-soldiers/.

Alvarez, L. (2008, October 30). Army and agency will study rising suicide rate among soldiers. *New York Times.* Retrieved from http://www.nytimes.com/2008/10/30/us/30soldiers.html.

Alvarez, L., & Sontag, D. (2008, February 15). When strains on military families turns deadly. *New York Times.* Retrieved from http://www.nytimes.com/2008/02/15/15vets.hmtl.

Amen, D. G., & Jellen, L. (1988). Minimizing the impact of deployment separation on military children: Stages, current preventative efforts, and system recommendations. *Military Medicine, 9,* 441–446.

American Council on Education. (2008, November). *Serving those who serve: Higher education and America's veterans* [Issue brief]. Washington, DC: Author.

American Foundation for Suicide Prevention. (2011). *Facts and figures.* Retrieved from http://www.afsp.org/index.cfm?.

American Psychiatric Association. (1980). *Diagnostic and statistical manual of mental disorders: DSM-III-TR* (3rd ed.). Arlington, VA: Author.

American Psychiatric Association. (2000). *Diagnostic and statistical manual of mental disorders: DSM-IV-TR* (4th ed.). Arlington, VA: Author.

Araujo, D. C. (2010, March). *Repealing "Don't Ask, Don't Tell."* (Working paper). Washington, DC: Center for Inquiry Office of Public Policy.

Armstrong, K., Best, S., & Domenici, P. (2006). *Courage after fire: Coping strategies for troops returning from Iraq and Afghanistan and their families.* Berkeley, CA: Ulysses Press.

Autry, D. (2008, March–April). Female veterans' care. *Disabled American Veterans Magazine*, 19, 28.

Bain, A. (1978). The capacity of families to cope with transitions: A theoretical essay. *Human Relations, 3*8(2), 675–688.

Barker, L. H., & Berry, K. D. (2009). Developmental issues impacting military families with young children during single and multiple deployments. *Military Medicine, 174*(10), 1033–1041.

Barnes, V. A., Davis, H., & Treiber, F. A. (2007). Perceived stress, heart rate, and blood pressure among adolescents with family members deployed in Operation Iraqi Freedom. *Military Medicine, 172*, 40–43.

Bartelt, E. S. (2007). Army covenant signed by Secretary Geren. *Pointer View, 64*(43), 1–3.

Basham, K. (Ed.). (2009). [Editorial.] *Smith College Studies in Social Work, 79*, 239–243.

Batres, A. R. (2010, April 23). *The RCS mission.* Briefing presented at the meeting of the Advisory Committee for the Readjustment of Veterans, Washington, DC.

Batten, S. J., Drapalski, A. L., Decker, M. I., DeViva, J. C., Morrie, L. J., Mann, M. A., et al. (2009). Veterans' interest in family involvement in PTSD treatment. *Psychological Services, 6*(3), 184–189.

Beck, A. T. (1991). *Cognitive therapy and emotional disorders.* New York: Penguin Books.

Beck, A. T., & Steer, R. A. (1991). *Manual for Beck scale for suicide ideation.* San Antonio, TX: Psychological Corporation.

Beck, A. T., Steer, R. A., & Brown, G. K. (1996). *Manual for Beck Depression Inventory* (2nd ed.). San Antonio, TX: Psychological Corporation.

Belkin, A. (2008). Don't ask, don't tell: Does the gay ban undermine the military's reputation? *Armed Forces and Society, 34*(2), 276–291.

Ben Arzi, N., Solomon, Z., & Dekel, R. (2000). Secondary traumatization among wives of PTSD and post-concussion casualties: Distress, caregiver burden and psychological separation. *Brain Injury, 14*(8), 725–736.

Bender, B. (2010, February 2). Admiral Mullen: "Allowing gays and lesbians to serve openly would be the right thing to do." *Boston Globe*. Retrieved from http://www.boston.com/news/politics/politicalintelligence/2010/02/nations_top_off.html.

Benedict, H. (2009). *The lonely soldier: The private war of women serving in Iraq.* Boston: Beacon Press.

Biank, T. (2006). *Under the sabers: The unwritten code of Army wives.* New York: St. Martin's Press.

Black, W. (1993). Military-induced family separation: A stress reduction intervention. *Social Work, 38*, 273–280.

Blount, W., Curry, A., & Lubin, G. I. (1992). Family separations in the military. *Military Medicine, 157*, 76–80.

Bonds, T. M., Baiocchi, D., & McDonald, L. L. (2010). *Army deployments to OIF and OEF.* Santa Monica, CA: RAND.

Booth, B., Segal, M. W., Bell, B. D., Martin, J. A., Ender, M. G., Rohall, D. E., et al. (2007). *What we know about Army families: 2007 update.* Washington, DC: Department of Army Family and Morale, Welfare and Recreation Command.

Boss, P. (1980). Normative family stress: Family boundary changes across the life span. *Family Relations, 29*, 445–450.

Boss, P. (1999). *Ambiguous loss: Learning to live with unresolved grief.* Cambridge, MA: Harvard University Press.

Boss, P. (2007). Ambiguous loss theory: Challenges for scholars and practitioners. *Family Relations, 56*(2), 105–110.

Bowen, G. L. (1989). Satisfaction with family life in the military. *Armed Forces and Society, 15*(4), 571–592.

Bride, B. E., & Figley, C. R. (2009). Secondary trauma and military veteran caregivers. *Smith College Studies in Social Work, 79*, 314–329.

Briere, J., & Scott, C. (2006). *Principles of trauma therapy.* Thousand Oaks, CA: Sage.

Broz, C. (2009, February 9). Record suicide rate. *Army Times*, p. 10.

Bumiller, E. (2010, March 16). Sexual assault reports rise in military. *New York Times*. Retrieved from http://www.nytimes.com/2010/13/17/us17assault.html.

Burnam, M. A., Meredith, L. S., Helmus, T. C., Burns, R. M., Cox, R. A., D'Amico, E., et al. (2008). Systems of care: Challenges and opportunities to improve access to high-quality care. In T. Tanielian & L. H. Jaycox (Eds.), *Invisible wounds of war: Psychological and cognitive injuries, their consequences, and services to assist recovery* (pp. 245–428). Santa Monica, CA: RAND Corporation Center for Military Policy and Research.

Burnam, M. A., Meredith, L. S., Sherbourne, C. D., Valdez, R. B., & Vernez, G. (1992). *Army families and soldier readiness*. Santa Monica, CA: RAND.

Burrell, L. M., Adams, G. A., Durand, D. B., & Castro, C. A. (2006). The impact of military lifestyle demands on well-being, Army, and family outcomes. *Armed Forces and Society, 33*(1), 43–58.

Burton, D. L. (2009). Commentary to reaction panel in response to keynote lecture presented by Drs. B. E. Bride and C. R. Figley titled "Secondary traumatic stress and military veteran caregivers." *Smith College Studies in Social Work, 79*, 330–334.

Butler, S. D. (1935). *War is a racket.* Los Angeles: Feral House.

Calhoun, P. S., Beckham, J. C., & Bosworth, H. B. (2002). Caregiver burden and psychological stress in partners of veterans with chronic posttraumatic stress disorder. *Journal of Traumatic Stress, 15*(3), 205–212.

Campagna, H., & Cohen, J. A. (2010, November 16). Child traumatic grief: Issues and interventions related to military children. [Webinar]. Retrieved from http://www.TAPS.org.

Campbell, C. I., Brown, E. J., & Okwara, L. (2011). Addressing sequelae of trauma and interpersonal violence in military children: A review of the literature and case illustration. *Cognitive and Behavioral Practice, 18*, 131–143.

Carroll, B. (2009, Fall). Out of tragedy. *Tragedy Assistance Program for Survivors, 15*, 6–7.

Caruso, K. (2004). Suicide rates on the rise in the Air Force. Retrieved from http://www.suicide.org/suicide-rateus-air-force.html.

Castille, R. D. (n.d.). A special court for veterans. *New York Times.* Retrieved from http://www.nadcp.org/VTCinNYT.

Castro, C. (2009). Impact on combat on the mental health of Soldiers and Marines. *Smith College Studies in Social Work, 79*, 247–262.

Castro, C., & McGurk, D. (2008). The intensity of combat and behavioral health. *Traumatology, 13*(4), 6–23.

Cavallaro, G. (2007, August 27). Army suicides spike; war zone accounts for one-third. *Army Times*, p. 8.

Cavallaro, G. (2008, September 22). Repugnant record: Army starts top-down campaign to end rampant sexual assault. *Army Times*, pp. 8–9.

Cavallaro, G. (2009, May 18). Vice chief's plan: Restore discipline, stop suicides. *Army Times*, p. 22.

Century Foundation. (2008). Legions stretched thin: The U.S. Army's manpower crisis. Retrieved from http://www.tcf.org/Publications/Homeland Security/legions.pdf.

Chamberlain, H., Stander, V., & Merrill, L. L. (2003). Research on child abuse in the U.S. armed forces. *Military Medicine, 168*, 257–260.

Chandra, A., Lara-Cinisomo, S., Jaycox, L. H., Tanielian, T., Burns, R. M., Ruder I., et al. (2010). Children on the home front: The experience of children from military families. *Pediatrics, 125*, 16–25.

Chartrand, M. M., Frank, D. A., White, L. F., & Shope, T. R. (2008). Effect of parents' wartime deployment on the behavior of young children in military families. *Archives of Pediatric and Adolescent Medicine, 162*(11), 1009–1014.

Chartrand, M. M., & Siegel, G. (2007). At war in Iraq and Afghanistan: Children in U.S. military families. *Ambulatory Pediatrics, 7*(1), 1–2.

Childers, T. (2009). *Soldier from the war returning.* New York: Houghton Mifflin, Harcourt.

Church, T. E. (2009). Returning veterans on campus with war-related injuries and the long road back home. *Journal of Postsecondary Education and Disability, 22*(1), 59–60.

Cline, L. S. (1989). *Today's military wife: Meeting the challenges of service life.* Harrisburg, PA: Stackpole Books.

Cogan, J. (2010, January 6). *Suicide claims more U.S. military lives than Afghan war.* Retrieved from http://www.wsws.org/articles/2010Jan2010/Suic-jo6.shmtl.

Collins, E. M. (2009, October 8). Army psychiatrist: Military children have increased mental health risk. *Army Military News.* Retrieved from http://www.army.mil/-news/2009/10/08/28555.

Commander shuts down Fort Campbell because of suicides. (2009, May 29). *Newsmax.* Retrieved from http://www.newsmax.com/printTemplate.html.

Comprehensive Soldier Fitness Program. (2009, May). *2009 U.S. Army posture statement to the committees and subcommittees of the United States Senate and the House of Representatives.* Washington, DC: Headquarters, U.S. Army. Retrieved from http://www.army.mil/aps/09/information_papers/comprehensive_soldier_fitness_program.

Corrigan, P. W., & Penn, D. L. (1999). Lessons from social psychology on discrediting psychiatric stigma. *American Psychologist, 54,* 765–766.

Corrigan, P. W., & Watson, A. C. (2002). The paradox of self-stigma and mental illness. *Clinical Psychology, 9,* 35–53.

Council on Social Work Education. (2009, October). *A joint task force on Veteran's affairs: Final report.* Retrieved from http://www.cswe.org/Search.aspx?qsearch=veterans.

Cozza, S. J., Guimond, J. M., McKibben, J. B., Chun, R. S., Arata-Maiers, T. L., Schneider, B., et al. (2010). Combat-injured service members and their families: The relationship of child distress and spouse-perceived family distress and disruption. *Journal of Traumatic Stress, 23*(1), 112–115.

Crossley, A. (1990). *The Army wife handbook: A complete social guide.* Sarasota, FL: ABI.

Crossley, A., & Keller, C. A. (2004). *The Army wife handbook: Updated and expanded.* Sarasota, FL: ABI.

Crouch, K. (2010). *Army covenant delivers programs, services.* Retrieved from http://www.army.mil/-news/2010/01/11/32756.

Cucullu, G. (2010). The dry Army. Retrieved from http://supportamericansoldiers.com/Articles/Dry_No_Alcohol_Army.html.

Curley, B. (2009, June 15). *Wounds of war: Drug problems among Iraq, Afghan vets could dwarf Vietnam.* [Fact sheet]. Retrieved from http://www.drugfree.org/join-together/alcohol/wounds-of-war-drug problems.

Curtin, T. R., & Cahalan, M. W. (2005). *A profile of the Veterans Upward Bound Program: 2000–2001.* Washington, DC: U.S. Department of Education, Office of Postsecondary Education.

Cvetanovich, B., & Reynolds, L. (2009). Joshua Omvig Veterans Suicide Prevention Act of 2007. *Harvard Journal on Legislation, 45*(2), 619–645.

Daley, J. G. (Ed.). (1999). *Social work practice in the military.* New York: Haworth Press.

Darwin, J. (2009). Families: "They also serve who only stand and wait." *Smith College Studies in Social Work, 79,* 433–442.

Dekel, R., Solomon, Z., & Bleich, A. (2005). Emotional distress and marital adjustment of caregivers: Contribution of the care recipient's level of impairment and of the caregiver's appraised burden. *Anxiety Stress Coping, 18*, 71–82.

Dennett, D. E. (1988). Suicide in the Naval service. Part II. Incidence and rate. *Navy Medicine, 79*, 24–28.

Domenech, O. (2010, March 10). Many returning veterans feel stigmatized in asking for psychological help. *Brooklyn Daily Eagle*. Retrieved from http://www.brooklyneagle.com/categories/category.php?categoru-id= 10&id=34018.

Donnelly, J. (2011, February 22). More troops lost to suicide. Retrieved from http://www.Congress.org/news/2011/01/24/more troops lost to suicide.

Driscoll, J. (2009, November 3). Opening statement at the VA Summit to end veteran homelessness. Retrieved from http://www.nchv.org/news_article .cfm?id=633.

Drug Policy Alliance. (2009, November 4). *Healing a broken system: Veterans battling addiction and incarceration.* [Issue brief]. New York: Author.

Dublin, L. I., & Bunzel, M. A. (1933). *To be or not to be: A study of suicide.* New York: Quinn and Boden.

Durkheim, E. (1951). *Suicide: A study in sociology.* New York: Free Press. (Originally published 1897).

Eberstadt, M. (2010, January–February). Mothers in combat boots. *Policy Review*, 33–44.

Eliot, T. S. (1943). *Four quartets.* Orlando, FL: Harcourt Brace Jovanovich.

Engel, C. C. (2003). Managing depression in primary care using the VA/DoD major depressive disorder clinical practice guidelines. Retrieved from http://www./PDHealth.mil/video/clinical_training_series/mdd_engel/pdf/ slides.pdf.

Fairweather, A. (2006, December 6). *Risk and protective factors for homelessness among OIF/OEF veterans.* San Francisco: Swords to Plowshares' Iraq Veteran Project.

Fehrenbach, T. R. (1963). *This kind of war: A study in unpreparedness.* New York: Macmillan.

Figley, C. R. (Ed.). (1995). *Compassion fatigue: Coping with secondary traumatic stress disorder in those who treat the traumatized.* Bristol, PA: Brunner/ Mazel.

Figley, C. R., & Nash, W. P. (Eds.). (2007). *Combat stress injury: Theory, research, and management.* New York: Routledge.

Finkel, L. B., Kelley, M. L., & Ashby, J. (2003). Geographic mobility, family, and maternal variables as related to the psychosocial adjustment of military children. *Military Medicine, 168*(12), 1019–1024.

Firestone, J. M., & Harris, R. J. (Eds.). (2009). Sexual harassment in the U.S. military reserve component: A preliminary analysis. *Armed Forces and Society, 36*(1), 86–102.

Fontana, A., Rosenheck, R., & Brett, E. (1992). War zone traumas and post-traumatic stress disorder symptomatology. *Journal of Nervous and Mental Disease, 180*, 748–755.

Franciskovic, T., Stevanovic, A., Jelusic, I., Roganovic, B., Klaric, M., & Grkovic, J. (2007). Secondary traumatization of wives of war veterans with posttraumatic stress disorder. *Croatian Medical Journal, 48*, 177–184.

Freeman, S. M., Moore, B. A., & Freeman, A. (2009). *Living and surviving in harms way: A psychological treatment handbook for pre- and post-deployment of military personnel.* New York: Routledge.

Gambill, G. (2010, May 11). A mounting social crisis: Veterans of Iraq and Afghanistan at the crossroads of justice. Retrieved from http://www.ejfi.org/courts/courts-39.htm.

Gates, R. M. (2009, May 23). U.S. Military Academy Commencement Address. Retrieved from http://www.defense.gov/speeches/speech.aspx?speedchid=1354.

Geren, P., & Casey, G. (2008, September 22). A sacred trust: Soldiers must unite to create climate of zero tolerance for sexual assault. *Army Times*, p. 62.

Gerhart, A. (2010). Suicide of four soldiers in a week stun Fort Hood. *Washington Post.* Retrieved from http://www.washingtonpost.com/wp-dyn/content/article/2010/09/30/Ar2010093006496.

Gibbs, D. A., Martin, S. L., Kupper, L. L., & Johnson, R. E. (2007). Child maltreatment in enlisted soldiers' families during combat related deployment. *Journal of the American Medical Association, 298*(5), 528–535.

Goldsmith, S. K., Pellmar, T. C., Kleinman, A. M., & Bunney, W. (Eds.). (2002). *Reducing suicide: A national imperative.* Washington, DC: National Academies Press.

Goldstein, A. (2008, May 5). Post-war suicides may exceed combat deaths, U.S. says. Retrieved from http://www.bloomberg.com/appsnews?sid=a2_71.

Gordon, D. M., Gordon, M., & Smith, D. M. (Eds.). (n.d.). *Uniformed services almanac.* Falls Church, VA: Uniformed Services Almanac.

Gould, J. (2011, January 31). A tough stand on sexual assault. *Army Times*, p. 16.

Gray, J. G. (1970). *The warriors: Reflections on men in battle.* New York: Harcourt, Brace.

Green-Shortridge, T. M., Britt, M. W., & Castro, A. (2007). The stigma of mental health problems in the military. *Military Medicine, 172*(2), 157–161.

Grossman, D. A. (1995). *On killing: The psychological cost of learning to kill in war and society.* Boston: Little, Brown.

Guerra, V. S., & Calhoun, P. S. (2010). Examining the relation between post-traumatic stress disorder and suicidal ideation in an OEF/OIF veteran sample. *Journal of Anxiety Disorders, 25*(1), 12–18.

Gunnell, D., & Lewis, G. (2005). Studying suicide from the life course perspective: Implications for prevention. *British Journal of Psychiatry, 1187*, 206–208.

Hall, L. K. (2008). *Counseling military families: What mental health professionals need to know.* New York: Routledge

Hames, J. (2009, October 6). *Resiliency training to be given Army wide.* Retrieved from http://www.army.mil.

Hampton, T. (2007). Research, law address veteran's suicide. *Journal of the American Medical Association, 298*(23), 27–32.

Harkness, L., & Zandor, N. (2001). Treatment of PTSD in families and couples. In J. P. Wilson, M. J. Friedman, & J. D. Lindy (Eds.), *Treating psychological trauma and PTSD* (pp. 335–353). New York: Guilford Press.

Harman, J. (2008, March 31). Rapists in the ranks: Sexual assaults are frequent and frequently ignored, in the Armed Services. *L.A. Times*, pp. 1–2. Retrieved from http://www.latimes.com/news/printededition/asection/la=-oe-harman31mar31,0,2039956.print.story.

Harrell, M. C. (2002). Current Army officers: Wives compelled to volunteer. *National Council on Family Relations Report, 47*(1), F18–F19.

Hayes, P. (2010, April 23). *Women veterans' health care.* Presentation at the Advisory Committee on the Readjustment of Veterans, Washington, DC.

Hefling, K. (2009a, July 7). More military children seeking mental health care. *Marine Corps Times.* Retrieved from http://www.marinecorpstimes.com/news/2009/07/ap_children_mental_health_070709/.

Hefling, K. (2009b, July 14). Privacy deemed lacking at some VA hospitals. *Navy Times.* Retrieved from http://www.navytimes.com/news/2009/07/ap_women_va_hospitals_071409.

Hendin, H., & Haas, A. P. (1991). Suicide and guilt as manifestations of PTSD in Vietnam combat veterans. *American Journal of Psychiatry, 148,* 586–591.

Henry J. Kaiser Family Foundation (2004). *Military families survey, March 2004.* Menlo Park, CA: Author.

Hoge, C. W., Castro, C. A., & Eaton, K. M. (2006). Impact of combat duty in Iraq and Afghanistan on family functioning: Findings from the Walter Reed Army Institute of Research Land Combat Study. In *Human dimensions in military operations: Military leaders' strategies for addressing stress and psychological support* (pp. 5-1–5-6). [Meeting proceedings RTO-MP-HFM-134, Paper No. 5]. Neuilly-sur-Sein, France: Research Technology Organization. Retrieved from http://www.rto.natio.int/abstracts.asp.

Hoge, C. W., Castro, C. A., Messner, D., McGurk, D., Cotting, D. I., & Koffman, R. L. (2004). Combat duty in Iraq and Afghanistan, mental health problems and barriers to care. *New England Journal of Medicine, 351*(1), 13–23.

Holbrook, J. (2011). Veterans' courts and criminal responsibility: A problem-solving history and approach to the liminality of combat trauma. In D. C. Kelley, S. Howe-Barksdale, & D. Gitelson (Eds.), *Treating young veterans: Promoting resilience through practice and advocacy* (pp. 259–300). New York: Springer.

Huebner, A. J., Mancini, J. A., Wilcox, R. M., Grass, S. R., & Grass, G. A. (2007). Parental deployment and youth in military families: Exploring uncertainty and ambiguous loss. *Family Relations, 56*(2), 112–123.

Hunter, E. J., & Nice, D. S. (Eds.). (1978). *Military families: Adaptation to change.* New York: Praeger.

Huseman, S. (2008, January 3). Battlemind prepares soldiers for combat, returning home. *Army News Service.* Retrieved from http://www army.mil/article/6829/battlemind-prepares-soldiers-cor combat-returning-home.

Institute of Medicine, Committee on Gulf War and Health (2008). *Long-term consequences of traumatic brain injury.* Retrieved from http://www .iom.edu/Reports/2008/Gulf-War-and-Health_Volumne7-Long-Term-consequences-of-Traumatic-Brain-Injury.aspx.

Isay, R. A. (1968). The submariners' wives syndrome. *Psychiatric Quarterly, 42,* 647–652.

Ivanoff, A., & Riedel, M. (1996). Suicide. In *The encyclopedia of social work.* Washington, DC: National Association of Social Workers Press.

Jacobs, J. (2006, May 12). An Iowa couple's son killed himself while suffering from post traumatic stress disorder. "We can't ignore others," they say. Retrieved from http://joshua-omvig.memory-of.com/Legacy.apx.

Jacobson, I. G., Ryan, M. A. K., Hooper, T. I., Smith, T. C., Amoroso, P. J., Boyko, E. J., et al. (2008). Alcohol use and alcohol-related problems before and after military combat deployment. *Journal of the American Medical Association, 300*(6), 663–675.

Jarrett, T. A. (2008). *Warrior Resilience and Thriving.* [Training module]. Fort Sill, OK: Social Work Service and Outreach Program.

Jelinek, P. (2008, March 2). Military divorce rate steady. *Tuscaloosa News*, pp. 1A, 15A.

Joiner, T. (2005). *Why people die by suicide.* Cambridge, MA: Harvard University Press.

Jowers, K. (2009, May 18). Marine widow describes pain that suicide brings. *Army Times*, p. 11.

Jowers, K. (2011, February 28). Gates now supports laws to protect child custody. *Army Times*, p. 35.

Jowers, K., & Tilghman, A. (2011, January 2). Military kids taking more psychiatric drugs. *Army Times*, p. 12.

Kang, H. D., & Bullman, T. A. (2008). Risk of suicide among U.S. Veterans after returning from the Iraq or Afghanistan war zones. *Journal of the American Medical Association, 300*(6), 652–653.

Kaplan, M. S., Huguet, N., McFarland, B. H., & Newsom, J. T. (2007). Suicide among male veterans: A prospective population based study. *Journal of Epidemiology and Community Health, 61*(7), 619–624.

Karney, K. R., & Crown, J. S. (2007). *Families under stress: An assessment of data, theory, and research on marriage in the military.* Santa Monica, CA: RAND National Defense Research Institute.

Kaslow, F. W. (Ed.). (1993). *The military family in peace and war.* New York: Springer.

Kaslow, F. W., & Ridenour, R. I. (Eds.). (1984). *The military family: Dynamics and treatment.* New York: Guilford Press.

Katz, I. (2010a, February 24). *Statement to the U.S. House of Representatives Committee on Veterans' Affairs.* Washington, DC: Government Printing Office.

Katz, I. (2010b, March 23). *Statement to the U.S. House of Representatives Appropriations Committee*. Washington, DC: Government Printing Office.

Keegan, J. (1976). *The face of battle*. Suffolk, UK: Chaucer Press.

Kelley, M. L. (1994). The effects of military-induced separation on family factors and child behavior. *American Journal of Orthopsychiatry, 64*, 103–111.

Kelley, M. L., Hock, E., Smith, K. M., Jarvis, M. S., Bonney, J. F., & Gaffney, M. A. (2001). Internalizing and externalizing behavior of children with enlisted Navy mothers experiencing military-induced separation. *Journal of the American Academy of Child and Adolescent Psychiatry, 40*, 454–471.

Kelley, M. M., Vogt, D. S., Scheiderer, E. M., Ouimette, P., Daley, J., & Wolfe, J. (2008). Effects of military trauma exposure on women veterans' use and perception of Veterans Health Administration care. *Journal of General Internal Medicine, 23*(6), 741–747.

Kennedy, K. (2007, September 10). War-zone stress revealing itself in suicidal thoughts. *Army Times*, pp. 20–21.

Kennedy, K. (2008a, June 9). All the warning signs were there, but could anyone have saved 1st Sgt. Jeff McKinney? *Army Times*, pp. 30–33.

Kennedy, K. (2008b, June 9). Soldier suicides increase in 2007. *Army Times*, p. 10.

Kennedy, K. (2008c, September 10). War-zone stress revealing itself in suicidal thoughts. *Army Times*, p. 20.

Kennedy, K. (2010a, August 9). Report links suicide spike to Army's focus on war. *Army Times*, p. 20.

Kennedy, K. (2010b, December 20). Study finds "hidden epidemic" of female vet suicides. *Army Times*, p. 20.

Kerr, J. C. (2007, May 30). *Post-deployment suicide: A closer look*. Retrieved October 4, 2007, from http://www.vawatchdog.org/07/nfo07/nfmay07/nfo53007-5.htm.

Keteyian, A. (2007, November 13). Suicide epidemic among veterans. Retrieved from http://www.cbsnews.com/stories/2007/11/13/cbsnews_investigates/main3496471shtml.

Keteyian, A. (2008, April 21). *VA hides suicide risk, internal e-mails show*. Retrieved from http://www.cbsnews.com/stories/2008/04/21/cbsnews_investigates/main4032921.shtml.

Knox, J. G. (1990). *Coping during pregnancy: A longitudinal study among Air Force spouses*. Unpublished doctoral dissertation, University of California, Berkeley.

Knox, J. G., & Price, D. H. (1995). The changing American military family: Opportunities for social work. *Social Service Review, 69*(3), 479–498.

Knox, J. G., & Price, D. H. (1999). Total force and the new American military family: Implications for social work practice. *Families in Society: The Journal of Contemporary Human Services, 40,* 128–136.

Knox, K. L., Litts, D. A., Talcott, G. W., Feig, J. C., & Caine, E. D. (2003). Risk of suicide and related adverse outcomes after exposure to a suicide prevention programme in the U.S. Air Force: Cohort study. *British Medical Journal, 327,* 1376–1378.

Knox, K. L., Pflaz, S., Talcott, G. W., Campise, R. L., Lavigne, J. E., Bajorska, A., et al. (2010). The U.S. Air Force Suicide Prevention Program: Implications for Public Health Policy. *American Journal of Public Health, 100*(12), 2457–2463.

Koic, E., Franciskovic, T., Muzinic-Masle, L., Dordevic, V., & Vondracek, S. (2002). Chronic pain and secondary traumatization in the wives of Croatian veterans treated for posttraumatic stress disorder. *Acta Clinica Croatica, 41,* 295–306.

Krug, E. G., Dahlberg, L. L., Mercy, J. A., Zwi, A. B., & Lozano, R. (Eds.). (2002). *Self-directed violence. World report on violence and health.* Geneva: World Health Organization.

Krupnick, J. L. (2008). *Major depressive disorder: A condition that frequently co-occurs with PTSD.* Retrieved from http://www.giftfromwithin.org/html/mdd.hmtl.

Kudler, H. (2010). *Painting a moving train: Working with veterans of Iraq and Afghanistan and their families.* [A PowerPoint presentation sponsored by the Veterans Integrated Service Network 6 VHA, DVA]. Retrieved from http://www.mirecc.va.gov/visn6/paint-moving-train.asp.

Kulka, R. A., Schlenger, W. E., Fairbank, J. A., Hough, R. L., Jordan, B. K., Marmar, C. R., et al. (1990). *Trauma and the Vietnam war generation.* New York: Brunner/Mazel.

Lagrone, D. M. (1978). The military family syndrome. *American Journal of Psychiatry, 135*(9), 1040–1043.

Lambrecht, M. (2009). The aftermath: Supporting and counseling suicide survivors. *TAPS Magazine.* Retrieved from http://www.TAPS.org/magazine.aspx.

LaMorie, J. H. (2010, Winter). Hope in the face of military suicide death. *TAPS Magazine,* 28–29.

Langdale, T. (2009, July 9). Drug use and addiction in war. Retrieved from http://www.highestfive.com/combat/drug-use-and-addiction-in-war.

Lindsey, T. M. (2007, November 6). Bush signs Joshua Omvig Suicide Prevention Bill into law. *Iowa Veterans Blog.* Retrieved from http://iowavetsblog .blogspot.com/2007/111)bush-signs-joshua-omvig-veterans.html.

Lindstrom, K. E., Smith, T. C., Wells, T. S., Wang, L. Z., Smith, B., Reed, R. J., et al. (2006). The mental health of U.S. military women in combat support operations. *Journal of Women's Health, 15*(2), 162–172.

Litz, B. T., Stein, N., Delany, E., Lebowitz, L., Nash, W. P., Silva, C., et al. (2009). Moral injury and moral repair in war veterans: A preliminary model and intervention strategy. *Clinical Psychological Review, 29*, pp. 695–706.

Lorge, E. M. (2007). Army leaders sign covenant with families. Retrieved from http://www.army.mil.news/2007/10/17/5641-army-leaders-sign-covenant-with-families.

Lothian, D. (2011). White house lifts ban on military condolences. *CNN.* Retrieved from http://articles.cnn.com/2010-07-15/us/army.suicides/us/military.suicides .condolences.

MacArthur, D. (1962). *General Douglas MacArthur's farewell speech: Given to the corps of cadets at West Point, May 12, 1962.* Retrieved from http://www.nationalcenter.org/MacArthur Farewell.hmtl.

Madaus, J. W. (Guest Ed.). (2009). From the special issue editor. *Journal of Post-secondary Education and Disability, 22*(1), 2–3.

Magee, D. (2006). *Parents push for soldier's story to continue beyond suicide.* Retrieved from http://joshua-omvig.memory-of.com/Legacy.apx.

Maguen, S., Luxton, D. D., Skopp, N. A., Gahn, G. A., Reger, M. A., Melzer, T. J., et al. (2011). Killing in combat, mental health symptoms and suicidal ideation in Iraq war veterans. *Journal of Anxiety Disorders, 25*, 293–301.

Malbran, P. (2007, December 4). Veteran suicides: How we got the numbers. http://www.cbs.news.com/stories/2007/11/13/cbsnews_investigates/main 3496471.shtml.

Mansfield, A. J., Kaufman, J. S., Marshall, S. W., Gaynes, B. N., Morrissey, J. P., & Engel, C. C. (2010). Deployment and the use of mental health services among U.S. Army wives. *New England Journal of Medicine, 362*(2), 101–109.

Marine Corps Community Services. (2008). *The Marine Corps, a young and vigorous force: Demographics update.* Washington, DC: Headquarters, Marine Corps, Personal and Family Readiness Division.

Marshall, R. D., Olfson, M., Hellman, F., Blanco, C., Guardino, M., & Struening, E. L. (2001). Comorbidity, impairment and suicidality in threshold PTSD. *American Journal of Psychiatry, 158,* 1467–1473.

Marshall, S. L. A. (1978). *Men against fire.* Gloucester, MA: Peter Smith.

Martin, J. A. (1984). Life satisfaction for military wives. *Military Medicine, 149,* 512–514.

Martin, J. A., Rosen, L. N., & Sparacino, L. R. (Eds.). (2000). *The military family: A practice guide for human service providers.* Westport, CT: Praeger.

Maxwell, B. D. (2005). *Army profile FY05.* Washington, DC: Office of Army Demographics.

Maze, R. (2010, January 25). Still a waiting game for post-9/11 GI Bill students. *Army Times,* p. 13.

Maze, R. (2011, February 28). DOD sex assault lawsuit seeks stronger prosecution efforts. *Army Times,* p. 12.

McCann, I. L., & Pearlman, L. A. (1990). *Psychological trauma and the adult survivor.* New York: Brunner/Mazel.

McFarland, B. H., Kaplan, M. S., & Huguet, N. (2010). Self-inflicted deaths among women in the U.S. military service: A hidden epidemic? *Psychiatric Services, 61*(12), 1177.

McMichael, W. H. (2008, December 15). Military divorce rates the highest in four years. *Army Times,* p. 25.

McMichael, W. H. (2010, April 15). Do tell: Pentagon "don't ask" panel will seek wide variety of views. *Army Times,* p. 8.

McMichael, W. H., & McGarry, B. (2010, February 15). Troops speak out on gays serving openly. *Air Force Times.* Retrieved from http://www.airforcetimes.com/news/2010/02/military_don't_ask_don't tell_02150w.

Medal of Honor Citation. (2008). Retrieved from http://www.army.mil/medalof honor/mcginnis/citation/index.html.

Meyers, S. L. (2009, August 19). Living and fighting alongside men, and fitting in. *New York Times,* pp. 1, A6.

Miles, D. (2010). Shinseki: VA tackles root causes of homelessness. *Armed Forces Information Services.* Retrieved from http://elitestv.com/pub/2010/04/shinseki-va-tackles-root-causes-of-homelessness.

Military Rape Litigation. (2011, February 15). *Service Women's Action Network.* Retrieved from http://www.servicewomen.org/our_work/litigation/military-rape-litigation.

Moore, B. A., & Reger, G. M. (2007). Historical and contemporary perspectives of combat stress and the Army combat stress control team. In C. R. Figley & W. P. Nash (Eds.), *Combat stress injury: Theory, research, and management* (pp. 161–181). New York: Routledge.

Morrison, J. (1981). Rethinking the military family syndrome. *American Journal of Psychiatry, 38*(3), 354–357.

Mozon, A. L. (1987). *Marital satisfaction, stress and coping patterns among wives of deployed Navy men.* Unpublished doctoral dissertation, University of California, Berkeley.

National Center for PTSD, U.S. Department of Veterans Affairs. (2010). *How deployment stress affects children and families: Research findings.* Retrieved from http://www.ptsd.va.gov/professional/pages/pro_deployment_stress_children.asp.

National Coalition for Homeless Veterans. (2010). *Facts and media.* Washington, DC: Author.

National Coalition for the Homeless. (2009). *Homeless veterans.* Washington, DC: Author.

National Survey on Drug Use and Health. (2008, November 6). *Major depressive episode and treatment for depression among veterans aged 21 to 39.* Retrieved from http://www.samhsa.gov/2k8/veteransDepressed/veteransDepressed.html.

National Veterans Upward Bound Program. (2009). *Welcome to the National Association of Veterans Upward Bound Project Personnel Website.* Retrieved from http:/navub.org/programinformation/index.php.

Oquendo, M., Brent, D. A., Birmaher, B., Greenhill, L., Kolko, D., Stanley, B., et al. (2005). Posttraumatic stress disorder comorbid with major depression: Factors mediating the association with suicidal behavior. *American Journal of Psychiatry, 162,* 560–566.

Orthner, D. K., Bowen, G. L., & Beare, V. G. (1990). The organization family: A question of work and family boundaries. *Marriage and Family Review, 115,* 15–36.

Ostendorff, J., & Bompey, N. (2011). VA boosts medical care for female veterans. Retrieved from http?//www.usatoday.com/news/military/2011-03-01-womenva01_ST_N.htm.

Oxendine, L. (2005). *Foreword: A profile of the veterans upward bound program: 2000–2001.* Washington, DC: U.S. Department of Education.

Padden, D. L. (2006). *The effect of perceived stress, coping behavior, previous deployment separation, and defined health promoting behaviors on general well being in female spouses of active duty military during deployment separation.* Unpublished doctoral dissertation, Catholic University, Washington, DC.

Parker, A. (2011, February 15). Lawsuit says military is rife with sexual abuse. *New York Times*, p. A18.

Paton, D., Violanti, J. M., & Smith, L. M. (2003). *Promoting capabilities to manage posttraumatic stress.* Springfield, IL: Charles C Thomas.

Pavlicin, K. M. (2003). *Surviving deployment: A guide for military families.* St. Paul, MN: Elva Resa.

Peebles-Kleiger, M. J., & Kleiger, J. H. (1994). Re-integration stress for Desert Storm families: Wartime deployments and family trauma. *Journal of Traumatic Stress, 7*(2), 173–194.

Perconte, S. T., Wilson, A. T., Pontius, A. B. Dietrick, A. L., & Spiro, K. J. (1993). Psychological and war stress symptoms among deployed and undeployed reservists following the Persian Gulf War. *Military Medicine, 158*, 516–521.

Perl, L. (2007, May 31). Veterans and homelessness. *CRS report for Congress.* Washington, DC: Congressional Research Service.

Petriccione, L. L. (2001). *A study of demographic characteristics and postsecondary experiences of Montana Veterans Upward Bound participants.* Unpublished doctoral dissertation, Montana State University.

Philpot, T. (2010, April). "Don't ask, don't tell" under scrutiny. *American Legion Magazine*, 18.

Pierce, M. M. (1982). *Psychological distress and needs among wives of an Air Force community.* Unpublished doctoral dissertation, University of Maryland.

Pincus, S. H., House, R., Christenson, J., & Adler, L. E. (2001, April–June). The emotional cycle of deployment: A military family perspective. *U.S. Army Medical Department Journal.* Retrieved from http://www.hooah4health.com/deployment/Familymatters/emotionalcycle.htm.

Pryce, J. G., Ogilvy-Lee, D., & Pryce, D. H. (2000). The "citizen-soldier" and reserve component families. In J. A. Martin, L. N. Rosen, & L. R. Sparacino (Eds.), *The military family: A practice guide for human service providers* (pp. 25–42). Westport, CT: Praeger.

Pryce, J., Shackelford, K., & Pryce, D. H. (2007). *Secondary traumatic stress and the child welfare professional.* Chicago: Lyceum Books.

Quarles, F. (1635). *Emblems*. In R. D. Heinl, *Dictionary of military and naval quotations* (p. 298). Annapolis, MD: U.S. Naval Institute.

Ramchand, R., Karney, B. R., Osilla, K. C., Burns, R. M., & Calderone, L. B. (2008). Prevalence of PTSD, depression, and TBI among returning service members. In T. Tanielian & L. H. Jaycox (Eds.), *Invisible wounds of war: Psychological and cognitive injuries, their consequences, and services to assist recovery* (pp. 54–56). Santa Monica, CA: RAND Center for Health Policy Research.

Rentz, E. D., Marshall, S. W., Loomis, D., Casteel, C., Martin, S. L., & Gibbs, D. A. (2007). Effect of deployment on the occurrence of child maltreatment in military and nonmilitary families. *American Journal of Epidemiology, 165,* 1199–1206.

Riemer, J. W. (1998). Durkheim's "heroic suicide" in military combat. *Armed Forces and Society, 25*(1), 103–120.

Riggs, D. S. (2000). Marital and family therapy. In E. Foa, T. M. Keane, & M. J. Friedman (Eds.), *Effective treatments for PTSD: Practice guidelines from the International Society for Traumatic Stress Studies* (pp. 354–355). New York: Guilford Press.

Rosen, L. N., & Carpenter, C. J. (1989). Impact of military life stress on the quality of life of military wives. *Military Medicine, 154,* 116–120.

Rosen, L. N., & Teitelbaum, J. M. (1993). Children's reactions to Desert Storm deployment: Initial findings from a survey of Army families. *Military Medicine, 158,* 465–469.

Rosen, L. N., Westhuis, D. J., & Teitelbaum, J. M. (1994). Patterns of adaptation among Army wives during operations Desert Shield and Desert Storm. *Military Medicine, 154,* 116–120.

Rothberg, J. M., & Koshes, R. J. (1994). Desert Shield deployment and social problems on a U.S. Army combat support post. *Military Medicine, 159,* 246–248.

Ryan-Wenger, N. A. (2001). Impact of the threat of war on children in military families. *American Journal of Orthopsychiatry, 71*(12), 236–244.

Salzer, D. (2011, February). Army Guard troops suicides spike in 2010. *National Guard,* 22.

Sareen, J., Joulahan, T., Cox, B. J., & Asmundson, G. J. G. (2005). Anxiety disorders associated with suicidal ideation and suicide attempts in the National Comorbidity Survey. *Journal of Nervous and Mental Disease, 193,* 450–454.

Savitsky, L., Illingworth, M., & DuLaney, M. (2009). Civilian social work: Serving the military and veteran population. *Social Work, 54*(4), 327–339.

Scarborough, R. (2011, February 24). Combat troops to get gay sensitivity training. *Washington Times.* Retrieved from http://www.washingtontimes.com/news/2011/feb/24/combat-troops-to-get-gay-sensitivity-training/.

Schaffer Library of Drug Policy. (n.d.). *Marijuana—The first twelve thousand years.* Retrieved from http://www.druglibrary.org/Schaffer/hemp/history/first12000/1.htm.

Schneider, R. J., & Martin, J. A. (1995). Military families and combat readiness. In F. Jones (Ed.), *Combat stress: Textbook for military medicine* (Vol. 6, pp. 19–30). Washington, DC: Office of the Surgeon General, Government Printing Office.

Schneidman, E. S. (1996). *The suicidal mind.* New York: Oxford University Press.

Seal, K. H., Maguen, S., Cohen, B., Gima, K. S., Metzler, T. J., Li Ren, et al. (2010). VA mental health services utilization in Iraq and Afghanistan veterans in the first year of receiving new mental health diagnoses. *Journal of Traumatic Stress, 23*(1), 5–16.

Segal, M. W. (1989). The nature of work and family linkages: A theoretical perspective. In G. L. Bowen & D. K. Orthner (Eds.), *The organization family: Work and family linkages in the U.S. military* (pp. 3–36). New York: Praeger.

Segal, M. W. (1995). Women's military roles cross-nationally: Past, present, and future. *Gender and Society, 9*(6), 757–775.

Selby, E. A., Anestis, M. D., Bender, T. W., Riberio, J. D., Nock, M. K., Rudd, M. D., et al. (2010). Overcoming fear of lethal injury: Evaluating suicidal behavior in the military through the lens of the interpersonal-psychological theory of suicide. *Clinical Psychology Review, 30,* 298–307.

Shay, J. (1994). *Achilles in Vietnam: Combat trauma and the undoing of character.* New York: Atheneum.

Shay, J. (2008, June 27). Presentation at Smith College School of Social Work symposium on deployment in Iraq and Afghanistan, Northampton, MA.

Shay, J. (2009). The trials of homecoming: Odysseus returns from Iraq/Afghanistan. *Smith College Studies in Social Work, 79,* 286–298.

Shinseki, E. K. (2003). *The Army family.* Retrieved from http://www.whs.mil/library/Dig/AR-M620U_20080912.pdf.

Slone, L. B., & Friedman, M. J. (2008). *After the war zone: A practical guide for returning troops and their families.* Philadelphia: Da Capo Press.

Solaro, E. (2006). *Women in the line of fire: What you should know about women in the military.* Emeryville, CA: Seal Press.

Soldier suicide rate may set record again. (2008, September 4). *Associated Press.* Retrieved from http://www.msnbc.msncom/id/26548448.

Sontag, D. (2008, January 20). An Iraq veteran's descent; a prosecutor's choices. *New York Times.* Retrieved from htt://www.nytimes.com/2008/01/20/us/20vets.html.

Sontag, D., & Alvarez, L. (2008a, January 27). In more cases trauma is taking the stand. *New York Times.* Retrieved from http://www.militarydefense.con/news_combat_trauma.php.

Sontag, D., & Alvarez, L. (2008b, January 30). War torn: Across America, deadly echoes of foreign battles. *New York Times.* Retrieved from http://query.nytimes.com/gst/fullpage.html.

Stander, V. A., Hilton, S. M., Kennedy, K. R., & Robbins, D. L. (2004). Surveillance of completed suicide in the Department of the Navy. *Military Medicine, 169,* 301–306.

Studenicka, E. (2007). *Suicide seen as a major threat to National Guard soldiers.* Retrieved from http://www.state.nj.us/military/admin/highlightsarchieve/highlights13Sept07.htm.

Sun Tzu (1971). *The art of war* (S. B. Griffith, Trans.). Oxford, UK: Oxford University Press.

Tan, M. (2008, February 11). Despite Army efforts, officials concerned about suicide trend. *Army Times,* p. 22.

Tan, M. (2009a, February 16). Suicides surpass combat deaths in January. *Army Times,* p. 14.

Tan, M. (2009b, July 20). Up to nine soldiers died by suicide in June: Eighty-eight such deaths reported this year. *Army Times,* p. 25.

Tanielian, T., & Jaycox, L. H. (Eds.). (2008). *Invisible wounds of war: Psychological and cognitive injuries, their consequences, and services to assist recovery.* Santa Monica, CA: RAND Center for Military Health Policy Research.

Tarabay, J. (2010). Suicide rivals the battlefield in toll on U.S. military. Retrieved from http://www.npr.org/templates/story/story.php?storyId=127860466.

Thompson, M. (2008, June 5). America's medicated Army. *Time.* Retrieved from http://www.time.com/time/nation/article/0,8599,1811858,00.html.

Tick, E. (2005). *War and the soul: Healing our nation's veterans from post-traumatic stress disorder.* Wheaton, IL: Quest Books.

Travis, A. (2009, September 24). Revealed: The hidden army in UK prisons: More veterans in justice system than soldiers serving in Afghanistan-study. *Guardian*. Retrieved from http://www.guardian.co.uk/uk/2009/sep/24/jail.

Two months of war, two years of Walter Reed: Guardsman contributed to medical center exposé. (April 20, 2007). *Army Times*. Retrieved from http://www.armytimes.com/news/2007/04/ap_mississippiguardsman_ walterreed_070420/.

University of Michigan Depression Center. (2009, January 5). *Vets and depression: Returning from war to fight new battle*. Retrieved from http://www2.med.umich.edu/prmc/media/newsroom/details.cfm?ID=972.

Ursano, R. J., & Norwood, A. E. (Eds.). (1996). *Emotional aftermath of the Persian Gulf War: Veterans, families, communities, and nations*. Washington, DC: American Psychiatric Press.

U.S. Air Force Suicide Prevention Program. (2005). *AFPAM 44-160: A description of program initiatives and outcomes*. Washington, DC: U.S. Air Force.

U.S. Army. (2005). *The Army: Our Army at war, relevant and ready, today and tomorrow* (Field Manual No. 1). Washington, DC: Headquarters, Department of the Army.

U.S. Army. (2007). *Army suicide event report for calendar year 2007*. Madigan Army Medical Center, Tacoma, WA: Suicide Risk Management and Surveillance Office.

U.S. Army Center for Health Promotion and Preventive Medicine. (2007). *A guide to female soldier readiness* (Technical Guide No. 281). Aberdeen Proving Ground, MD: Author.

U.S. Army Community and Family Support Center. (1993). *Operation R.E.A.D.Y.: Program materials for education about deployment*. Alexandria, VA: Author.

U.S. Army Community and Family Support Center. (2002). *Operation R.E.A.D.Y.: Program materials for education about deployment*. Alexandria, VA: Author.

U.S. Army Community and Family Support Center. (2006). *Operation R.E.A.D.Y.: Program materials for education about deployment*. Alexandria, VA: Author.

U.S. Army Sexual Assault Prevention and Response Program. (2010). *Headquarter of U.S. Army Regulation 600-20 (2010). Army Command Policy. U.S. Army Equal Opportunity Program, Prevention of Sexual Harassment and the Army Sexual Assault Prevention and Response Program*. Washington, DC: U.S. Army.

U.S. Department of Defense. (2009, December 4). *DoD Task Force on Sexual Assault Submits Findings, Recommendations: Executive Summary*. Washington, DC: Author.

U.S. Department of Defense. (2010, November 30). *Report of the comprehensive review of the issues associated with a repeal of "don't ask, don't tell."* [Executive Summary]. Washington, DC: Author.

U.S. Department of Defense Manpower Data Center. (2009). *Demographics 2009: Profile of the military community*. Arlington, VA: Author. Retrieved from http://militaryhomefront.dod.mil.

U.S. Department of Defense Task Force on Mental Health. (2007). *An achievable vision: Report of the Department of Defense Task Force on Mental Health*. Falls Church, VA: Defense Health Board.

U.S. Department of Education. (2009). *Veterans upward bound program*. Retrieved from http://www.ed.gov/print/programs/triovub/index.html.

U.S. Department of Labor, Veterans Employment and Training Services. (2010). *Incarcerated Veterans' Transition Program (IVTP) Competitive Grants for FY 2010 or between the period of July 1, 2010, to June 30, 2011*. Washington, DC: Author.

U.S. Department of Veterans Affairs. (2008, May 13). *Incarcerated veterans re-entry services and resources.* [Fact sheet]. Retrieved from http://www1.va.gov/homeless/page.cfm?pg=38.

U.S. Department of Veterans Affairs. (2009a). *Yellow Ribbon Program*. Retrieved from http://www.gibill.va.gov/GI_Bill_infor/ch33/yellow_ribbon.htm.

U.S. Department of Veterans Affairs. (2009b, November 6). *G.I. Bill history*. Retrieved from http://www.gibill.va.gov/GI_Bill_Info/history.htm.

U.S. Department of Veterans Affairs. (2010a, March 9). *VA history: A fact sheet*. Retrieved from http://www4.va.gov/about_va/vahistory.asp.

U.S. Department of Veterans Affairs. (2010b). *Homelessness*. Retrieved from http://www1.va.gov/HOMELESS/Programs.asp.

U.S. Department of Veterans Affairs. (2011, May 31). *New services for family caregivers of post-9/11 veterans*. Retrieved from http://www.caregiver.va.gov/support_benefit.asp.

U.S. Government Accountability Office. (2008a). *Report to congressional addressees: Mental health and traumatic brain injury implemented but consistent pre-deployment medical record review policies needed* (GAO-08-615). Washington, DC: Author.

U.S. Government Accountability Office. (2008b). *Report to congressional requesters: Military personnel, DOD's and the Coast Guard's sexual assault prevention and response programs face implementation and oversight challenges* (GAO-08-924). Washington, DC: Author.

U.S. Government Accountability Office. (2008c, October 22). *VA national initiatives and local programs that address education and support for families of returning veterans* (GAO-09-22R). Washington, DC: Author.

U.S. Interagency Council on Homelessness. (2009). *Our mission.* Retrieved from http://www.ich.gov/mission/index.html.

U.S. Marine Corps. (2000). *Combat stress* (FM 90-44/6-22.5, NTTP 1-15M, MCRP 6-11C). Washington, DC: Author.

U.S. Uniform Code of Military Justice. (2006), U.S. Code, title 10, article 120, chapter 47 (effective October 2007).

Walker, M. (2008, February 13). *Combat Marine suicides doubled in 2007.* Retrieved from http://www.leatherneck.com/forums/showthread.php?t= 60860.

Walker, M. (2010, July 14). Marine Corps sees big drop in monthly suicide statistics. *North County Times.* Retrieved from http://www.nctimes.com/news/local/military/article_cf693bdd-19dd-5d0b-8d29-dff2590fce.

Watkins, S., & Sherk, J. (2008, August 21). *Who serves in the U.S. Military? The demographics of enlisted troops and officers* (Center for Data Analysis Report #08-05). Washington, DC: Heritage Foundation.

Welton, R. S., & Blackman, L. R. (2006). Suicide and the Air Force mental health provider: Frequency and impact. *Military Medicine, 171,* 844–848.

Wertsch, M. E. (1991). *Military brats: Legacies of childhood inside the fortress.* New York: Harmony Books.

Wheeler, A. R. (2009). *While they are at war: Stress and coping in Army National Guard spouses.* Unpublished doctoral dissertation, Graduate College, University of Nebraska.

Wickham, J., Gen. (1983). *The Army family.* Washington, DC: Author. Retrieved from http://www.whs.mil/Library/Dig/AR-M62011_20080911.pdf.

Williams, K. (2006). *Love my rifle more than you: Young and female in the U.S. Military.* New York: W. W. Norton.

Wilson, R. (2009). The difficulties one veteran has had to overcome to obtain an education beyond high school. *Veterans Upward Bound Guardian, 3*(4), 7. Retrieved from http://navub.org/newsletter/downloadPdf.pip.

Wortzel, H. S., & Arciniegas, D. B. (2010). Combat veterans and the death penalty: Forensic neuropsychiatric perspective. *Journal of the American Academy of Psychiatry and the Law, 38*, 407–414.

Wortzel, H. S., Binswanger, I. A., Anderson C., & Adler, L. E. (2009). Suicide among incarcerated veterans. *Journal of the American Academy of Psychiatry and the Law, 37*, 82–91.

Wright, A. (2008). *U.S. military keeping secrets about female soldiers' "suicides."* Retrieved from http://www.truthdig.com/report/item/20080826_us_military _keeping_secrets_about_female_soldiers_suicides/.

Wright, A. (2009, July 22). Majority of colleges offer services for veterans, report says. *Chronicle of Higher Education*. Retrieved from http://chronicle.com/ article/Majority-of-Colleges-Offer/47426/.

Yancey, D. (2007, April 8). A soldier's story: Fighting Walter Reed after fighting the war. *Washington Post*. Retrieved from http://www.washingtonpost .com/wp-dyn/content/article/2007/04/06/AR2007040601788.html.

Zinzow, H. M., Grubaugh, A. L., Monnier, J., Suffolette-Maierte, S., & Vrueh, C. B. (2007). Trauma among female veterans: A critical review. *Trauma, Violence, and Abuse, 8*(7), 384–400.

Zivin, K. (2007). Suicide mortality among individuals receiving treatment for depression in the Veterans Affairs health system: Association with patient and treatment setting characteristics. *American Journal of Public Health, 97*(12), 2193–2198.

Zoroya, G. (2008, December 2). Divorce rates rise for soldiers, Marines. *Army Times*. Retrieved from http://www.armytimes.com/news/2008/12/gns_ divorcerates_120308w/.

Zoroya, G. (2010a, May 14–16). Mental care stays are up in the military: Disorders outpaced injuries in 2009. *USA Today*, p. 1.

Zoroya, G. (2010b, June 8). Marine suicide attempts at record-high rate. Retrieved from http://abcnews.go.com/Politics/marine-suicide-attempts-record-rate/ story?id=10855079.

Zoroya, G. (2011). Army efforts don't stem Fort Hood suicides. *USA Today*. Retrieved from http://www.usatoday.com/news/military/2011-01-06- suicides06_ST_N.htm.

Zwerdling, D. (2009, July 21). Soldiers say Army ignores, punishes mental anguish. *National Public Radio*. Retrieved from http://www.npr.org/templates/story/ story.php?storyId=6576505.

Index

About the Authors

Josephine G. Pryce earned her MSW at Our Lady of the Lake University and her PhD at University of California, Berkeley. She is associate professor of social work at the University of Alabama. She was a military spouse for twenty-two years and has been a combat veteran's spouse for fifteen years. Her teaching specialties are social work research, practice, and traumatic stress. Pryce has published extensively on military families and is coauthor of three books.

Colonel David H. Pryce, MA (history) from the University of Nebraska, MSSW from the University of Texas, Arlington, is a retired infantry officer. He served two tours in Vietnam in attack helicopter and air cavalry units, earning three Silver Star medals for gallantry and two Purple Heart medals for wounds received in combat. He served on the faculty of the U.S. Air Force Academy developing and teaching courses in American military history. Since his retirement in 1987, he has published extensively on warriors and their families. This is his second book.

Kimberly K. Shackelford earned her MSW from the University of Southern Mississippi and her PhD from the University of Mississippi. She is associate professor of social work at the University of Mississippi. She conducted the interviews with warriors and family members for this book. Her teaching specialties are human behavior in the social environment, child welfare, social work practice and policy, social work supervision, and traumatic stress. This is her second book.